Collins

Science Expert

Chemistry 8

Series Editor
Lipika Dutta

Preface

Collins Science Expert is a series of 14 coursebooks for Classes 1 to 8. The coursebooks for grades 1 and 2 are aligned with Environmental Studies (EVS) and grades 3 to 5 with Science. For Classes 6 to 8, there are separate coursebooks for Physics, Chemistry and Biology. This series, which is the revised edition of *Science Panorama*, is based on the **latest curriculum** prescribed by the **Council for the Indian School Certificate Examinations** and adheres to the guidelines of the *National Education Policy* (NEP) 2020.

In line with the curriculum, a thematic, coherent and structured approach has been followed and all new topics suggested in the curriculum have been included. The series also caters to the three domains of learning—**cognitive** (*intellectual nature*), **affective** (*attitudinal nature*) and **psychomotor** (*actionable nature*).

Aimed to answer a learner's cry: '*Teach me the way I want to learn*', this series adopts a method—**visual**, **auditory**, **kinesthetic** and **tactile** (**VAKT**)—that caters to all kinds of learners. Keeping in mind the saying 'I hear – I forget, I see – I understand and I do – I remember', a lot of hands-on activities have been incorporated. This would enable learners to understand and learn scientific concepts through experiential learning.

This series also emphasizes on developing *scientific skills* such as **observation**, **data collection**, **investigation**, **estimation**, **prediction**, **analysis** and **drawing inferences**. This would help in developing a scientific temperament in learners from a young age. The series also draws a connection between cause and effect; and focuses on the application of concepts in real-life situations. The language used is child-friendly and age-appropriate. Sufficient examples from everyday life have been given to help learners understand the concepts. A lot of colourful illustrations and well-labelled diagrams have been included to engage learners and aid in their understanding.

We would like to take this opportunity to thank all the teachers who reviewed the books and provided their valuable feedback, which helped in improving the quality of the content.

Any suggestions or constructive criticism from the users are welcome. We shall try to incorporate those in the future editions.

Authors

Key Features

The key features of ***Collins Science Expert*** series are completely aligned with *National Education Policy* (NEP) 2020. These meticulously designed key features, based on VAKT (visual, auditory, kinesthetic and tactile) learning style and the three domains of Bloom's Taxonomy which include **cognitive (intellectual skills)**, **affective (attitudinal nature)** and **psychomotor (actionable nature)**, can be used as learning strategies to help in the development of scientific and 21st Century Skills in students. These key features also aim to help students shift from rote-learning to competency-based learning.

Bloom's Taxonomy

Cognitive Domain

- Focuses on intellectual skills such as critical thinking, problem solving, and creating a knowledge base
- Expects learners to progress linearly, beginning at "remember" and ending at "create."

Features:
- Prior Knowledge
- Learning Objectives
- Let's Get Started
- Quick Revision
- Talk Time
- Concept Map
- Keywords
- Exercise
- Word to know
- Review Corner

Affective Domain

- Focuses on the attitudes, values, interests and appreciation of learners
- Focuses on allowing learners to understand what their own values are and how they have developed

Features:
- Greenathon
- Skill Booster
- Worksheets
- My Environment, My Responsibility!
- Happy Accidents
- Innovation: The Steppingstone
- Role of Science in Benefitting the Society

Psycho motor Domain

- Encompasses the ability of learners to physically accomplish tasks and perform movement and skills
- Expects learners to progress from using reflexes and basic movement to non-discursive communication and meaningfully expressive activity

Features:
- Do It Yourself
- Activities
- Skill Booster
- Worksheets
- My Eco Craft
- Innovation: The Steppingstone
- STEAM Worksheets

Skills and Learnings

Colour-coded tags and icons are used to easily identify the types of skills and learnings being addressed.

NEP Aligned Skills

21st Century Skills (21CS)

Learning Skills
- Critical Thinking
- Creativity and Innovation
- Collaboration
- Communication

Life Skills
- Flexibility and Adaptability
- Leadership and Responsibility
- Initiative and Self-direction
- Productivity and Accountability
- Social and Cross-cultural Interaction

Literacy Skills
- Information Literacy
- Media Literacy
- Technology Literacy

SUSTAINABLE DEVELOPMENT GOALS

Experiential Learning (EL)

Cross Curricular (CC)

Bloom's Taxonomy (BT)

Art Integration (AI)

India Focus (IF)

SEE Learning

About the Features

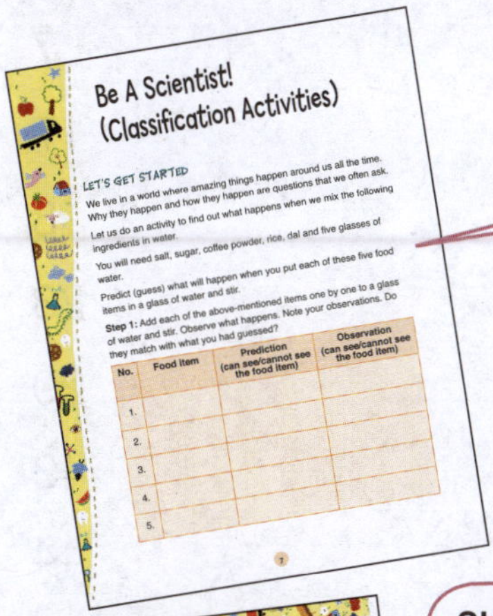

Be a Scientist! (Classes 3 to 5):
Introduction to science process skills to help develop scientific attitudes

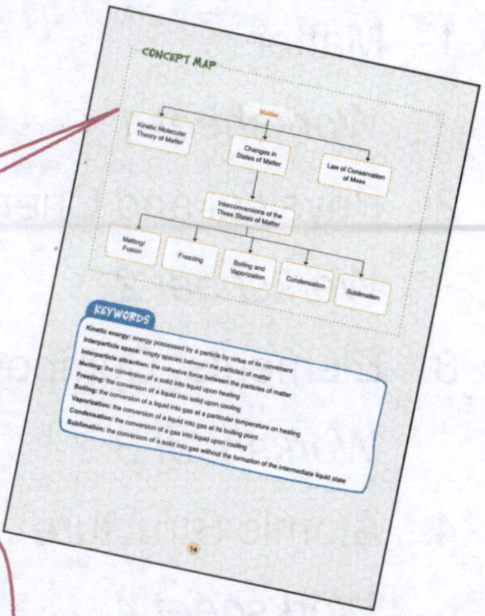

- **Concept Map:** Snapshot of the chapter in the form of a graphic organizer for quick recapitulation
- **Keywords:** Definitions of important terms

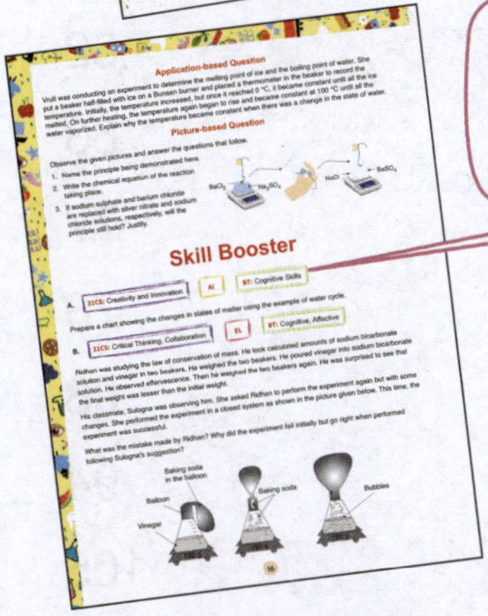

Skill Booster: Section aimed at imparting 21st Century Skills alongwith a focus on Cross-curricular Links, India Focus, Art Integration, Experiential Learning and Bloom's Taxonomy

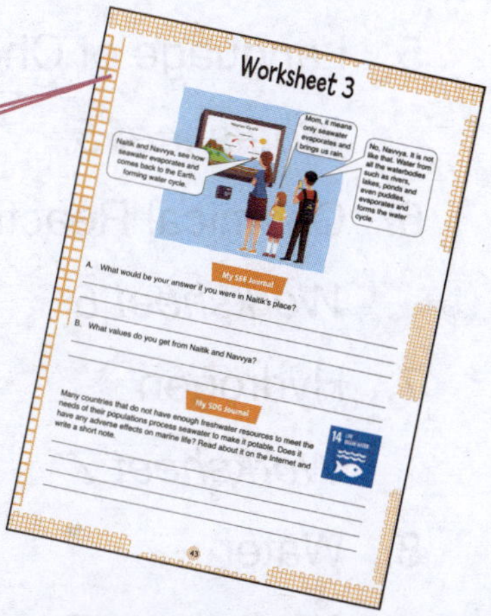

Worksheet: Interesting questions imparting skills catering to social, emotional and ethical (SEE) needs and United Nations' sustainable development goals (SDGs)

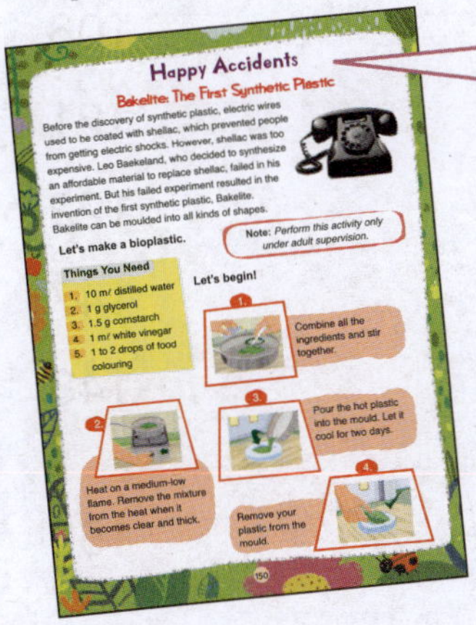

My Environment, My Responsibility! (Classes 1 and 2): Special pages to spread awareness and a sense of responsibility towards the environment

Happy Accidents (Classes 3 to 8): Interesting snippets on discoveries and inventions by chance/accidents that led to beneficial ways

STEAM Worksheets (Physics 6 to 8): Interesting project ideas integrating Science, Technology, Engineering, Arts and Mathematics to solve real-world problems

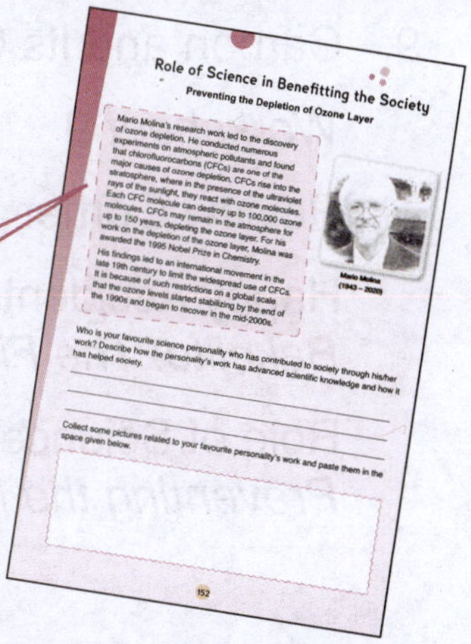

My Eco Craft (Classes 1 and 2): Hands-on activities to enhance learning beyond the classroom

Innovation: The Steppingstone (Classes 3 to 5): Ideas to guide students to solve real-life problems in innovative ways

Role of Science in Benefitting the Society (Classes 6 to 8): Snippets on the contributions made by various scientists for the development of the society

Find Out: Research-oriented questions requiring learners to look beyond the classroom

What do we call the person who treats our pet dog when it falls sick? FIND OUT

Contents

1 Matter

Prior Knowledge	**Learning Objectives**
• Definition of matter • Classification of matter with examples • Composition of matter	• Postulates of the kinetic molecular theory of matter • Changes in states of matter • Law of conservation of mass

LET'S GET STARTED

Carefully observe the given images and answer the following questions.

1. In which state of matter are the particles closest together?
2. In which state of matter are the particles least tightly packed?

We know that matter is anything that has mass and occupies space. A piece of bread, a book, aerated soft drinks, air and steam all possess mass and occupy space. Thus, they are known as matter. It is evident from the examples we considered here that matter can exist in three different states, that is, solid, liquid and gas. We have learned in previous classes that all matter is made up of tiny particles. The particles in matter are in constant motion and therefore possess energy. Let us learn about this concept in detail in this chapter.

KINETIC MOLECULAR THEORY OF MATTER

Based on the state of matter, solid, liquid or gas, the particles have different amounts of energy, are arranged differently and move in different ways. The kinetic molecular theory of matter explains the properties of the different states of matter. The main postulates of this theory are as follows:

1. Matter is made up of tiny particles called atoms or molecules. These particles are so tiny that they cannot be seen with unaided eyes.
2. In a particular substance, the constituent particles are identical in all aspects.
3. These particles have spaces or gaps between them. These gaps are called **interparticle spaces**.
4. The particles of matter attract each other through a cohesive force called the **interparticle force of attraction**. This force holds the particles in a substance together.
5. The constituent particles of matter are always in a state of random motion by virtue of which they possess **kinetic energy**.

The average kinetic energy of all the particles gives the measure of the temperature.

DO YOU KNOW?

The random motion of particles in liquids and gases was first discovered by Robert Brown. Hence, it is called the **Brownian movement**.

STATES OF MATTER

The interparticle space and the interparticle force of attraction decide the state of matter and the kinetic energy possessed by its constituent particles.

Solids

Solids have the least interparticle space and the maximum interparticle force of attraction. These particles cannot move freely. As a result, solids have well-defined boundaries, which give them fixed shapes and volumes.

As the constituent particles in solids are fixed, they can only vibrate to and fro about their fixed positions. Thus, particles in solids possess the least kinetic energy.

Liquids

In comparison with solids, the interparticle space is greater and the interparticle force of attraction is less among the constituent particles in liquids. As a result, the particles in liquids are loosely packed as compared to solids. The weaker interparticle force of attraction allows the liquid particles to move more freely and randomly than solid particles. This force, however, is strong enough to limit their movement to the bulk of the matter. That is, the particles can only roll over each other but cannot fly away like gas particles. Hence, liquids do not have fixed shapes, but they do have fixed volumes.

As the particles in liquids are not fixed and can move more freely as compared to solid particles, liquid particles possess more kinetic energy than solid particles.

Gases

The constituent particles in gases have the maximum interparticle space and the least interparticle force of attraction. These particles can move freely in all directions. As a result, gases do not have fixed shapes or volumes. A gas fills the whole container it is poured into.

As the particles in gases are not fixed and can randomly move in any direction, the gas particles possess the maximum kinetic energy.

Refer to Table 1.1 to compare and contrast the properties of constituent particles in different states of matter.

Table 1.1 Characteristics of the particles in the three states of matter

Characteristic	State of Matter		
	Solid	**Liquid**	**Gas**
Shape	Definite shape	No definite shape. It takes the shape of the container.	No definite shape. It takes the shape of the container.
Volume	Definite volume	Definite volume	No definite volume. It fills the entire volume of the container.
Ability to flow	Cannot flow	Flows from a higher level to a lower level	Flows in all directions
Compressibility	Incompressible	Can be compressed to some extent	Highly compressible
Diffusion	Negligible	Can occur easily	Can occur quickly
Free surface	Many	One	None
Density	High	Medium	Least
Arrangement of particles	Closely and orderly packed 	Closely but randomly packed 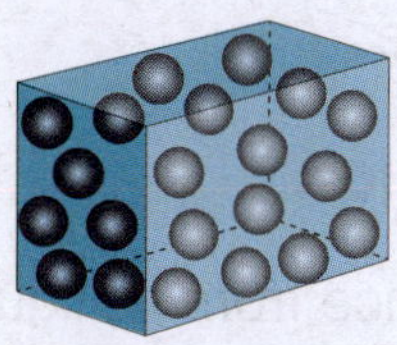	Loosely and randomly packed 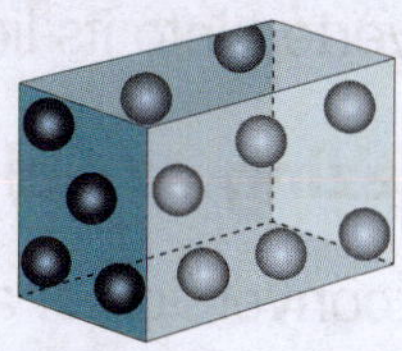
Interparticle space	Minimum	More than that in solids	Maximum
Interparticle attraction	Strongest	Less than that of solids	Weakest
Movement of particles	Restricted movement	Easy movement	Free movement

CHANGES IN THE STATES OF MATTER

Matter can change its state by changing the pressure and temperature. For example, water at 0 °C exists as ice (solid). When heated, ice melts into water (liquid) and upon continuous heating, water is converted into steam (gas). Fig. 1.1 depicts various processes that change the state of matter.

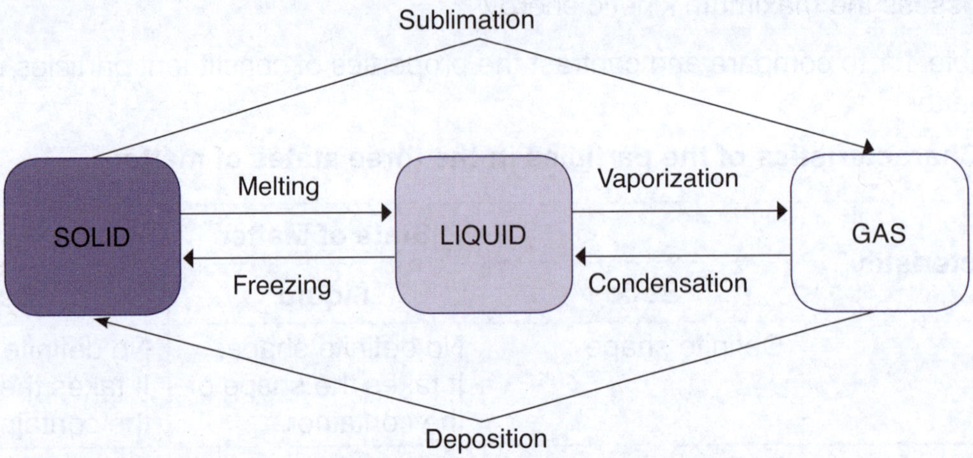

Fig. 1.1 Interconversions of the three states of matter

Let us discuss some processes that involve changes in the states of matter.

Melting or Fusion

The conversion of a substance from its solid state to its liquid state at a particular temperature and constant pressure is called **melting/fusion**. Particles in a solid tend to move faster when the solid is heated. This increases the kinetic energy of the particles and the same can be recorded on a thermometer as rise in temperature. At a certain temperature, the particles gain sufficient energy to overcome the forces of attraction between them. This temperature is called the **melting point** of the solid. On further heating, the particles in the solid move apart without any change in their kinetic energy. This movement increases the interparticle space between the particles. The temperature remains the same until the solid is completely converted into its liquid state.

Freezing or Solidification

The conversion of a substance from its liquid state to its solid state at a particular temperature and constant pressure is called **freezing/solidification**. Particles in a liquid possess some kinetic energy and the same can be recorded on a thermometer as temperature. When a liquid is cooled, the speed of its particles slows down, with a direct proportional decrease in its temperature. At a certain temperature, the speed of the particles is minimum. This temperature is called the **freezing point** of the liquid. On further cooling, the particles in the liquid move closer without any change in their kinetic energy. This movement decreases the interparticle space between the particles. The temperature remains the same until the liquid is converted into its solid state.

Fig. 1.2 represents the reversibility of melting and solidification.

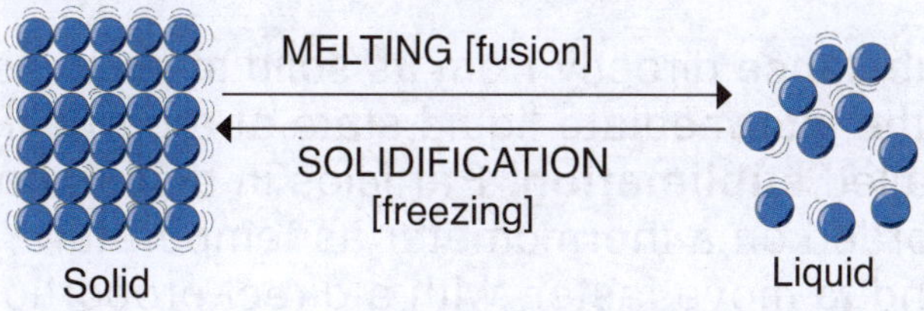

Fig. 1.2 Melting and freezing of matter

Vaporization

The conversion of a substance from its liquid state to its gaseous state is called **vaporization**. When this conversion occurs at a particular temperature and constant pressure, it is called **boiling**. Particles in a liquid possess some kinetic energy which can be recorded on a thermometer as temperature. When a liquid is heated, its particles begin to move faster, with a direct proportional increase in its temperature. At a certain temperature, the particles gain sufficient kinetic energy to overcome the forces of attraction between them. This temperature is called the **boiling point** of the liquid. On further heating, the particles in the liquid move further apart from each other without any change in their kinetic energy. This movement increases the interparticle space between the particles. The temperature remains the same until the entire liquid is converted into its gaseous state.

Evaporation is the same as vaporization. The only difference between evaporation and vaporization is that evaporation is a continuous process that occurs at room temperature without the supply of any external heat. In evaporation, the surface particles of a liquid absorb the heat energy from the surroundings, which increases their kinetic energy. When the kinetic energy of the surface particles is sufficient enough, the particles from their liquid state break free and evaporate, exposing particles in the bulk of the liquid to come to the surface. This process continues until all the liquid evaporates. Water spilled on the floor disappears after some time due to evaporation.

Condensation

The conversion of a substance from its gaseous state to its liquid state at a particular temperature and constant pressure is called **condensation**. Particles in a gas tend to move slower when the gas is cooled. This decreases the kinetic energy of the particles which gets recorded on a thermometer as temperature. At a certain temperature, the speed of the particles is minimum. This temperature is called the **dew point** of the gas. On further cooling, the particles in the gas move closer without any change in their kinetic energy. This movement decreases the interparticle space between the particles. The temperature remains the same until the gas is completely converted into its liquid state.

Fig. 1.3 shows the reversibility of vaporization and condensation.

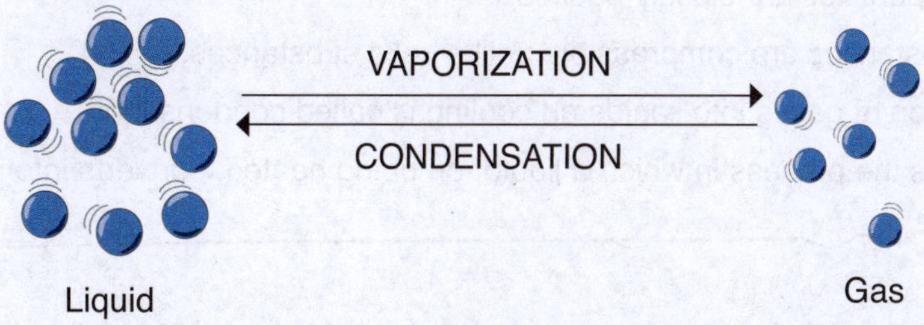

Fig. 1.3 Vaporization and condensation of matter

Sublimation

The conversion of a substance directly from its solid state to its gaseous state without going through the intermediate liquid state at a particular temperature and constant pressure is called **sublimation**. Particles in a solid possess some kinetic energy which gets recorded on a thermometer as temperature. When a solid is heated, its particles tend to move faster, with a direct proportional increase in its temperature. At a certain temperature, the particles gain sufficient energy to overcome the forces of attraction between them. This temperature is called the **sublimation point** of the solid. On further heating, the particles in the solid move farther apart without any change in their kinetic energy. This movement increases the interparticle space between the particles. The temperature remains the same until the solid is completely converted into gaseous state.

Deposition

The conversion of a substance directly from its gaseous state to its solid state without going through the intermediate liquid state at a particular temperature and pressure is called **deposition**. When the particles of a gaseous substance are cooled, they lose their kinetic energy and tend to move slower. Due to this, the interparticle distance between the particles decreases. At a certain temperature and constant pressure, the particles have the minimum kinetic energy that can be recorded on a thermometer. This temperature is called the **deposition point**. On further cooling, the interparticle space reduces to the minimum without any change in their kinetic energy. The temperature remains the same until the gaseous state of the substance is changed into its solid state. Frost formation is an example of deposition in which water vapour in the air changes directly from a gaseous to a solid state.

Fig. 1.4 shows the reversibility of sublimation and deposition.

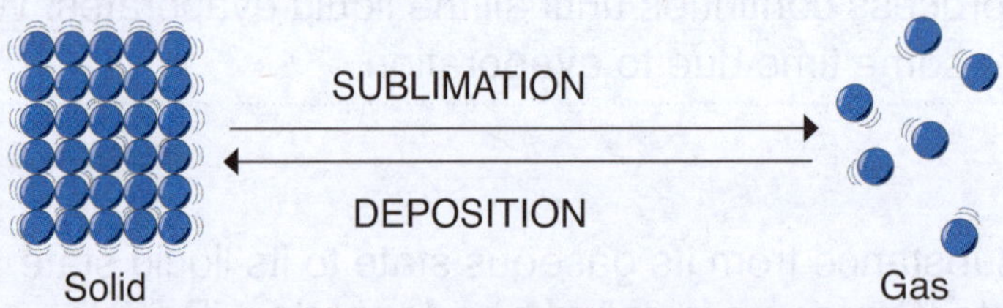

Fig. 1.4 Sublimation and deposition of matter

QUICK REVISION

Write T for True and F for False.

1. In a solid, diffusion takes place very slowly.
2. In a gas, the particles are closely packed.
3. Gaseous substances are compressible unlike solid substances.
4. The conversion of gases into liquids on cooling is called condensation.
5. Sublimation is the process in which a liquid, on being heated, converts into its solid state.

LAW OF CONSERVATION OF MASS

The **law of conservation of mass** states that mass can neither be created nor destroyed by chemical reactions or physical transformations.

In other words, in any chemical reaction, the total mass of the reactants is equal to the total mass of the products formed, provided the masses are measured under similar conditions.

For example, if A and B react to form C and D, then according to the law of conservation of mass,

Mass of A + Mass of B = Mass of C + Mass of D

Consider the reaction of sodium chloride (NaCl) with silver nitrate ($AgNO_3$) which results in the formation of silver chloride (AgCl) and sodium nitrate ($NaNO_3$) (Fig. 1.5). The mass of each element is written below in the chemical equation for this reaction. We can see that the total mass on both sides of the equation comes out to be equal.

$$NaCl + AgNO_3 \rightarrow AgCl(\downarrow) + NaNO_3$$
$$(23 + 35.5) + (108 + 14 + 48) = (108 + 35.5) + (23 + 14 + 48)$$
$$228.5 = 228.5$$

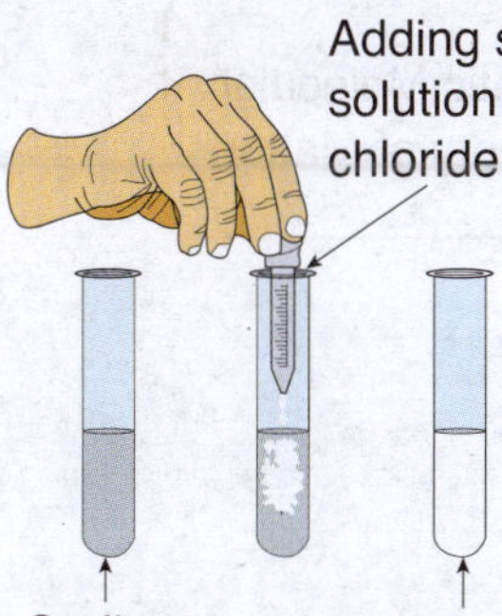

Fig. 1.5 Precipitation reaction between sodium chloride and silver nitrate

ACTIVITY 1

Aim: To show that mass is neither gained nor lost in a reaction

Materials required: A conical flask, an ignition tube, a measuring cylinder, a cork, a weighing balance, barium chloride solution and sodium sulphate solution

Procedure:

1. Take 15 mℓ of sodium sulphate solution in a conical flask.
2. Take 5 mℓ of barium chloride solution in an ignition tube.
3. Place the ignition tube carefully in the conical flask as shown in Fig. A. Cork the conical flask without disturbing the two solutions.
4. Weigh the whole setup.
5. Tilt the conical flask so that barium chloride solution mixes with sodium sulphate solution.
6. Weigh the whole set up again.

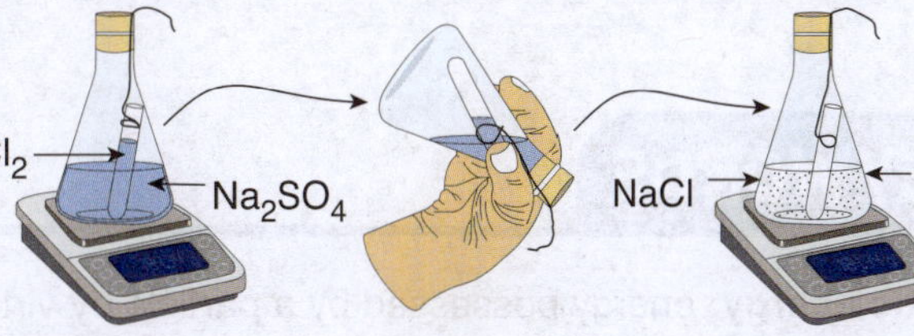

Fig. A Fig. B Fig. C

(**Note:** *Perform the experiment with the assistance of a teacher. Wear a lab coat and protection glasses. Wash the hands thoroughly after the experiment.*)

Observation:

1. On mixing barium chloride with sodium sulphate, a white precipitate of barium sulphate is formed.
2. Weight of the setup remains the same.

Conclusion: The mass of the products (barium sulphate and sodium chloride) formed is equal to the mass of the reactants (barium chloride and sodium sulphate). Thus, we conclude that mass is conserved during a chemical reaction.

$$\underset{\text{Barium chloride}}{BaCl_2} + \underset{\text{Sodium sulphate}}{Na_2SO_4} \longrightarrow \underset{\text{Barium sulphate (White precipitate)}}{BaSO_4} + \underset{\text{Sodium chloride}}{2NaCl}$$

CONCEPT MAP

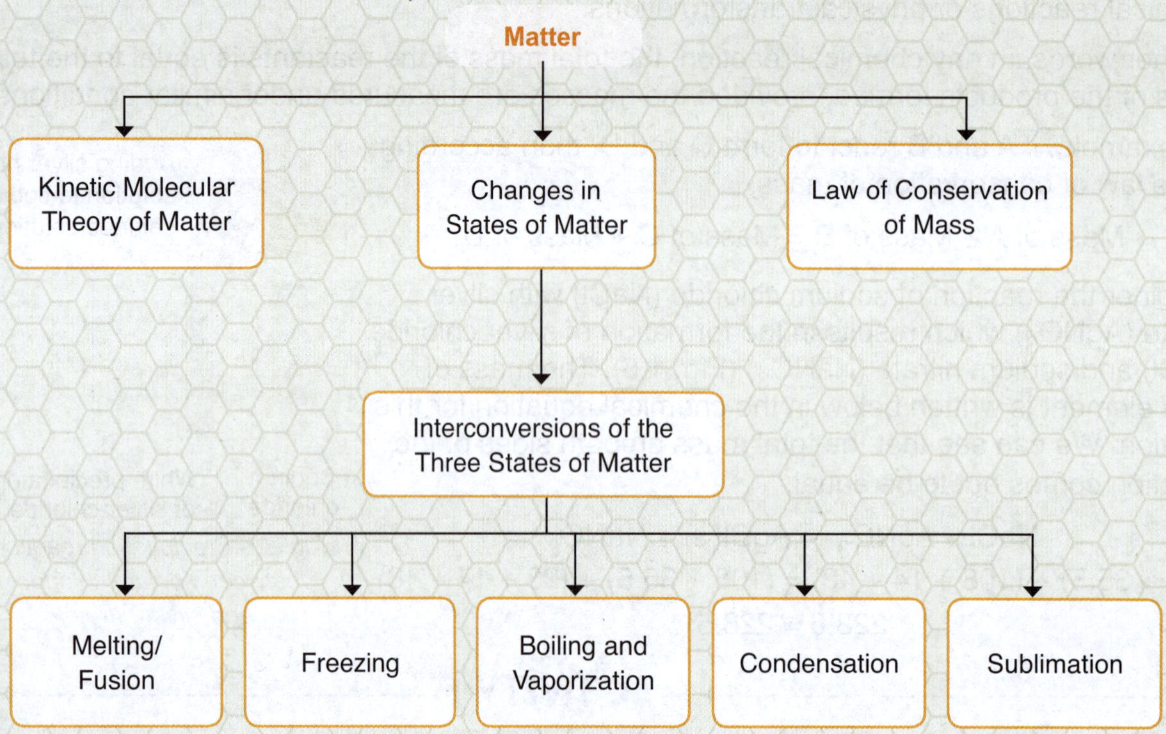

KEYWORDS

Kinetic energy: energy possessed by a particle by virtue of its movement

Interparticle space: empty spaces between the particles of matter

Interparticle attraction: the cohesive force between the particles of matter

Melting: the conversion of a solid into liquid upon heating

Freezing: the conversion of a liquid into solid upon cooling

Boiling: the conversion of a liquid into gas at a particular temperature on heating

Vaporization: the conversion of a liquid into gas at its boiling point

Condensation: the conversion of a gas into liquid upon cooling

Sublimation: the conversion of a solid into gas without the formation of the intermediate liquid state

Exercise

Objective Type Questions

A. Choose the correct answer.

1. Which of the following has a definite volume and a definite shape?
   a. Chair b. Apple juice
   c. Oil d. Shampoo
2. Gases occupy all the available space because their particles are ___________.
   a. strong
   b. weak
   c. very loosely packed
   d. tightly packed
3. The process in which a liquid converts into solid upon cooling is called ___________.
   a. vaporization b. condensation
   c. melting d. freezing
4. The boiling point of a substance is the temperature at which a substance changes from ___________.
   a. a liquid to solid
   b. a solid to liquid
   c. a liquid to gas
   d. a gas to solid
5. The law of conservation of mass states that mass cannot be ___________.
   a. changed or created
   b. burnt or destroyed
   c. dissolved or disposed
   d. created or destroyed

B. Fill in the blanks.

1. Solidification is also termed as ___________ (fusion/freezing).
2. The ___________ (potential/kinetic) energy of particles in a solid is very low.
3. The force of ___________ (attraction/repulsion) between particles of matter in gases is negligible.
4. The interparticle ___________ (space/force) is the maximum between the particles of gases.
5. Interparticle space between the particles of a solid is ___________ (minimum/maximum).

C. Write T for True and F for False.

1. On heating a solid to its melting point, the interparticle space increases.
2. On heating a sublimable solid, the interparticle force of attraction is lost.
3. The interparticle attraction between the particles of gases is maximum.
4. A substance changes from its liquid state to gaseous state at its melting point.
5. Atoms are the only minute particles that make up matter.

D. Name the following.

1. The constant temperature at which a liquid changes to solid ___________
2. The force of attraction between the particles of matter ___________
3. The process in which a liquid is converted into gas ___________
4. The process in which a solid changes its state to gas ___________
5. The temperature at which a liquid is formed from solid ___________

Subjective Type Questions

A. Define the following.

1. Melting
2. Freezing
3. Vaporization
4. Condensation
5. Sublimation

B. Answer the following questions in brief.

1. State the law of conservation of mass.
2. What is the difference between vaporization and boiling?
3. What is sublimation? Explain.
4. How are melting point and boiling point of a substance different from each other?
5. Differentiate between evaporation and vaporization with an example of each.

C. Answer the following questions in detail.

1. Write the postulates of the kinetic theory of matter.
2. Explain the law of conservation of mass with the help of an experiment.
3. Write a short note on the interparticle changes that occur when a solid changes into a liquid.
4. What are the characteristics of liquids?
5. Explain briefly the changes in states of matter on heating or cooling.

Application-based Question

Vruti was conducting an experiment to determine the melting point of ice and the boiling point of water. She put a beaker half-filled with ice on a Bunsen burner and placed a thermometer in the beaker to record the temperature. Initially, the temperature increased, but once it reached 0 °C, it became constant until all the ice melted. On further heating, the temperature again began to rise and became constant at 100 °C until all the water vaporized. Explain why the temperature became constant when there was a change in the state of water.

Picture-based Question

Observe the given pictures and answer the questions that follow.

1. Name the principle being demonstrated here.
2. Write the chemical equation of the reaction taking place.
3. If sodium sulphate and barium chloride are replaced with silver nitrate and sodium chloride solutions, respectively, will the principle still hold? Justify.

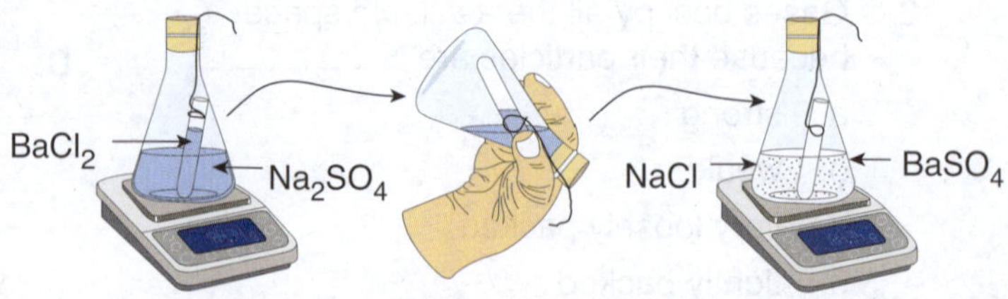

Skill Booster

A. **21CS:** Creativity and Innovation | **AI** | **BT:** Cognitive Skills

Prepare a chart showing the changes in states of matter using the example of water cycle.

B. **21CS:** Critical Thinking, Collaboration | **EL** | **BT:** Cognitive, Affective

Ridhan was studying the law of conservation of mass. He took calculated amounts of sodium bicarbonate solution and vinegar in two beakers. He weighed the two beakers. He poured vinegar into sodium bicarbonate solution. He observed effervescence. Then he weighed the two beakers again. He was surprised to see that the final weight was lesser than the initial weight.

His classmate, Sulogna was observing him. She asked Ridhan to perform the experiment again but with some changes. She performed the experiment in a closed system as shown in the picture given below. This time, the experiment was successful.

What was the mistake made by Ridhan? Why did the experiment fail initially but go right when performed following Sulogna's suggestion?

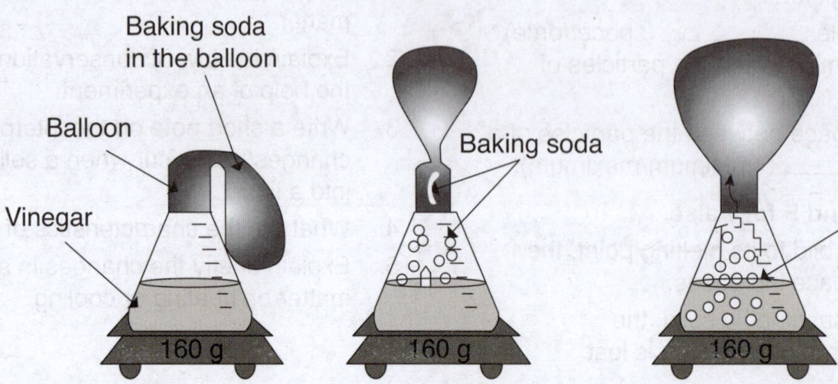

Worksheet 1

Rahul is a student of class 8. During his vacation, he went to his aunt's house. One afternoon, he noticed that the numbers on the water meter were increasing. He closed all taps and water-using appliances and checked the reading on the water meter again. He was surprised that even when there was no usage of water, the numbers on the meter were rising. He was sure that some water pipes were leaking. Rahul informed his aunt of this. His aunt called a plumber to inspect the pipes. The plumber confirmed the leakage of water and fixed the leaking pipes. His aunt appreciated Rahul for taking the initiative and using his cognitive skills to solve the problem.

My SEE Journal

Have you ever used your cognitive skills to identify a problem and solve it like Rahul? What was the problem and how did you solve it?

____

____

____

____

____

My SDG Journal

12 RESPONSIBLE CONSUMPTION AND PRODUCTION

A. List the various ways of preventing water leaks.

____

____

____

____

____

B. Create catchy slogans to raise awareness about water conservation.

2 Physical and Chemical Changes

Prior Knowledge

- Definition of a change
- Different types of changes with examples

Learning Objectives

- Types of changes
- Physical changes
- Chemical changes

LET'S GET STARTED

Most of us like eating popcorn while watching a movie at the cinema. Is the popping of popcorn a physical or a chemical change? Justify your answer.

Almost everything around us undergoes change. Some changes are easy to detect while some changes occur so slowly that they are very difficult to identify. A change in the shape of play dough when pressure is applied to it, a change in the direction of a moving ball when a batsman hits it with his bat and a change in the colour of water when a few drops of food colour are added to it are a few examples of changes that are easy to detect. Growth in plants and animals, the formation of curd from milk and the rusting of iron are a few examples of slow changes.

TYPES OF CHANGES

We have already learned about the different types of changes in Class 7. Refer to Table 2.1 to recall these changes.

Table 2.1 Different types of changes

Natural and Artificial Changes	
Changes that occur in nature on their own are known as **natural changes**. For example, growth of a plant or a baby, ripening of a fruit, change in seasons, change of day into night, weathering of rocks, formation of fossil fuels, and greying of hair.  *Growth of a plant (natural change)*	Changes that are made to occur or are caused by human activities are known as **artificial changes**. For example, making a pot from clay, a dress from fibres and furniture from wood, cooking of food, construction of dams and bridges, and cutting down of trees to set up factories and cities (leading to pollution and global warming). 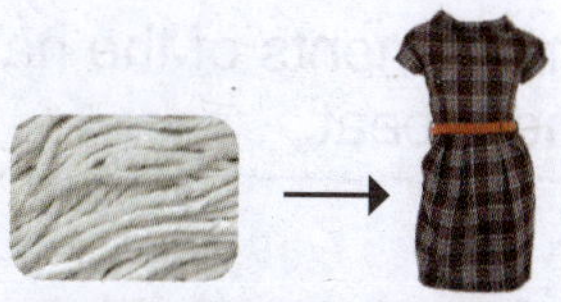 *Making of a dress from fibres (artificial change)*
Fast and Slow Changes	
Changes that take place in a very short period of time are known as **fast changes**. For example, burning of matchsticks, burning of paper into ash, occurrence of landslides, breaking of glass mirrors, bursting of firecrackers and lightning during a thunderstorm.  *Lightning during thunderstorm*	Changes that take place over a long period of time are known as **slow changes**. For example, growth of a baby into an adult, formation of fossil fuels, germination of seeds, rusting of iron, growth of fingernails and decay of dead plants.  *Germination of seeds (slow change)*
Reversible and Irreversible Changes	
Changes that can be reversed, that is, we can get back the original substance by changing the conditions that brought about the change, are known as **reversible changes**. For example, melting of ice, stretching of a rubber band, folding and unfolding of paper, blowing of air into a balloon, boiling of water and dissolving of salt or sugar in water.  *Melting of ice (reversible change)*	Changes that cannot be reversed, that is, we cannot get back the original substance by changing the conditions that brought about the change, are known as **irreversible changes**. For example, growth of living things, cooking of rice, ripening of fruits, burning of wood, digestion of food and withering of leaves.  *Growth of a baby into an adult (irreversible change)*

Periodic and Non-Periodic Changes

Changes that repeat after a fixed interval of time are known as **periodic changes**.

For example, changes in seasons, appearance of different phases of the moon, cycle of day and night, rotation and revolution of Earth, movements of the hands of a clock and our heartbeat.

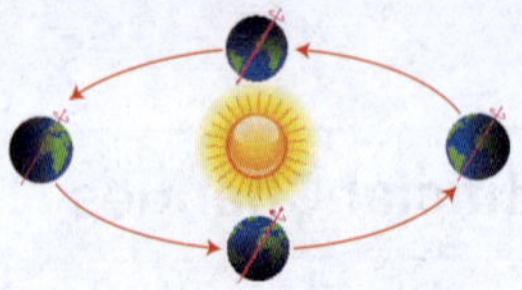

Revolution of Earth (periodic change)

Changes that do not repeat after a fixed interval of time and can occur any time are known as **non-periodic changes**.

For example, occurrence of cyclones, earthquakes, tsunamis, volcanic eruptions, accidents and rain showers, and sneezing.

Volcanic eruption (non-periodic change)

Exothermic and Endothermic Changes

Changes that involve a release of energy in the form of heat are known as **exothermic changes**.

For example, burning of fuels, bursting of crackers, condensation of water vapour and freezing of water to form ice cubes.

Bursting of crackers (exothermic change)

Changes that involve the absorption of energy in the form of heat are known as **endothermic changes**.

For example, photosynthesis in green plants, cooking of food, evaporation of water and melting of ice cubes.

Photosynthesis (endothermic change)

Desirable and Undesirable Changes

Changes that are useful to us are known as **desirable changes**.

For example, fermentation of grape juice into wine, formation of curd from milk, cooking of food, ripening of fruits and blooming of flowers.

Cooking of food (desirable change)

Changes that are harmful to us are known as **undesirable changes**.

For example, spoilage of food, occurrence of earthquakes, storms and floods, rotting of fruits and vegetables, soil erosion and rusting of iron.

Flood (undesirable change)

Physical and Chemical Changes

Changes in which the chemical composition of the substances undergoing the change remains the same are called **physical changes**.

For example, melting of ice, tearing of paper, boiling of water, folding of clothes and breaking of glass.

Broken glass

Changes in which the chemical composition of the substances undergoing the change does not remain the same are called **chemical changes**.

For example, burning of paper, cooking of food, curdling of milk and rusting of iron.

Rusted iron lock

PHYSICAL CHANGES

Changes in which no new substances are formed are known as **physical changes**. Such changes might alter the physical properties of the original substance, but the chemical properties remain the same.

Changes in states of matter, resulting from processes such as boiling, melting, freezing, condensation, sublimation and deposition are all physical changes.

ACTIVITY 1

Aim: To prove that evaporation and condensation are physical changes

Materials required: Two beakers, a Bunsen burner, water, tripod stands, a wire gauze, matchbox, tongs and a stainless steel plate

Procedure:

1. Take a beaker containing water.
2. Place the beaker on a wire gauze placed on a tripod stand. Heat the beaker with the help of a Bunsen burner.
3. Set up the apparatus as in the figure given alongside.

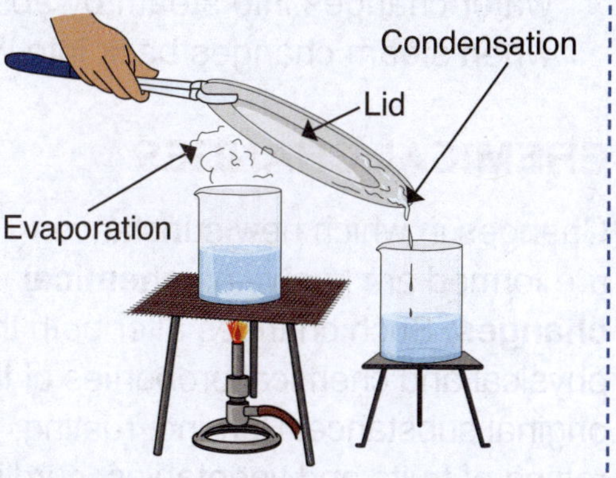

Observation: Upon heating, the water gradually converts into water vapour. When the vapour comes into contact with the cool surface of the plate, it condenses and changes back into water.

Conclusion: Both evaporation and condensation are physical changes as no new product is formed.

From Activity 1, it is clear that evaporation is a physical change. Water molecules do not lose their chemical identity. They only gain kinetic energy and leave the bulk and escape to form steam (gaseous state). The process can be reversed by condensing the vapours to form the water again. This shows that physical changes are generally reversible. Melting of ice cream, dissolution of sugar in water, sublimation of camphor, and folding of clothes are a few more examples of reversible physical changes.

Physical changes can be irreversible as well. Breaking of glass, tearing of paper, chopping of fruits and vegetables, cutting of wood, and breaking the shell of an egg are some of the examples of irreversible physical changes. In any of these cases, the pieces cannot be put together to give back the initial material.

Fig. 2.1 represents physical changes in the three states of matter.

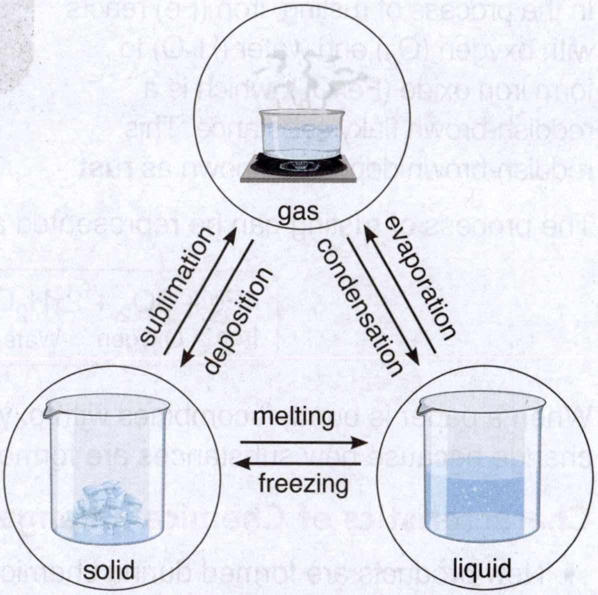

Fig. 2.1 Physical changes in states of matter

Characteristics of Physical Changes

- No new products are formed in physical changes.
- In physical changes, there might be change in one or more physical properties of the substance, such as shape, size, state, colour and density.
- Chemical properties and composition of the original substance do not change at all in physical changes.
- Physical changes can be reversible or irreversible in nature. For example, melting of ice is a reversible change, whereas breaking of glass is an irreversible change.
- During reversible physical changes, there is no net gain or loss of energy. For example, water changes into steam by absorbing a certain amount of energy, which is given out when steam changes back into water.

CHEMICAL CHANGES

Changes in which new substances are formed are known as **chemical changes**. Such changes alter both the physical and chemical properties of the original substance. Burning, rusting, rotting of fruits and vegetables, curdling of milk and formation of curd from milk are a few examples of chemical changes.

Fig. 2.2 Rusting of iron

In the process of rusting, iron (Fe) reacts with oxygen (O_2) and water (H_2O) to form iron oxide (Fe_2O_3), which is a reddish-brown flaky substance. This reddish-brown deposit is known as **rust**.

The process of rusting can be represented as:

$$\underset{\text{Iron}}{4Fe} + \underset{\text{Oxygen}}{3O_2} + \underset{\text{Water}}{2xH_2O} \longrightarrow \underset{\text{Rust}}{2Fe_2O_3 \cdot xH_2O}$$

When a paper is burnt, it combines with oxygen to form ash and smoke. It is a chemical change because new substances are formed.

Characteristics of Chemical Changes

- New products are formed during chemical changes.
- During chemical changes, the chemical composition and properties of the original substance change.
- Chemical changes are irreversible and permanent in nature.
- Energy change involved is more during chemical changes than during physical changes.
- During a chemical change, energy is either absorbed or released.

Table 2.2 lists the differences between physical and chemical changes.

Table 2.2 Differences between physical and chemical changes

Physical changes	Chemical changes
Only the physical properties of substances are changed.	Both the physical and the chemical properties of substances are changed.
Physical changes can either be reversible or irreversible in nature.	All chemical changes are permanent and cannot be reversed by simple physical methods.
No new products are formed.	New products are formed with properties different from the original substances.
The amount of energy absorbed or released is small.	A significant amount of energy is absorbed or released.

Signs of a Chemical Change

Given below are a few indicators for a chemical change. If two or more of these signs are observed, the change occurring is a chemical change.

- Change in colour
- Change in odour
- Change in temperature
- Production of heat and light
- Production of gas
- Formation of a precipitate

Here are some examples to understand these changes.

Change in colour: Some changes alter the colour of the reactants, that is, the colour of the product may differ from that of the reactants. For example, when an acid is added to the red cabbage indicator, the colour of the indicator changes from purple to pink. When a base is added to the indicator, its colour changes to blue.

Change in odour: In some changes, when two or more substances are mixed, a distinct odour is produced. Then it is a result of a chemical change.

Change in temperature: When carbon dioxide is bubbled through calcium hydroxide solution, a considerable amount of heat is produced during the reaction. The heat produced warms up the water.

$$\underset{\text{Calcium hydroxide}}{Ca(OH)_2} + \underset{\text{Carbon dioxide}}{CO_2} \longrightarrow \underset{\text{Calcium carbonate}}{CaCO_3} + \underset{\text{Water}}{H_2O} + \text{heat}$$

Production of heat and light: When a hydrocarbon reacts with oxygen to form carbon dioxide and water vapour, heat and light are produced. This type of chemical reaction is called a **combustion reaction**.

$$\underset{\text{Methane}}{CH_4} + \underset{\text{Oxygen}}{2O_2} \longrightarrow \underset{\text{Carbon dioxide}}{CO_2} + \underset{\text{Water}}{2H_2O} + \text{heat} + \text{light}$$

Production of gas: When dilute hydrochloric acid is added to a test tube containing granulated zinc, hydrogen gas is evolved.

$$\underset{\text{Zinc}}{Zn} + \underset{\text{Hydrochloric acid}}{2HCl} \longrightarrow \underset{\text{Zinc chloride}}{ZnCl_2} + \underset{\text{Hydrogen}}{H_2\uparrow} + \text{heat}$$

Formation of precipitate: When a solution of silver nitrate is added to the solution of sodium chloride, a white precipitate of silver chloride is formed.

$AgNO_3$	+	$NaCl$	$\longrightarrow$	$AgCl$	+	$NaNO_3$
Silver nitrate		Sodium chloride		Silver chloride (precipitate)		Sodium nitrate

A **precipitate** is an insoluble solid that forms during a chemical reaction and separates out from the solution.

Physical Changes that Show Signs of Chemical Changes

Some changes can be easily classified as a physical change or a chemical change. For example, the melting of ice is a physical change, while the boiling of an egg is a chemical change. But some changes are not easy to classify. The evidences for a chemical change are change in colour, change in temperature, production of gas and formation of precipitate. But sometimes, these indications may be the result of a physical change. Here are some examples of physical changes where signs of chemical changes are observed.

- **Change in colour:** Dissolving food-colouring agents in water results in a colour change. This colour change is caused due to the dissolution of the colouring agents. Moreover, no new products are formed, and hence, this is a physical change and not a chemical change.
- **Change in temperature:** When water is heated, there will be a change in temperature. However, as the chemical property of water is not affected due to heating, this is a physical change and not a chemical change.
- **Production of gas:** When a carbonated drink is poured into a glass, bubbles of carbon dioxide gas rise to the surface (Fig. 2.3). This could be misunderstood for a chemical change but the formation of bubbles is only a physical phenomenon in this case.

Fig. 2.3 Formation of bubbles in carbonated drinks

Burning of a Candle

When a candle burns, both physical and chemical changes occur (Fig. 2.4). The melting of the solid wax to form liquid wax and the evaporation of liquid wax to form wax vapour are physical changes. When this wax vapour burns, it gives heat, light and carbon dioxide. Thus, burning of a candle involves both physical and chemical changes taking place at the same time.

Fig. 2.4 A burning candle

QUICK REVISION

Classify the following changes as physical or chemical.

1. Beating a piece of aluminium to make foil
2. Sublimation of camphor
3. Formation of water vapour
4. Pickling of *amla*
5. Heating of an iron rod to soften it
6. Digestion of chocolate

CONCEPT MAP

Changes

- **Types of Changes**
  - Natural and Artificial
  - Fast and Slow
  - Reversible and Irreversible
  - Periodic and Non-periodic
  - Exothermic and Endothermic
  - Desirable and Undesirable
  - Physical and Chemical
- **Characteristics of Physical Changes**
  1. Changes in physical properties
  2. Do not involve the formation of a new substance
  3. Can be reversible or irreversible
- **Characteristics of Chemical Changes**
  1. Changes in chemical properties
  2. Involve the formation of one or more new substances
  3. Are irreversible

KEYWORDS

Periodic changes: changes that repeat after a fixed time interval

Non-periodic changes: changes that occur any time and do not repeat after a fixed time interval

Physical changes: changes in which no new substances are formed

Chemical changes: changes in which new substances with different properties are formed

Precipitate: an insoluble solid that forms during a chemical reaction and separates out from the solution

Exercise

Objective Type Questions

A. Choose the correct answer.

1. Which of the following is a reversible change?
   a. Melting of wax
   b. Boiling of vegetables
   c. Baking of biscuits
   d. Frying of food products
2. The occurrence of which of the following is a periodic change?
   a. Cyclone   b. Phases of moon
   c. Accident   d. Tsunami
3. Which of these is a physical change?
   a. Rusting of iron
   b. Burning of paper
   c. Folding of paper
   d. Cooking of food
4. Identify the characteristic of a chemical change.
   a. Change in both physical and chemical properties
   b. No formation of new products
   c. Temporary and reversible
   d. Minimal energy change
5. Which of the following statements is correct?
   a. Most of the chemical changes are reversible.
   b. Volume is a chemical property of a substance.
   c. Rusting of iron is an example of a physical change.
   d. A precipitate is the insoluble solid that is formed during a chemical reaction.

B. Fill in the blanks.

1. Cutting down of trees is a/an __________ (natural/artificial) change.
2. Germination of seeds is a __________ (fast/slow) change.
3. __________ (Boiling of water/Baking a cake) is a physical change.
4. Curdling of milk is a __________ (physical/chemical) change.
5. Rusting of iron is a/an __________ (desirable/undesirable) change.

C. Write T for True and F for False.

1. Burning of a matchstick is a fast change.
2. All changes in nature are reversible.
3. In a physical change, only one or more physical properties of a substance change.
4. Evaporation is a physical change.
5. Temperature change is the only feature of a chemical change.
6. During a chemical change, new products are formed.

Subjective Type Questions

A. Define the following.

1. Desirable changes
2. Exothermic changes
3. Physical properties
4. Chemical properties
5. Rusting

B. Differentiate between the following.

1. Natural and artificial changes
2. Fast and slow changes
3. Reversible and irreversible changes
4. Periodic and non-periodic changes

C. Answer the following questions in brief.

1. Define the term change. Give any two examples of a fast change.
2. What is a physical change? Give examples.
3. What is a chemical change? Give examples.
4. Why do materials rust?
5. Give an example of a physical change that shows signs of a chemical change.
6. Burning of a candle is both a physical and a chemical change. Why?

D. Answer the following questions in detail.

1. Distinguish between exothermic and endothermic changes. Explain with examples.
2. A change can be desirable at one time or undesirable at another time. Justify this statement with examples.
3. List the characteristics of physical and chemical changes.
4. What are the different indicators for a chemical change? Give examples.

Application-based Question

Observe and record all the changes happening in your daily life for a week. Classify the changes according to the parameters studied in this chapter.

Picture-based Question

Ashish took a potato and peeled a portion of it. He then added a few drops of iodine to the peeled portion of the potato with a dropper. He noticed that the colour of the peeled portion of the potato had turned blue-black. Now, answer the following questions.

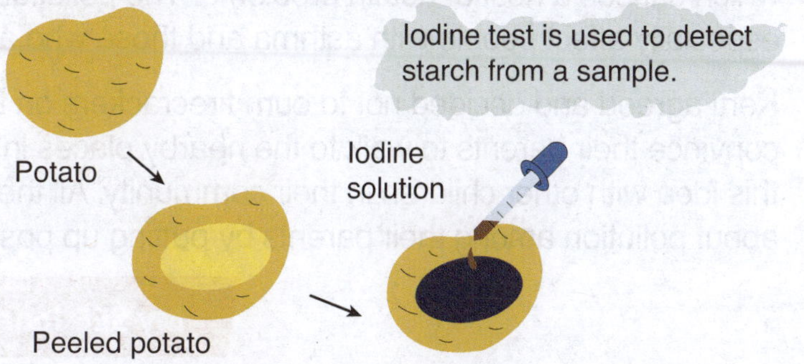

1. Is the peeling of a potato a physical or a chemical change?
2. Is the changing of the colour of the peeled potato to blue-black on addition of iodine, a physical or a chemical change?
3. If a peeled potato is left out in the open for some time, its surface turns brown. Is it a chemical change or a physical change?
4. Name a few more vegetables or fruits that turn brown when their cut surfaces are left in the open for some time.

Skill Booster

A. **21CS:** Critical Thinking, Life Skills | **EL** | **BT:** Cognitive, Affective

Sparsh made a supersaturated solution of sugar and water. He then recovered the sugar from this solution by applying the crystallization method. He claimed that dissolving sugar is a physical change. He then dissolved salt in water and evaporated all the water. He recovered the salt also. He concluded that the dissolution of both sugar and salt in water are physical changes. Udoy, Sparsh's classmate argued that dissolving sugar in water is a physical change but dissolving salt in water is a chemical change.
Who is correct and why?

B. **21CS:** Critical Thinking | **EL** | **BT:** Cognitive, Psychomotor

Materials required: Steel wool (wire sponge) and vinegar

Procedure:

1. Place steel wool in a cup and add 100 mℓ of vinegar into it.
2. Wait for 20 minutes and record your observations.

Did you observe any change? If yes, what is the type of change: physical or chemical? What evidence will you provide to prove it as a physical or a chemical change?

C. **21CS:** Critical Thinking, Information Literacy | **BT:** Cognitive

Lipakshi's uncle from Kerala gifted her a box of wafers and a box of her favourite coconut cookies. Lipakshi immediately opened the box of cookies and started eating. She wanted to open the box of wafers also. However, her mother stopped her and advised her to open the sealed box of wafers only after she finished the cookies.

1. Why do you think Lipakshi's mother asked her not to open the sealed box of wafers?
2. How are readymade snacks preserved for a longer time?

Worksheet 2

Sam and Kerti were good friends and lived in a community building, where they used to play together along with other friends during play time. As Diwali was approaching, Kerti started dreaming of buying and bursting crackers. She shared the same excitement with Sam. Sam, being a naturalist, opposed it. He said that the bursting of firecrackers leads to air pollution, which causes a host of health problems. The pollution caused by burning of firecrackers can especially affect people with asthma and those who are recovering from COVID.

Kerti agreed and decided not to burn firecrackers on Diwali. She suggested that they should also convince their parents to walk to the nearby places instead of using their vehicles. They shared this idea with other children in their community. All the children decided to spread awareness about pollution among their parents by putting up posters and placards in the building.

My SEE Journal

Do you think Sam and Kerti did the right thing by deciding not to burn firecrackers on Diwali? Justify your answer.

My SDG Journal

3 GOOD HEALTH AND WELL-BEING

Should bursting of firecrackers inside society's premises be banned as a safety measure? List down the consequences of bursting firecrackers inside the society's premises.

3 Elements, Compounds and Mixtures

Prior Knowledge

- Composition of substances
- Classification of substances
- Types of pure substances and mixtures with examples

Learning Objectives

- Elements
- Compounds
- Mixtures
- Methods of separation of mixtures

LET'S GET STARTED

Complete the flowchart given below.

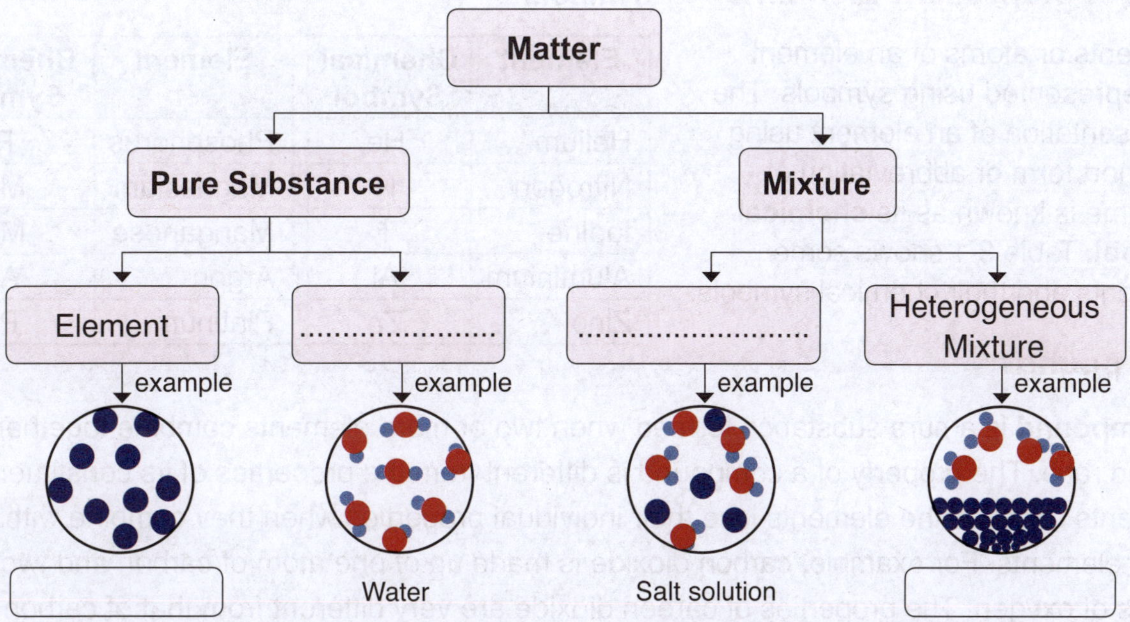

We use a variety of substances in our daily life. Each substance around us is made of matter. For example, the food we eat, the water we drink, the air we breathe, non-living objects such as table, chair, book, stars and clouds, and living things are all made of **matter**. All the things mentioned above have mass and occupy a certain space. Therefore, matter can be defined as anything that has mass and occupies space.

We have learned that each substance has a unique composition and substances have different properties due to differences in their state, size and shape. Based on their composition, all substances in nature can be broadly classified into pure and mixed substances. Mixed substances are also called **mixtures**. Most of the substances found in nature are mixtures. Let us revise the related concepts we have learnt in previous classes.

PURE SUBSTANCE

A substance that consists of only one kind of atoms or molecules is called a **pure substance**.

There are two types of pure substances: elements and compounds.

Elements

A substance that is made up of only one kind of atoms is called an **element**. Every element has its own unique properties. Some examples of elements are carbon, sodium, gold and oxygen.

Here are the characteristic features of elements.

- Elements consist of only one kind of atoms.
- Each element has its own unique, individual properties.
- The atoms of an element show the same properties as the element.
- Elements cannot be separated or broken down into simpler components by physical or simple chemical methods.

How to Represent Elements

Elements or atoms of an element are represented using symbols. The representation of an element using the short form or abbreviation of its name is known as its **chemical symbol**. Table 3.1 shows some elements and their chemical symbols.

Table 3.1 Some elements and their chemical symbols

Element	Chemical Symbol	Element	Chemical Symbol
Helium	He	Phosphorus	P
Nitrogen	N	Magnesium	Mg
Iodine	I	Manganese	Mn
Aluminium	Al	Argon	Ar
Zinc	Zn	Platinum	Pt

Compounds

A **compound** is a pure substance formed when two or more elements combine together in a fixed ratio. The property of a compound is different from the properties of its constituent elements because the elements lose their individual properties when they combine with other elements. For example, carbon dioxide is made up of one atom of carbon and two atoms of oxygen. The properties of carbon dioxide are very different from that of carbon and oxygen. Carbon is a solid but carbon dioxide is a gas.

Here are the characteristic features of compounds.

- Compounds are formed when two or more atoms of different elements combine together chemically in a fixed ratio.
- The properties of compounds are different from the properties of their constituent elements.
- Compounds exhibit their own physical and chemical properties.
- Compounds can be separated into their individual components by chemical methods.

How to Represent Compounds

We know that elements are represented by their symbols. Similarly, the representation of a compound using the symbols of its constituent elements is called its **chemical formula**.

When the number of atoms of an element in a molecule is one, then the subscript is not written.

For example, the chemical formula of magnesium chloride is $MgCl_2$. This indicates that it has one atom of magnesium and two atoms of chlorine. Table 3.2 gives the chemical formulae of some compounds.

Table 3.2 Some compounds and their chemical formulae

Compound	Chemical Formula	Compound	Chemical Formula
Water	H_2O	Magnesium oxide	MgO
Sodium chloride (common salt)	$NaCl$	Copper sulphate	$CuSO_4$
Hydrochloric acid	HCl	Ammonia	NH_3
Sodium carbonate	Na_2CO_3	Methane	CH_4

Significance of a Chemical Formula

A chemical formula gives the characteristics of a compound. The following information can be drawn from a chemical formula:

- The chemical name of the compound
- The elements present in the compound
- The number of atoms of each element present in each molecule of the compound

MIXTURES

A **mixture** is a substance that contains two or more different substances mixed together in any ratio. Different types of substances present in a mixture are called its components or constituents.

Types of Mixtures

Based on the state of substances that are mixed together, mixtures can be classified into the six types shown in Fig. 3.1.

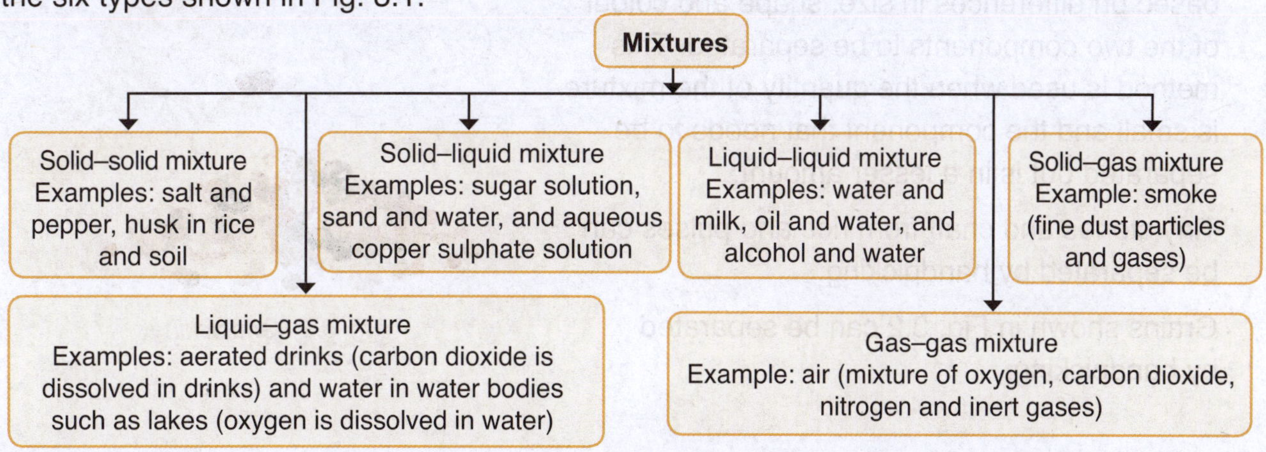

Fig. 3.1 Classification of mixtures

Based on the distribution of two or more substances that are mixed together, mixtures can be classified as homogeneous and heterogeneous.

- **Homogeneous mixtures:** The mixtures in which the components that make up the mixture are distributed uniformly are called **homogeneous mixtures**.

  Air is an example of a homogeneous mixture. We cannot see the different gases present in the air distinctly. Another example is a mixture of salt and water.

- **Heterogeneous mixtures:** The mixtures in which the components that make up the mixture are not distributed uniformly are called **heterogeneous mixtures**.

  A mixture of oil and water is an example of a heterogeneous mixture. We can see the oil and water distinctly in the mixture. Mud and water, sand and stones, rice and pulses are some other examples of heterogeneous mixtures.

SEPARATION OF MIXTURES

Separation of mixtures is necessary due to the following reasons:

- To separate useful components from a mixture. For example, by churning milk, the cream is separated from milk so that both the components can be used appropriately.
- To remove unwanted materials or impurities from a mixture. For example, separation of husk from rice grains, stones from rice grains or pulses before cooking and separation of unwanted leaves from raw leafy vegetables.
- To get desirable or pure substances. For example, in the preparation of tea, tea leaves are separated from brewed tea.

METHODS OF SEPARATION OF MIXTURES

Different components of a mixture have different chemical and physical properties. Hence, selecting the appropriate method of separation for a mixture depends on the characteristic properties of each component. Let us look at the various techniques used to separate the components of a mixture.

Separating Solid–Solid Mixtures

1. **Handpicking:** This method of separation is based on differences in size, shape and colour of the two components to be separated. This method is used when the quantity of the mixture is small and the component that needs to be separated out is in a lesser amount.

   Tiny stones and chaff from rice and pulses can be separated by handpicking.

   Grains shown in Fig. 3.2 can be separated by handpicking.

Fig. 3.2 Handpicking

2. **Threshing:** The process of separating grains from stalks of harvested crops either by beating the stalks against a hard surface or by using a threshing machine is called **threshing** (Fig. 3.3).

   Substances that can be separated by threshing are all types of stalks with grains such as wheat, oats, barley and rice.

Fig. 3.3 Threshing

3. **Winnowing:** The process of separating grains (heavier components) from chaff (lighter components) by the action of blowing wind is called **winnowing** (Fig. 3.4). This method of separation is based on the difference in weight of the two components to be separated.

   Substances that can be separated by winnowing are all types of grains which are covered by husk such as rice and wheat.

Fig. 3.4 Winnowing

ACTIVITY 1

Aim: To separate a mixture of paper bits and wheat by winnowing

Materials required: A mixture of wheat and small bits of paper, a sheet of cloth, a table fan and a plate or basket

Procedure:

1. Take the mixture in the plate or basket.
2. Spread the sheet of cloth on the floor.
3. Now, stand on a chair or stool and gradually drop the mixture on the piece of cloth. Ensure that the fan is placed in the direction as shown in the figure given alongside. Observe what happens.

   (**Note:** *The speed of the table fan should be kept at the lowest.*)

Observation: Wheat being heavy falls vertically on the sheet of cloth and forms a heap, whereas the paper bits being light get carried away and fall some distance away from the mixture.

Conclusion: Solid components with different densities can be separated by winnowing.

4. **Sieving:** The method of using a sieve to separate undesirable components from a mixture is called **sieving**. This method of separation is based on the difference in the sizes of the components to be separated.

   Either the desired component or the impurities to be separated should have particles of size smaller than the sieve pores. The larger component is left behind on the sieve, while the smaller component passes through the pores of the sieve.

   Substances that can be separated by sieving are substances that have bran or impurities in them such as flour and semolina. Wheat flour is sieved before making dough (Fig. 3.5). During construction of buildings, stones and pebbles are removed from sand by sieving.

Fig. 3.5 Sieving

ACTIVITY 2

Aim: To separate the components of a mixture by sieving

Materials required: A mixture of talcum powder, mustard seeds and resins, two sieves with different pore sizes and a big bowl

Procedure:

1. Put the mixture into the sieve with a small pore size.
2. Place a bowl below the sieve and shake the sieve to and fro.
3. Talcum powder will pass through the sieve pores but mustard seeds and resins will be left behind.
4. Transfer the mixture of mustard seeds and resins into the sieve with larger pore size and shake the sieve to and fro.
5. This time, mustard seeds will pass through the pores of the sieve but resins will be left behind on the sieve.

Observation: When the mixture is passed through the sieve with a small pore size, the talcum powder separates first, leaving behind mustard seeds and raisins. When the remaining mixture is passed through the sieve with a larger pore size, the mustard seeds separate from the mixture, leaving behind only raisins on the sieve. Thus, all the three components of the mixture are separated by sieving.

Conclusion: Solid components from a mixture can be separated using sieves of the right pore size.

5. **Magnetic separation:** The method of using a magnet to separate the magnetic components from a mixture is called **magnetic separation**. This method is based on the difference in the magnetic properties of the components to be separated, that is, a magnetic substance gets attracted to a magnet. In this method, a magnet is rotated over a mixture so that the magnetic components cling to the magnet, while the non-magnetic components are left behind. This method is used in industries to remove scrap iron from a garbage heap with the help of a large magnet fitted to a crane.

   Fig. 3.6 shows the separation of iron filings from a mixture of sulphur and iron filings using a magnet.

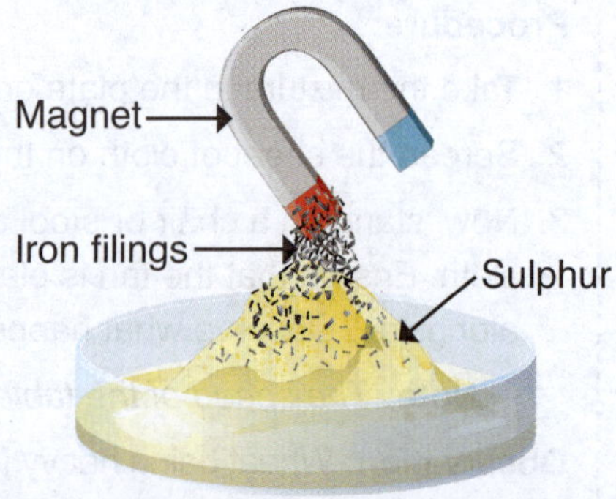

Fig. 3.6 Separation of iron filings and sulphur powder using a magnet

ACTIVITY 3

Aim: To separate a mixture of sand and iron filings by magnetic separation

Materials required: A mixture of sand and iron filings, a china dish and a magnet

Procedure:

1. Take the mixture of sand and iron filings in a china dish.
2. Now, hover and rotate the magnet over the mixture. What do you see?

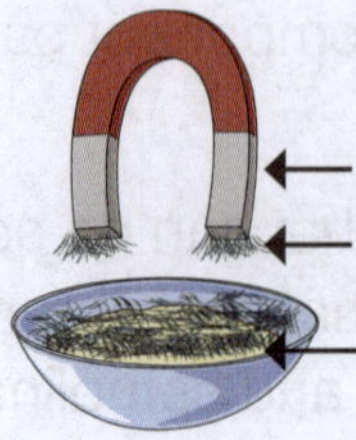

Observation: The iron filings get attracted and cling to the magnet leaving behind the sand.

Conclusion: Magnetic components of a mixture can be separated using a magnet.

6. **Sublimation:** The process in which a solid changes directly into its gaseous state without passing through its liquid state is called **sublimation**. This method is used when a mixture contains a component that can sublime.

In this method, the mixture is taken in an evaporating dish. When the mixture is heated, the solid component that sublimes evaporates as vapours, leaving behind the component that does not sublime in the dish. Then, the sublimed solid is obtained by cooling the vapours. Thus, the mixture is separated (Fig. 3.7).

Iodine, camphor and ammonium chloride are sublimable substances.

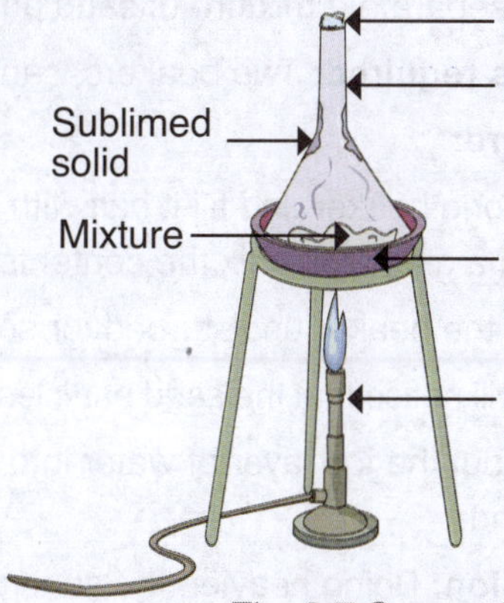

Fig. 3.7 Separation by sublimation

QUICK REVISION

Fill in the blanks using the correct words.

1. Pebbles and stones can be separated from sand by __________. (sieving/winnowing)
2. The method used by farmers to separate lighter husk particles from heavier seeds of grains is __________. (winnowing/handpicking)
3. Handpicking is a method to separate __________ mixtures. (solid–solid/solid–liquid)
4. The mixture of rice flour and husk can be separated by __________. (threshing/sieving)
5. Stones can be separated from pulses by __________. (handpicking/sieving)

Separating Solid–Liquid Mixtures

To separate solid–liquid mixtures, the selection of the appropriate method depends on whether the solid component is soluble or insoluble in the liquid.

The process of sedimentation can be speeded up by adding potash alum (*phitkari*). This process is called **loading**.

Methods to Separate Insoluble Solids from Solid–Liquid Mixtures

The following methods are used for separating a solid–liquid mixture when the solid is insoluble in the liquid.

Sedimentation and decantation: The settling down of heavier insoluble solid particles present in a solid–liquid mixture when left undisturbed is called **sedimentation**. The solid that settles down during sedimentation is called **sediment** while the clear liquid above is called the **supernatant**. This method is then followed by decantation in which the clear liquid is poured out without disturbing the sediment.

The process of pouring out the top clear liquid without disturbing the sediment is called **decantation**.

This method is used to separate the components of heterogeneous solid–liquid mixture where a solid component is insoluble and heavier than the liquid component.

Sedimentation and decantation are used at home while washing rice and pulses with water. The upper layer of water that contains the impurities is decanted and the sediments (pulses) are used further.

ACTIVITY 4

Aim: To separate a mixture of sand and water by sedimentation and decantation

Materials required: Two beakers, sand, water and a glass rod

Procedure:

1. Take one beaker and fill it half with water. Add a small amount of sand to it. Using a glass rod, mix the contents of the beaker.
2. Keep the beaker undisturbed for some time.
3. You will notice that the sand particles settle down at the bottom of the beaker.
4. Pour out the top layer of water into another beaker without disturbing the layer of sand.

Conclusion: Being heavier, the sand particles settle down at the bottom of the beaker, forming a layer of clear water on the top. Pouring the top layer carefully into another beaker separates the two components of this mixture.

Filtration: The process of separating the insoluble solids suspended in a liquid using a porous medium (filter) is called **filtration**. Filters with different pore sizes are available. The pores of the filter should be smaller than the size of the components that need to be removed. The insoluble solid component left in the filter is called the **residue**. The liquid that passes through the filter is called the **filtrate**. Straining tea using a tea strainer (Fig. 3.8) is a common example of filtration used in almost every household. Separating seeds from orange juice and lemon juice are some more examples of filtration used in homes.

Fig. 3.8 Filtration

ACTIVITY 5

Aim: To separate a mixture of sand and water by filtration

Materials required: Two beakers, sand, water, a glass rod, filter paper, a clamp, a stand and a funnel

Procedure:

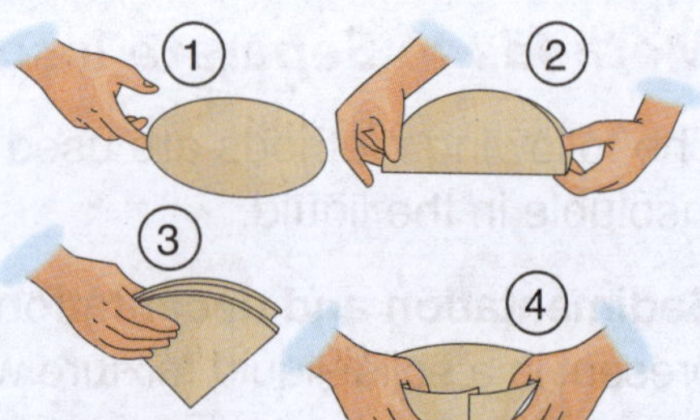

1. Take some sand in a beaker. Add some water to it and use a glass rod to mix the contents of the beaker.
2. Take a filter paper and make a cone as shown in the figure given alongside. Place the paper cone in the funnel and fix it using a clamp stand. Keep an empty beaker below the funnel.
3. Gently pour the mixture into the funnel.

Observation: You will notice that clear water collects in the beaker after passing through the filter paper and sand particles are left behind on the filter paper.

Centrifugation: The process that involves rotating a mixture rapidly in a closed container to separate very fine, insoluble solid components mixed in a liquid is called **centrifugation**.

The machine used for centrifugation is called a **centrifuge** (Fig. 3.9). A centrifuge consists of a rotating motor with holes to place centrifuge tubes. These tubes contain the mixture to be separated. When the centrifuge is switched on, the motor rotates the mixture at a very high speed due to which the heavier components settle down at the bottom of the tubes. The sediment in the tubes is then separated from the liquid by decantation. The lighter components of the mixture remain in the liquid. This method is used in laboratories to separate cells from blood and in dairies to separate cream from milk.

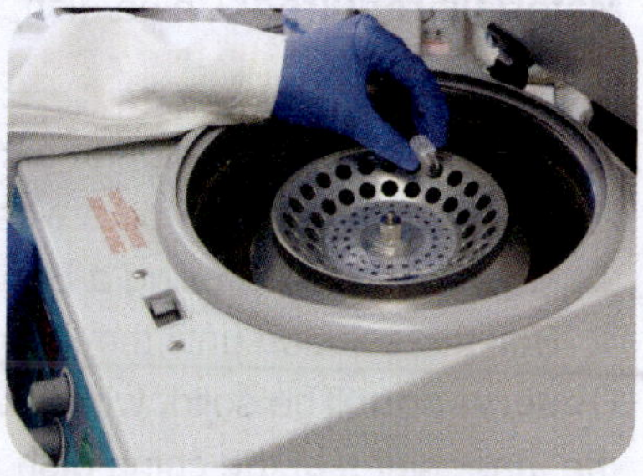

Fig. 3.9 A centrifuge

Methods to Separate Soluble Solids from Solid-Liquid Mixtures

The following methods are used for separating a solid–liquid mixture when the solid is soluble in the liquid.

Evaporation: The process in which a liquid converts into its gaseous state is called **evaporation**. This method is used to separate soluble solids from liquids.

Evaporation is the process used to obtain common salt from seawater. Seawater consists of a large amount of salts in it. It is allowed to flow through narrow channels near coastal areas and get collected in shallow ponds called **salt pans** (Fig. 3.10). The water in these salt pans is then allowed to evaporate by the heat of the sun. The solid salt is left behind as the water evaporates. The salt is then collected and sent for purification. The purified salt is used for various purposes.

Fig. 3.10 Separation of salt from seawater by evaporation

Distillation: The separation method used to separate a pure liquid from a solution by evaporation followed by condensation is called **distillation**. The process of distillation is carried out in special laboratory apparatus. The process involves the following steps:

- The mixture is heated in a round-bottomed flask. Due to heating, the liquid component in the mixture evaporates to form vapours and the solid component is left behind in the flask.
- A condenser is fitted to the flask. The vapour of the liquid rises and passes through this condenser where it cools down and condenses to form pure liquid.
- This pure liquid is collected in a separate flask.

TALK TIME

What kind of impurities can the salt contain that must be removed before use?

Distillation is used to obtain distilled water, which is considered to be the purest form of water as it does not contain any impurities. Distilled water is used in science laboratories, car batteries and medicines.

ACTIVITY 6

Aim: To demonstrate the separation of salt from salt solution by the evaporation

Materials required: China dish, salt solution, wire gauze, Bunsen burner and tripod stand

Procedure:

1. Take some salt solution in a china dish.
2. Place the china dish on a wire gauze kept on a tripod stand.
3. Heat the solution using a Bunsen burner.
4. Boil the solution until the liquid evaporates completely.

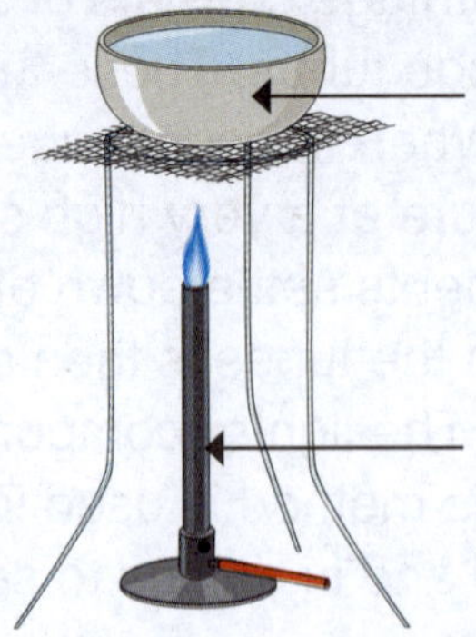

Observation: The solid, white particles of salt are left behind along the inner sides of the china dish after evaporation.

Conclusion: Soluble solids present in a solid–liquid mixture can be separated by evaporation method.

ACTIVITY 7

Aim: To demonstrate the separation of the components of a solid–liquid mixture by distillation method

Materials required: Round-bottom flask, solution of salt and water, beaker, condenser, Bunsen burner and laboratory stands

Procedure:

1. Set up the apparatus as shown in the figure given alongside.
2. Heat the mixture in the round-bottomed flask.
3. The mixture starts to boil and the liquid component (water) evaporates.
4. The vapour passes through the condenser, where it cools and condenses to form the pure liquid that gets collected in the beaker.
5. The solid component of the mixture (salt) is left behind.

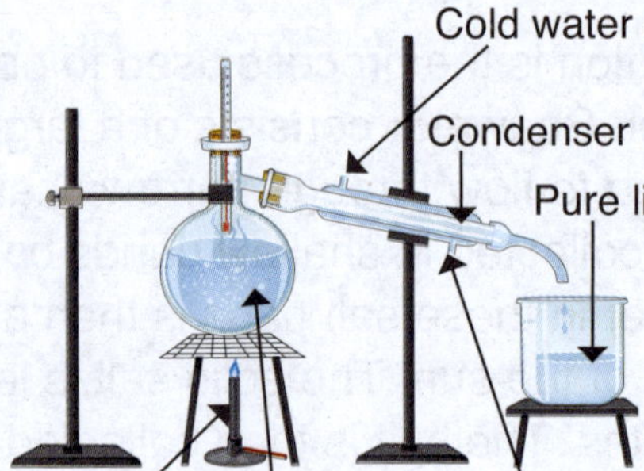

Observation: The liquid component is separated from the solid–liquid mixture leaving behind the solid component. The liquid thus obtained is in its pure form.

Conclusion: The components of a solid-liquid mixture can be separated by distillation method.

Crystallization: The process of separating a solid in its pure form from its solution by forming crystals is known as **crystallization**. Common salt obtained from seawater is purified by crystallization. Common salt (sodium chloride) is obtained from seawater by evaporation. The salt obtained by this process consists of many impurities such as sand and magnesium chloride. This impure salt is purified by crystallization.

For crystallization, a large amount of salt is dissolved in water. The solution is heated and, if needed, more salt is added to the solution till it becomes a saturated solution. The solution is then filtered to separate the insoluble impurities, such as sand, present in it. The filtrate is then allowed to cool and the salt present in the solution aggregates to form crystals. The salt crystals are separated by filtration and then dried.

Separating Liquid–Liquid Mixtures

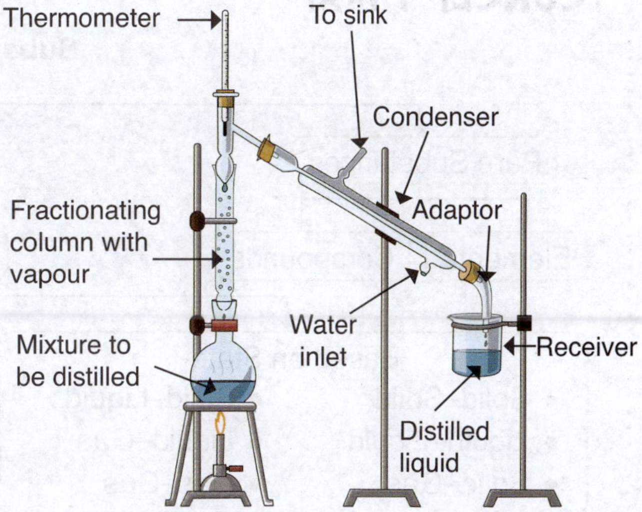

Fig. 3.11 Set-up of fractional distillation

Fractional distillation: Fractional distillation is the method used to separate a mixture of miscible liquids (liquids that completely mix together). This method is based on the difference in the boiling points of the liquid components to be separated. The apparatus used for this method consists of a distillation flask, fractionating column, a condenser and heat supply (Fig. 3.11). When a mixture of two or more liquids is heated in the distillation flask, the liquid with a lower boiling point vaporizes first, rises to the top of the column and passes through the condenser. Here, the vapour cools down and condenses to form a pure liquid, which is collected in a receiver. The temperature remains constant until the whole of that liquid distils over. Then the temperature is slowly increased and the second liquid starts vaporizing at its boiling point. Vapour of the second liquid rises through the fractionating column, gets condensed and is collected into another receiver. In a similar way, all the components of the liquid mixture are separated. This method is used in oil refineries to get petroleum products, such as petrol, kerosene, diesel, gasoline, petroleum gas and tar, from crude oil.

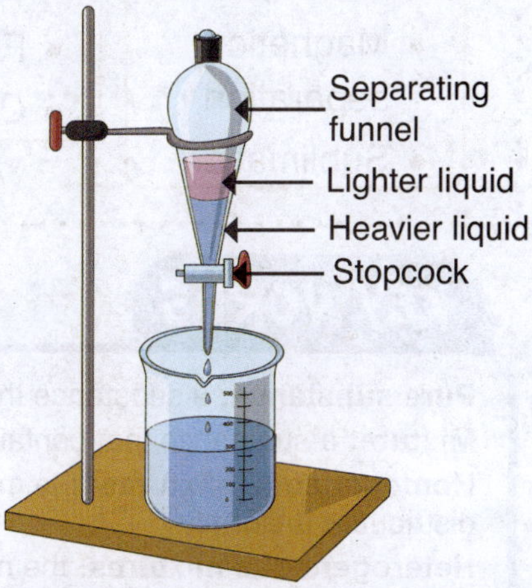

Fig. 3.12 Separation using a separating funnel

Separating funnel: A separating funnel (Fig. 3.12) is used to separate a mixture of immiscible liquids. This method is based on the principle that in immiscible liquids, the lighter liquid floats above the layer of the heavier liquid.

A separating funnel is a glass apparatus that is narrow at the bottom with a stopcock (like a tap). The funnel has an opening at the top to pour the liquid mixture. After the liquid mixture is poured, it is left undisturbed for some time. Immiscible liquids form separate layers with the heavier liquid at the bottom and the lighter liquid at the top. When the stopcock is opened, the heavier liquid at the bottom moves out first and is collected in a separate container. When the bottom layer flows out completely, the stopcock is closed. Only the lighter liquid remains in the separating funnel. Thus, the two liquids are separated.

A mixture of oil and water can be separated using this technique.

QUICK REVISION

Write T for True and F for False.

1. Decantation is the best process for removing tea leaves from tea.
2. A mixture of milk and water can be separated by sedimentation and decantation.
3. The preferred method to recover clear water from a bucket of muddy water is filtration.
4. Evaporation is used to obtain salt from seawater.

CONCEPT MAP

- **Substances**
  - Pure Substances
    - Elements
    - Compounds
  - Mixtures
    - Classification
      - Based on State
        - Solid–Solid
        - Solid–Liquid
        - Liquid–Liquid
        - Liquid–Gas
        - Solid–Gas
        - Gas–Gas
      - Based on Distribution of Components
        - Heterogeneous
        - Homogeneous
    - Separation
      - Solid–Solid
        - Handpicking
        - Threshing
        - Winnowing
        - Sieving
        - Magnetic separation
        - Sublimation
      - Solid–Liquid
        - Insoluble Solids
          - Sedimentation and decantation
          - Filtration
          - Centrifugation
        - Soluble Solids
          - Evaporation
          - Distillation
          - Crystallization
      - Liquid–Liquid
        - Fractional distillation
        - Separating funnel

KEYWORDS

Pure substance: a substance that consists of only one kind of atoms or molecules

Mixture: a substance that contains two or more different substances mixed together in any ratio

Homogeneous mixtures: the mixtures in which the constituents that make up the mixture are distributed uniformly

Heterogeneous mixtures: the mixtures in which the constituents that make up the mixture are not distributed uniformly

Threshing: the process of separation of grains from stalks by beating the stalks against a hard surface or by using threshing machines

Sieving: a method that uses a sieve to separate undesirable components from a solid–solid mixture

Winnowing: a method that uses the action of wind to separate undesirable components from a solid–solid mixture

Sedimentation: the process in which the insoluble, heavier particles of a solution settle down at the bottom of the container

Decantation: the process of transferring clear liquid collected at the top of a mixture without disturbing the sediment at the bottom

Filtration: the process of using a porous medium (filter) to separate the fine, insoluble solid components suspended in a liquid

Centrifugation: the process of separating very fine, insoluble solid components mixed in a liquid using a centrifuge

Distillation: the method of separating the components of a mixture through evaporation and condensation

Fractional distillation: the process of separating the miscible liquids present in a mixture based on the difference in their boiling points

Exercise

Objective Type Questions

A. Choose the correct answer.

1. A substance that contains two or more substances mixed together is a ________.
   a. compound b. mixture
   c. element d. molecule
2. Which of the following methods is used to separate stones from rice before cooking?
   a. Handpicking b. Threshing
   c. Winnowing d. Filtration
3. Which of the following parameters is used to separate a mixture of two solids by winnowing?
   a. Weight difference b. Size difference
   c. Colour difference d. All of these
4. The process of pouring out the upper layer of clear liquid without disturbing the sediment is called ________.
   a. sedimentation b. evaporation
   c. decantation d. distillation
5. The component of the mixture retained on the filter during filtration is called ________.
   a. residue b. filtrate
   c. sediment d. effluent
6. Sublimation can be used to separate a mixture of
   a. sand and ammonium chloride
   b. sand and sugar
   c. iron filings and salt
   d. stones and rice

B. Fill in the blanks.

1. A ________ (compound/mixture) is formed when two or more elements combine together chemically.
2. The mixtures in which the components are distributed uniformly are called ________ (homogeneous/ heterogeneous) mixtures.
3. The chemical formula for sodium carbonate is ________ ($NaCO_3$/Na_2CO_3).
4. Filtration is used when the substances to be separated are ________ (soluble/ insoluble) in a liquid.
5. While using a separating funnel, the first liquid to be collected in a beaker will be ________ (water/oil).

C. Write T for True and F for False.

1. Compounds are impure substances.
2. Salt water is a homogeneous mixture.
3. Sieving allows fine flour particles to remain in the sieve while the bigger impurities pass through the sieve.
4. Sedimentation is followed by decantation in the separation of solid–liquid mixtures.
5. A centrifuge is used to separate very fine, insoluble solid components from a solution.

Subjective Type Questions

A. Define the following.

1. Element
2. Winnowing
3. Threshing
4. Filtration
5. Crystallization

B. Choose the odd one out. Give reasons for the choice.

1. Iodine, camphor, sugar, ammonium chloride
2. Winnowing, distillation, handpicking, threshing
3. Sieving, evaporation, filtration, centrifugation
4. Distillation, centrifugation, evaporation, crystallization
5. Water, coffee, tea, lemon juice

C. Differentiate between the following.

1. Homogeneous mixture and heterogeneous mixture
2. Handpicking and winnowing
3. Sedimentation and decantation
4. Evaporation and crystallization
5. Distillation and fractional distillation

D. Answer the following questions in brief.

1. What is the difference between an element and a compound?
2. What is a homogeneous mixture? Give an example.
3. What is a heterogeneous mixture? Give an example.
4. How is sieving used at construction sites?

5. Mention the appropriate methods for the separation of the following mixtures:
   a. A solid–solid mixture in which the components have different sizes
   b. A mixture that has components with different magnetic properties
   c. A mixture of liquids with different boiling points
6. Name the methods used to separate a solid–liquid mixture.
7. Why is distilled water the purest form of water? Give its uses.

E. Answer the following questions in detail.

1. Define mixture. Mention the different types of mixtures.
2. What are the different methods used to separate a solid–solid mixture? Explain any two.
3. What is a centrifuge? What kind of mixture is separated using it and how?
4. Explain the method of distillation with the help of a diagram.
5. Describe the process of fractional distillation.
6. Explain how immiscible liquids are separated using a separating funnel.

Application-based Question

How will you separate the following mixtures? Name the methods that can be used.

1. Sugar, iron filings and wheat
2. $CaCO_3$ and NaCl
3. Kerosene and water

Picture-based Question

Look at the picture and answer the following questions.

1. Label the diagram.
2. Explain the principle behind this separation technique.
3. Give two combinations of mixtures that can be separated using this apparatus.

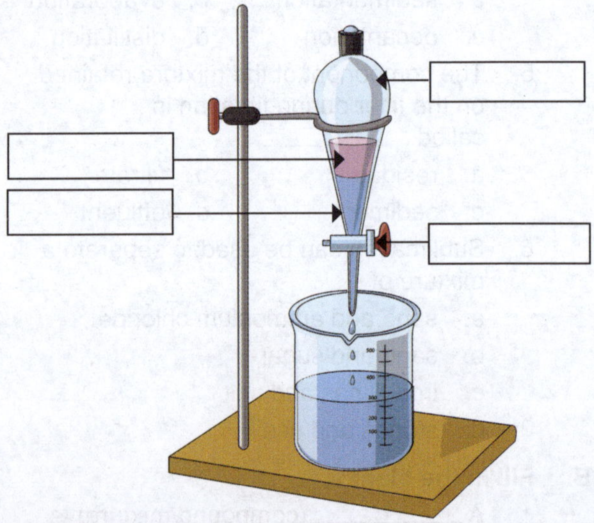

Skill Booster

A. 21CS: Information Literacy | CC: English | BT: Cognitive

Visit a water treatment plant and find out how many methods are used to treat the water before it is let into the taps for use. Write a report on the entire process involved in the cleaning of water.

B. 21CS: Critical Thinking, Technology Literacy | CC: Computer Science | BT: Cognitive, Affective

Iron and iron oxide content in waterbodies leads to adverse effects on aquatic animals and human beings. What happens if these toxic substances are not separated from industrial effluents? Collect more information on the effects and diseases caused by the presence of these toxic substances in water from the Internet.

Worksheet 3

My SEE Journal

A. What would be your answer if you were in Naitik's place?

____

____

____

B. What values do you get from Naitik and Navvya?

____

____

My SDG Journal

Many countries that do not have enough freshwater resources to meet the needs of their populations process seawater to make it potable. Does it have any adverse effects on marine life? Read about it on the Internet and write a short note.

____

____

____

____

4 Atomic Structure

Prior Knowledge

- Definition of atom
- Names of subatomic particles

Learning Objectives

- Earlier views on atomic structure
- Subatomic particles (electrons, protons and neutrons) and their discoveries
- Discovery of nucleus
- Atomic models
- Modern concept of the atom
- Atomic number and mass number
- Electronic configuration
- Valency and variable valency

LET'S GET STARTED

Observe the image of the subatomic particles and answer the following questions.

1. What is the charge carried by the electrons?

 ____

2. What is the charge carried by the neutrons?

 ____

3. The path that electrons will revolve is referred to as

 ______________________________.

4. Why is an atom neutral?

 ____

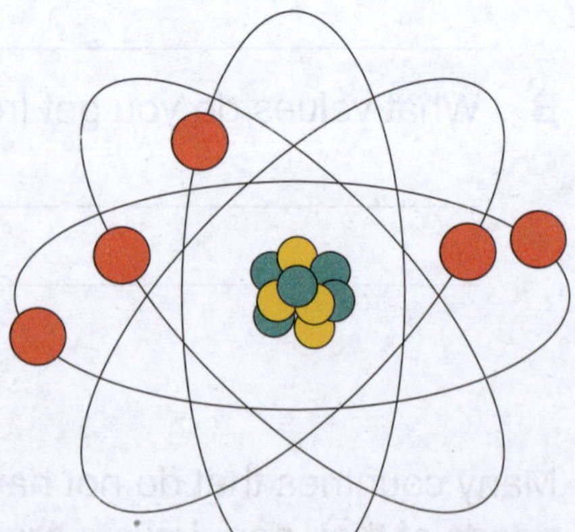

We have learnt in our previous classes that everything in this universe is made up of matter and all matter is made up of tiny particles called **atoms**. In other words, atoms are the building blocks of matter. Atoms were initially thought to be very small particles that cannot be further divided or split into smaller particles. Since then, many scientists from different generations have dedicated their lives to solve the mystery behind these atoms.

In this chapter, we will learn in detail about the contributions of various scientists who were involved in the study of the atom, its structure, properties and constituents.

EARLIER VIEWS ON ATOMIC STRUCTURE

Maharshi Kanada was an ancient Indian philosopher and scientist of 600 BC. He postulated that matter consists of very small particles, which he termed as *anu*. He also proposed that an *anu* may consist of subatomic particles, which he termed as *paramanu*, meaning a particle that cannot be further divided or broken down.

Democritus, a great Greek philosopher of 400 BC, stated that matter is made up of tiny particles called atoms and these atoms are invisible and indivisible. The word atom comes from the Greek word *atomos* in which *a* means 'not' and *tomos* means 'to cut'. That is, a particle that cannot be cut or divided anymore. Before Democritus, the concept of atom was originally proposed by the Greek philosopher Leucippus who was the teacher of Democritus. Democritus worked on his teacher's assumptions and put forward his ideas.

Dalton's Atomic Theory

John Dalton, an English chemist, postulated the atomic theory. His theory became the theoretical foundation in the field of chemistry. The postulates of Dalton's atomic theory are as follows:

- Matter is composed of tiny particles called atoms.
- Atoms are indivisible and cannot be created or destroyed.
- All atoms of an element are identical in all aspects, that is, all atoms of an element have the same mass, size and other properties.
- Atoms of different elements are different in all respects, that is, atoms of an element have different mass, size and other properties from atoms of other elements.
- Atom is the smallest unit of matter that takes part in a chemical reaction.
- Atoms of two or more elements combine together in small whole number ratios to form compounds.
- During a chemical reaction, atoms do not change but only rearrange themselves to form new compounds.

John Dalton's atomic theory was later modified as further discoveries were made in this field. Eventually, by the end of the 19th century, it was discovered that atoms are made up of tinier particles called **subatomic** or **fundamental particles**. These subatomic particles are called protons, neutrons and electrons.

Let us learn about how these particles were discovered and how these discoveries modified the views on atomic structure (Fig. 4.1).

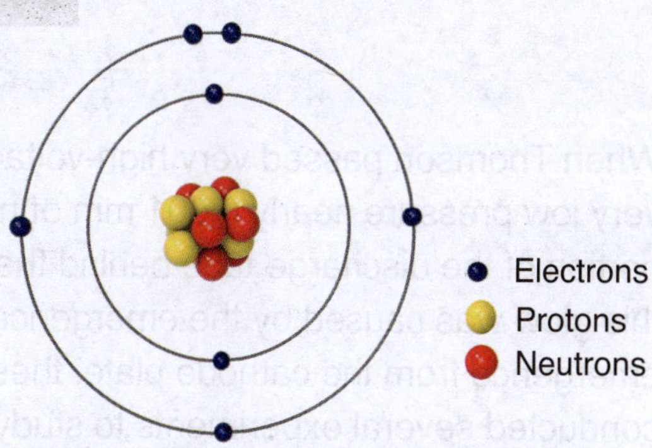

Fig. 4.1 Subatomic particles of an atom

DISCOVERY OF ELECTRONS

Electrons were the first subatomic particles to be discovered. In 1897, British scientist J.J. Thomson discovered the negatively charged particles known as electrons through the cathode ray-discharge tube experiment. He received the Nobel Prize in Physics in the year 1906 for his research on cathode rays.

J.J. Thomson's Cathode Ray Experiment

Thomson used a special tube called **discharge tube** for his experiment (Fig. 4.2). It is a hard, cylindrical glass tube that consists of two metal plates called **electrodes**, each sealed at the two ends of the tube. The metal plates are connected to the two terminals of a high-voltage battery.

The metal plate that is connected to the negative terminal acts as a cathode. The metal plate that is connected to the positive terminal acts as an anode. A vacuum pump is connected to one side of the tube to lower the pressure inside the tube.

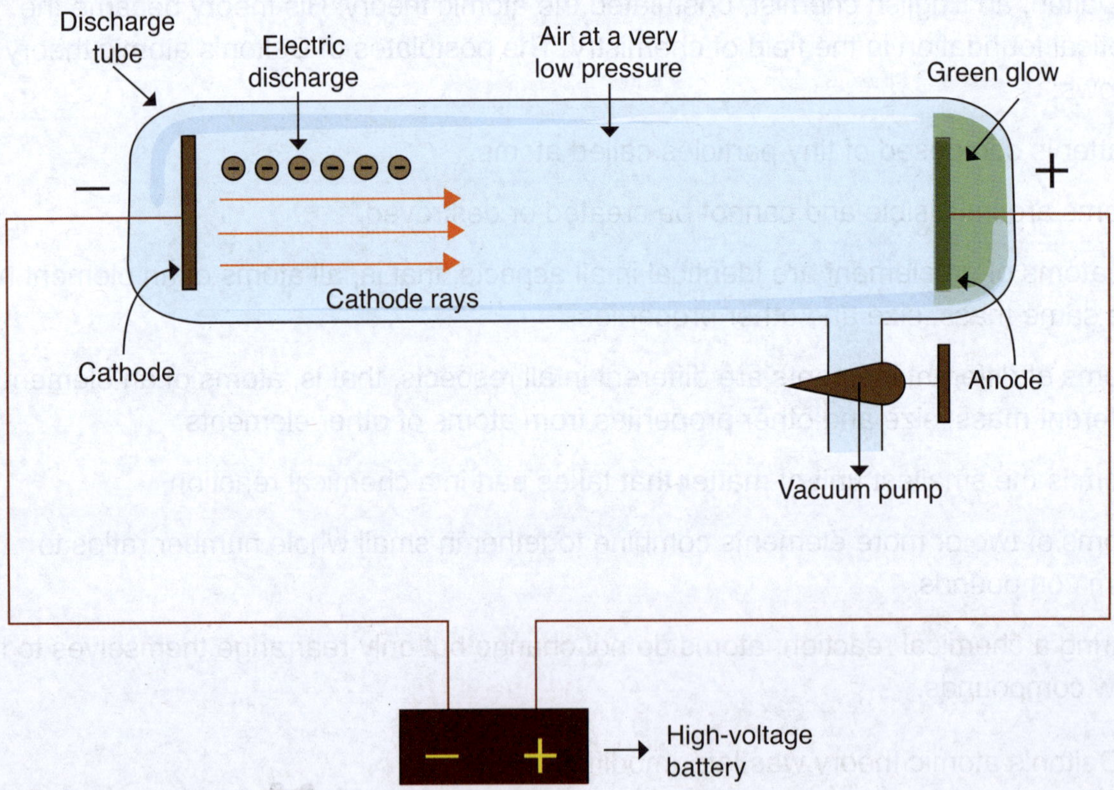

Fig. 4.2 Cathode ray experiment

When Thomson passed very high-voltage of 10,000 volts through the discharge tube at a very low pressure nearly 0.001 mm of mercury, he observed a fluorescent green glow on the portion of the discharge tube behind the anode plate. From this observation, he concluded that this glow was caused by the emergence of invisible rays from the cathode plate. Due to their emergence from the cathode plate, these rays were called **cathode rays**. Then, Thomson conducted several experiments to study the nature and composition of these rays and concluded that cathode rays consist of negatively charged particles that are present in atoms of all elements.

Characteristics of Cathode Rays

From the various experiments performed by J.J. Thomson, the following characteristics of cathode rays were identified.

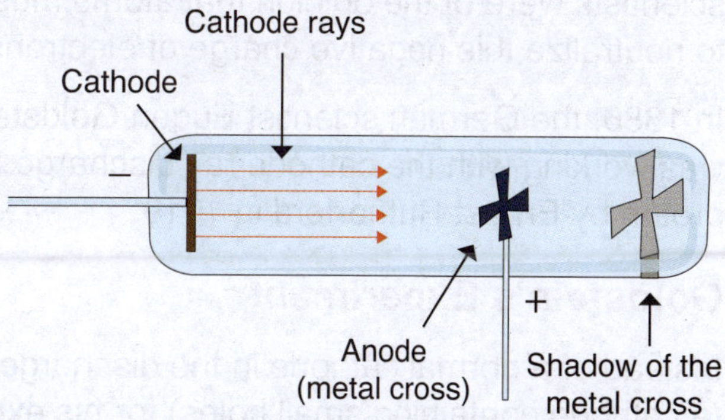

Fig. 4.3 Cathode rays form a shadow if an object is placed in their path

- **Cathode rays travel in straight lines:** When an object is placed in the path of cathode rays, a shadow of the object appears at the other end of the discharge tube (Fig. 4.3). This shows that the cathode rays travel in a straight line.
- **Cathode rays consist of fast-moving particles:** If a light paddle wheel is placed in the path through which cathode rays pass, it starts rotating (Fig. 4.4). This proves that the cathode rays consist of a stream of fast-moving particles.

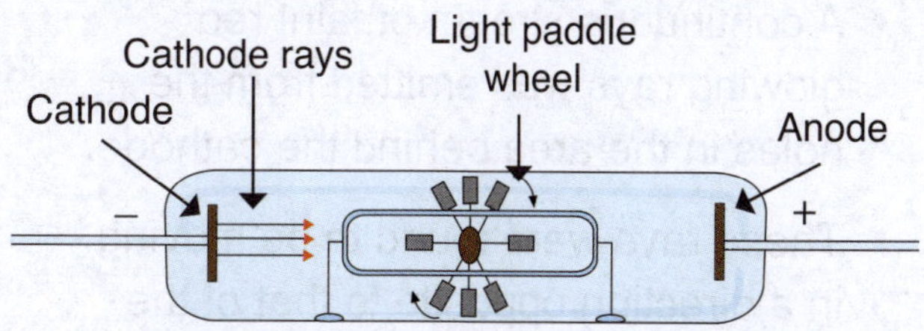

Fig. 4.4 Cathode rays can rotate a paddle wheel placed in their path

- **Cathode rays are negatively charged:** When an electric field is applied in the path of cathode rays, the rays tend to bend towards the positively charged plate (Fig. 4.5). This proves that cathode rays consist of negatively charged particles and these particles are termed as **electrons**. Thus, it was found that all matter or atoms contain negatively charged particles or electrons.

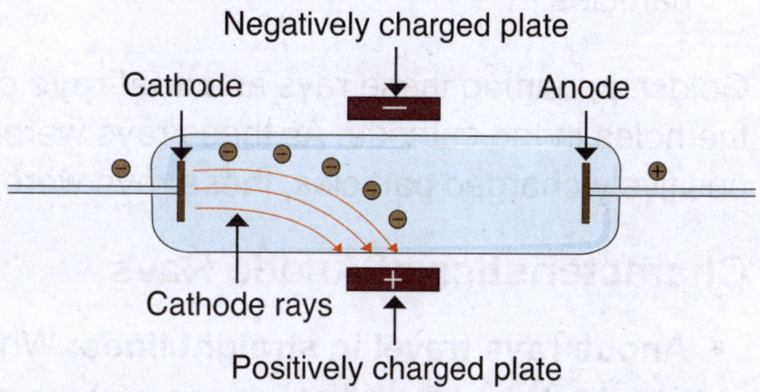

Fig. 4.5 The cathode rays bend towards the positively charged plate

- **Ratio of electric charge to mass (*e*/*m*) is constant:** Thomson also found out that the charge (*e*) to mass (*m*) ratio of the particles that constitute the cathode rays is constant, irrespective of the material of the electrodes or the gas used in the discharge tube. The ratio (*e*/*m*) was calculated to be 1.78×10^8 coulomb per gram (C/g).

Characteristics of an Electron

- The mass of an electron is 9.1×10^{-31} kg and is equal to 1/1837 times the mass of a hydrogen atom. The mass of an electron is negligible when compared to the mass of an atom.
- Electrons are particles with unit negative charge (*e*) which is equal to 1.6×10^{-19} coulombs (C).
- An electron is represented by the symbol ${}_{-1}e^0$, where '0' represents the mass and '–1' represents one unit negative charge.

DISCOVERY OF PROTONS

With the discovery that atoms consist of negatively charged particles called electrons, scientists were of the opinion that atoms must also contain some positively charged particles to neutralize this negative charge of electrons as all atoms are electrically neutral.

In 1886, the German scientist Eugen Goldstein discovered positively charged rays while he was working with the cathode ray discharge tube. This experiment led to the discovery of proton by Ernest Rutherford in 1919.

Goldstein's Experiment

Instead of a normal cathode in the discharge tube, Goldstein used a perforated cathode (a cathode containing small holes) for his experimental set-up (Fig. 4.6). When high-voltage electricity (10,000 volts) was applied across the terminals at a very low pressure of nearly 0.001 mm of mercury, he observed the following:

- A continuous stream of faint red glowing rays was emitted from the holes in the area behind the cathode.
- These rays were found to be moving in a direction opposite to that of the cathode rays. This proves that these rays consist of positively charged particles.

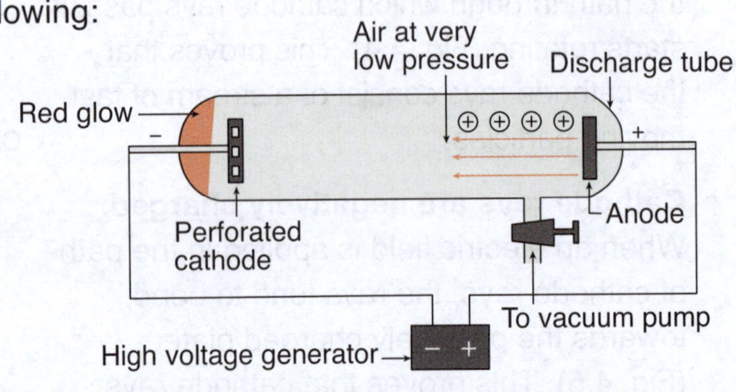

Fig. 4.6 Goldstein's experimental set-up

Goldstein named these rays as **canal rays** or **channel rays**, as they were produced through the holes in the cathode. As these rays were emitted from the anode and were composed of positively charged particles, these rays were also referred to as positive rays or **anode rays**.

Characteristics of Anode Rays

- **Anode rays travel in straight lines:** When an object is placed in the path of anode rays, the shadow of the object appears at the other end of the discharge tube. This shows that anode rays travel in straight lines.
- **Anode rays consist of fast-moving particles:** If a light paddle wheel is placed in the path through which anode rays pass, it starts rotating. This proves that anode rays consist of fast-moving particles.
- **Anode rays are positively charged:** When an electric field is applied in the path of anode rays, they tend to bend towards the negatively charged plate. This proves that anode rays consist of positively charged particles and these particles are termed as **protons**.
- **Ratio of electric charge to mass (*e*/*m*) is not constant:** The charge (*e*) to mass (*m*) ratio of particles that constitute the anode rays is not constant and varies with the gases used in the discharge tube. This proves that the nature of anode rays produced depends on the gas used in the discharge tube.

Characteristics of a Proton

- The mass of a proton is equivalent to the mass of a hydrogen atom, which is about 1 atomic mass unit (u) or 1.67×10^{-27} kg. It is about 1840 times heavier than an electron.
- Protons are particles with unit positive charge, which is equal to $+1.6 \times 10^{-19}$ coulombs (C). It is equal in magnitude to the charge on an electron but opposite in sign.
- A proton is represented by the symbol ${}_1p^1$, where subscript '1' represents the mass and superscript '1' represents one unit positive charge.

Thomson's Plum Pudding Model

J. J. Thomson proposed the first model of an atom in 1904. It was called the **plum pudding model** (Fig. 4.7) of the atom and shows how the subatomic particles protons and electrons are arranged inside an atom. He theorized the atom to be a positively charged spherical substance in which negatively charged electrons are dispersed just like plums or raisins in a pudding. Although this model described that atoms are electrically neutral, his theory was later on proved to be wrong by his former student Rutherford.

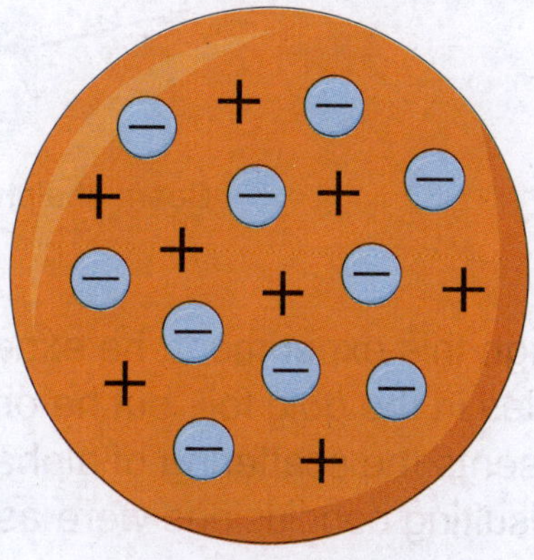

Fig. 4.7 Thomson's plum pudding model of the atom

DISCOVERY OF THE ATOMIC NUCLEUS

In 1911, Ernest Rutherford discovered that the nucleus is present at the centre of the atom while performing an experiment to find out the arrangement of protons and electrons inside an atom. This model is also known as the **nuclear atomic model**.

Rutherford's Alpha-Particle Scattering (Gold Foil) Experiment

The experimental setup used by Rutherford is shown in Fig. 4.8 given on the next page. It has the following components.

- A source of alpha (α) particles: a radioactive substance in a lead container with an aperture to let the emitted radioactive particles escape in the desired direction
- A thin gold foil (1000 atoms thick)
- A detector of alpha particles: a screen coated with zinc sulphide that glows when α-particles strike it

DO YOU KNOW?

An alpha particle is a helium nucleus. It consists of two protons and two neutrons with no electrons around it.

Rutherford placed a thin gold foil, surrounded by a zinc sulphide-coated screen, in the path of α-particles (positively charged helium ions). He bombarded the gold foil with α-particles.

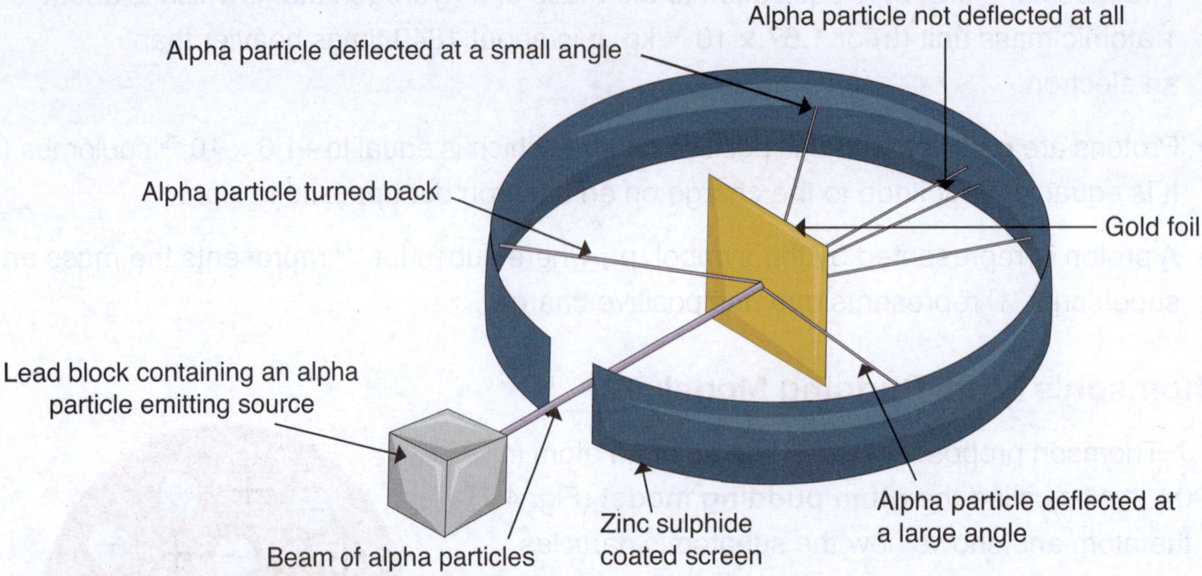

Fig. 4.8 Rutherford's alpha-particle scattering experiment

Through this experiment, he expected that α-particles would be deflected by the subatomic particles in the gold foil, but he observed some unexpected results. Fig. 4.9 pictorially represents the scattering of alpha particles through gold foil. Rutherford's observations and the resulting conclusions were as follows:

- Most of the α-particles passed in a straight line through the gold foil without any deflection from their path, indicating that the atom has a lot of empty space in it.
- A small number of α-particles were deflected by small angles, indicating that they approached some positively charged region within the atom, which repelled the positively charged α-particles. This region was called the **nucleus** by Rutherford.
- A very small number of α-particles were deflected by large angles. This indicated that all the mass and positive charge of an atom are concentrated in this very small region within the atom.

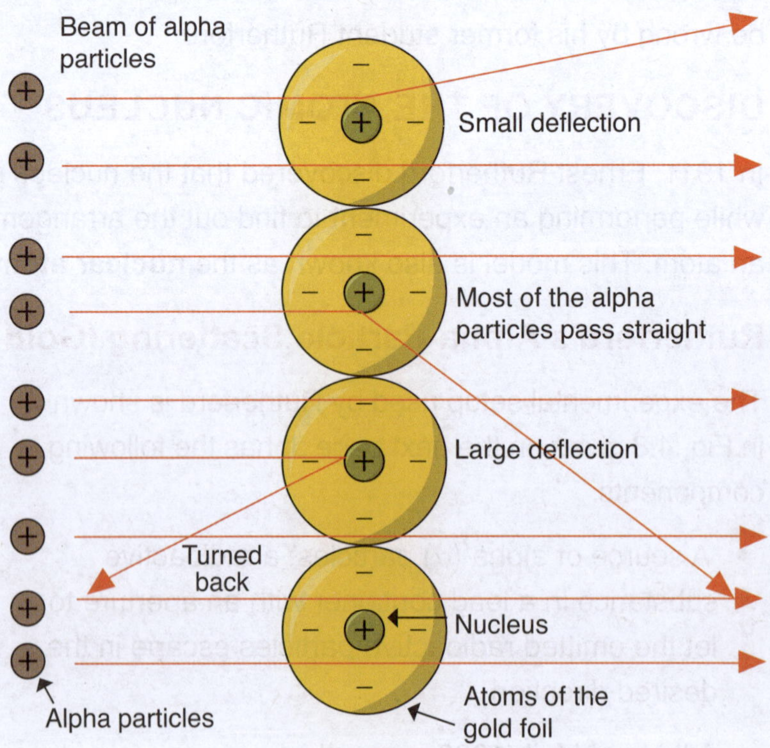

Fig. 4.9 Scattering of alpha particles through gold foil

Rutherford's Model of Atom

Rutherford proposed the following model of an atom (Fig, 4.10) based on his alpha-scattering experiment.

- An atom has a positively charged region at its centre, called the nucleus, which consists of protons (the positively charged particles).
- All the mass of an atom is concentrated in its nucleus.
- The size of the nucleus is very small as compared to the size of the atom.

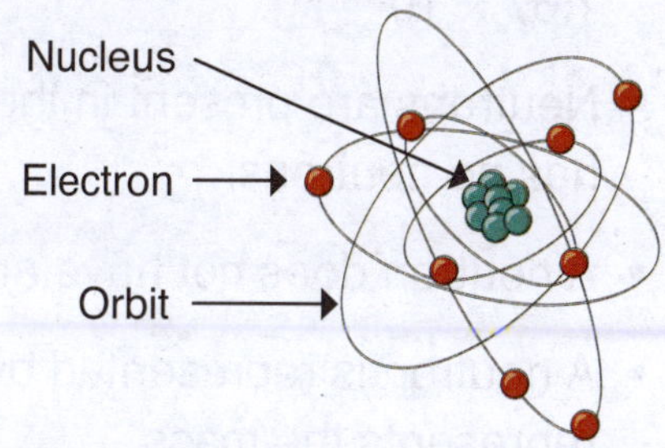

Fig. 4.10 Rutherford's model of atom

- The electrons revolve around the nucleus in well-defined paths called **orbits** in the same way as the planets move around the Sun.
- The electrons and the nucleus are held together by a strong electrostatic force of attraction.
- An atom is electrically neutral. This implies that the number of electrons revolving around the nucleus should be equal to the number of protons, so as to neutralize the positive charge in the nucleus.

Drawbacks of Rutherford's Model of Atom

- His model failed to explain the exact arrangement of electrons in an atom.
- As the electrons and the nucleus are held together by electrostatic forces of attraction, the electrons should fall into the nucleus eventually. But it does not happen and the atoms remain stable.

DISCOVERY OF NEUTRONS

Until 1920, an atom was considered to be the fundamental unit of matter, consisting of only positively charged protons and negatively charged electrons, thus making the atom electrically neutral.

Rutherford's gold foil experiment proved that the mass of an atom was concentrated in its positively charged nucleus as the mass of electrons was negligible. Later, it was discovered that the actual mass of the nucleus was twice that calculated from the number of protons present in it. This made Rutherford predict the presence of another subatomic particle inside the nucleus. He predicted that this unknown particle would be neutral, having a mass similar to that of a proton.

In 1932, James Chadwick conducted some experiments and discovered the neutral subatomic particles predicted by Rutherford. He named these particles neutrons. The mass of these particles was found to be almost equal to that of protons. These particles were electrically neutral, that is, they had no negative or positive charge.

Characteristics of a Neutron

- The mass of a neutron is nearly equal to that of a proton, that is, 1 u, that is, 1.67×10^{-27} kg.
- Neutrons are present in the nucleus of all atoms, with hydrogen being an exception, as it has no neutrons.
- A neutron does not have any charge.
- A neutron is represented by the symbol $_0n^1$, where '0' represents the charge and '1' represents the mass.

> **Electrons:** $_{-1}e^0$ — negligible mass and unit negative charge
> **Protons:** $_1p^1$ — 1 u mass and unit positive charge
> **Neutrons:** $_0n^1$ — 1 u mass and zero charge

Bohr's Model of Atom

To overcome the shortcomings of Rutherford's model, Danish physicist Neils Bohr postulated an atomic model (Fig. 4.11). It is known as **Bohr's model of atom**. He received the Nobel Prize in Physics in 1922 for his contribution towards this structure of atom. The significant features of the Bohr's atomic model are as follows:

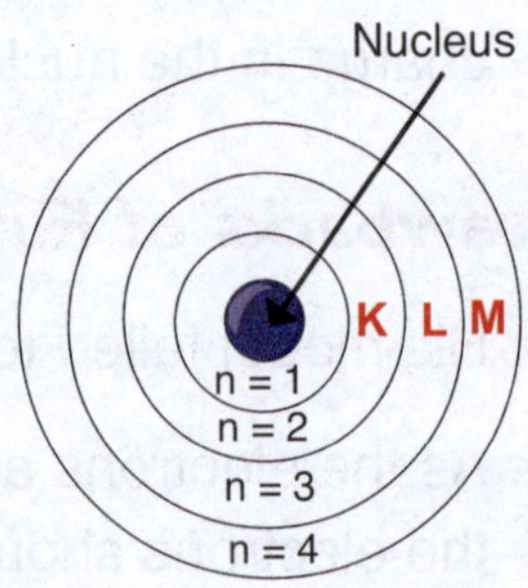

Fig. 4.11 Bohr's atomic model

- The electrons revolve around the nucleus in fixed paths called **orbits**, also known as **shells**.
- The shells or orbits are represented either by the numbers $n = 1, 2, 3, 4, \ldots$ or by the letters K, L, M, N, … (beginning from the innermost shell).
- Each orbit or shell has a fixed amount of energy associated with it. Thus, the shells are also known as **energy levels** or **energy shells**. Energy of each shell increases with its distance from the nucleus.
- The first orbit from the nucleus (K-shell) has the lowest energy, the second orbit (L-shell) has a higher energy than the K-shell, the third orbit is the M-shell and has a higher energy than the L-shell and so on.
- Electrons will not lose energy as long as they are revolving in their particular energy level.
- Electrons lose energy when they move from a higher energy level to a lower energy level.
- Electrons gain energy when they move from a lower energy level to a higher energy level.
- The outermost shell of an atom is called its **valence shell**.

QUICK REVISION

Fill in the blanks.

1. According to Dalton's theory, atoms __________ (can/cannot) be created or destroyed.
2. The charge to mass ratio of protons is __________ (constant/not constant).
3. Electrons __________ (gain/lose) energy when they move from a higher energy level to a lower energy level.
4. Neutrons were discovered by __________ (Rutherford/Chadwick).
5. The electrons and nucleus are held together by __________ (magnetic/electrostatic) forces of attraction.

MODERN CONCEPT OF THE ATOM

As per the modern concept of the atom, an atom has the following features:

- An atom is made up of three subatomic particles: electrons, protons and neutrons.
- All the positive charge and mass of the atom is concentrated in a small volume in the centre of the atom, which is called the nucleus.
- Protons and neutrons constitute the nucleus of the atom and are responsible for the entire mass of the atom.
- The nucleus is positively charged due to the presence of protons in it. Neutrons do not have any charge.
- Outside the nucleus, the electrons revolve in various fixed paths called orbits and do not contribute to the mass of the atom as the mass of electrons is negligible compared to that of protons and neutrons.
- Normally, an atom has equal number of electrons and protons, so it is electrically neutral in nature.

ATOMIC NUMBER

Atomic number is defined as the number of protons present in the nucleus of an atom of an element. It is denoted by the letter Z.

$$\text{Atomic number } (Z) = \text{Number of protons } (p)$$

We know that the number of protons in the nucleus of an atom is equal to the number of electrons revolving around the nucleus of that atom.

That is,

Number of protons (p) = Number of electrons (e)

or Atomic number (Z) = Number of protons (p) = Number of electrons (e)

MASS NUMBER

Mass number is defined as the total number of protons and neutrons present in the nucleus of an atom of an element. It is denoted by the letter A. For example, the mass of the element aluminium is 27, which contains 13 protons and 14 neutrons.

Mass number (A) = Number of protons (p) + Number of neutrons (n)

If we know the mass number and atomic number of an element, the number of protons, electrons and neutrons in the atom of that element can be calculated.

Mass number (A) = Number of protons (p) + Number of neutrons (n)

Number of protons (p) = Atomic number (Z)

So, Mass number (A) = Atomic number (Z) + Number of neutrons (n)

or, Number of neutrons (n) = Mass number (A) – Atomic number (Z)

Table 4.1 shows the calculation of the number of neutrons from the atomic and mass numbers of a few elements.

Table 4.1 Atomic number and mass number of some elements

Element	Atomic number (Z)	Mass number (A)	Number of neutrons ($n = A - Z$)
Hydrogen (H)	1	1	0
Boron (B)	5	11	6
Palladium (Pd)	46	106	60
Iodine (I)	53	126	73
Sulphur (S)	16	32	16
Antimony (Sb)	51	121	70
Cadmium (Cd)	48	112	64
Iron (Fe)	26	55	29

The representation of the mass number and atomic number of an element along with the symbol of that element is called its **atomic notation**.

An element is represented by ${}^{A}_{Z}X$ or ${}_{Z}X^{A}$ where X is the chemical symbol of the element, A is the mass number and Z is the atomic number. For example, helium, carbon and sulphur can be written as ${}^{4}_{2}He$ or ${}_{2}He^{4}$, ${}^{12}_{6}C$ or ${}_{6}C^{12}$ and ${}^{32}_{16}S$ or ${}_{16}S^{32}$, respectively.

ELECTRONIC CONFIGURATION

The systematic distribution or arrangement of electrons in various orbits or shells around the nucleus of an atom is called **electronic configuration**. It was explained by the scientists **Bohr** and **Bury**. The main rules suggested by them are known as **Bohr–Bury rules** and are as follows:

- The maximum number of electrons that can be accommodated in a given shell or orbit is $2n^2$, where n is the number of the energy shell.
- The maximum number of electrons that can be accommodated in the outermost or valence shell is 8, except for the K-shell (if it is the outermost shell) as it can hold only a maximum of 2 electrons. The shell just before the valence shell can hold only a maximum of 18 electrons.

Table 4.2 gives the maximum number of electrons in various shells.

Table 4.2 Maximum number of electrons in various shells

Shell or orbit name	Shell number, n	Maximum no. of electrons, $2n^2$
K-shell	1	$2 \times 1^2 = 2$
L-shell	2	$2 \times 2^2 = 8$
M-shell	3	$2 \times 3^2 = 18$
N-shell	4	$2 \times 4^2 = 32$

- The electrons will first try to occupy the shell that has the lowest energy. Electrons will not try to occupy the next shell until the lower energy shells are filled.
- If the outermost shell is K-shell and is filled with the maximum of two electrons, it is referred to as **duplet configuration**. In all the other cases, if the outermost shell is filled with the maximum of eight electrons, it is referred to as **octet configuration**. The atom of an element that has a duplet or an octet configuration is considered to be stable as compared to other elements that do not have these configurations. Table 4.3 gives the electronic configuration of the first 20 elements.

Table 4.3 Electronic configuration of the first 20 elements

Element	Symbol	Atomic no. (Z)	Mass no. (A)	No. of protons	No. of electrons	No. of neutrons ($A - Z$)	Electronic configuration			
							K	L	M	N
Hydrogen	H	1	1	1	1	1 – 1 = 0	1			
Helium	He	2	4	2	2	4 – 2 = 2	2			
Lithium	Li	3	7	3	3	7 – 3 = 4	2	1		
Beryllium	Be	4	9	4	4	9 – 4 = 5	2	2		
Boron	B	5	11	5	5	11 – 5 = 6	2	3		
Carbon	C	6	12	6	6	12 – 6 = 6	2	4		
Nitrogen	N	7	14	7	7	14 – 7 = 7	2	5		
Oxygen	O	8	16	8	8	16 – 8 = 8	2	6		
Fluorine	F	9	19	9	9	19 – 9 = 10	2	7		
Neon	Ne	10	20	10	10	20 – 10 = 10	2	8		
Sodium	Na	11	23	11	11	23 – 11 = 12	2	8	1	
Magnesium	Mg	12	24	12	12	24 – 12 = 12	2	8	2	
Aluminium	Al	13	27	13	13	27 – 13 = 14	2	8	3	
Silicon	Si	14	28	14	14	28 – 14 = 14	2	8	4	
Phosphorus	P	15	31	15	15	31 – 15 = 16	2	8	5	
Sulphur	S	16	32	16	16	32 – 16 = 16	2	8	6	
Chlorine	Cl	17	35	17	17	35 – 17 = 18	2	8	7	
Argon	Ar	18	40	18	18	40 – 18 = 22	2	8	8	
Potassium	K	19	39	19	19	39 – 19 = 20	2	8	8	1
Calcium	Ca	20	40	20	20	40 – 20 = 20	2	8	8	2

The arrangement of electrons for the first 20 elements are illustrated as follows.

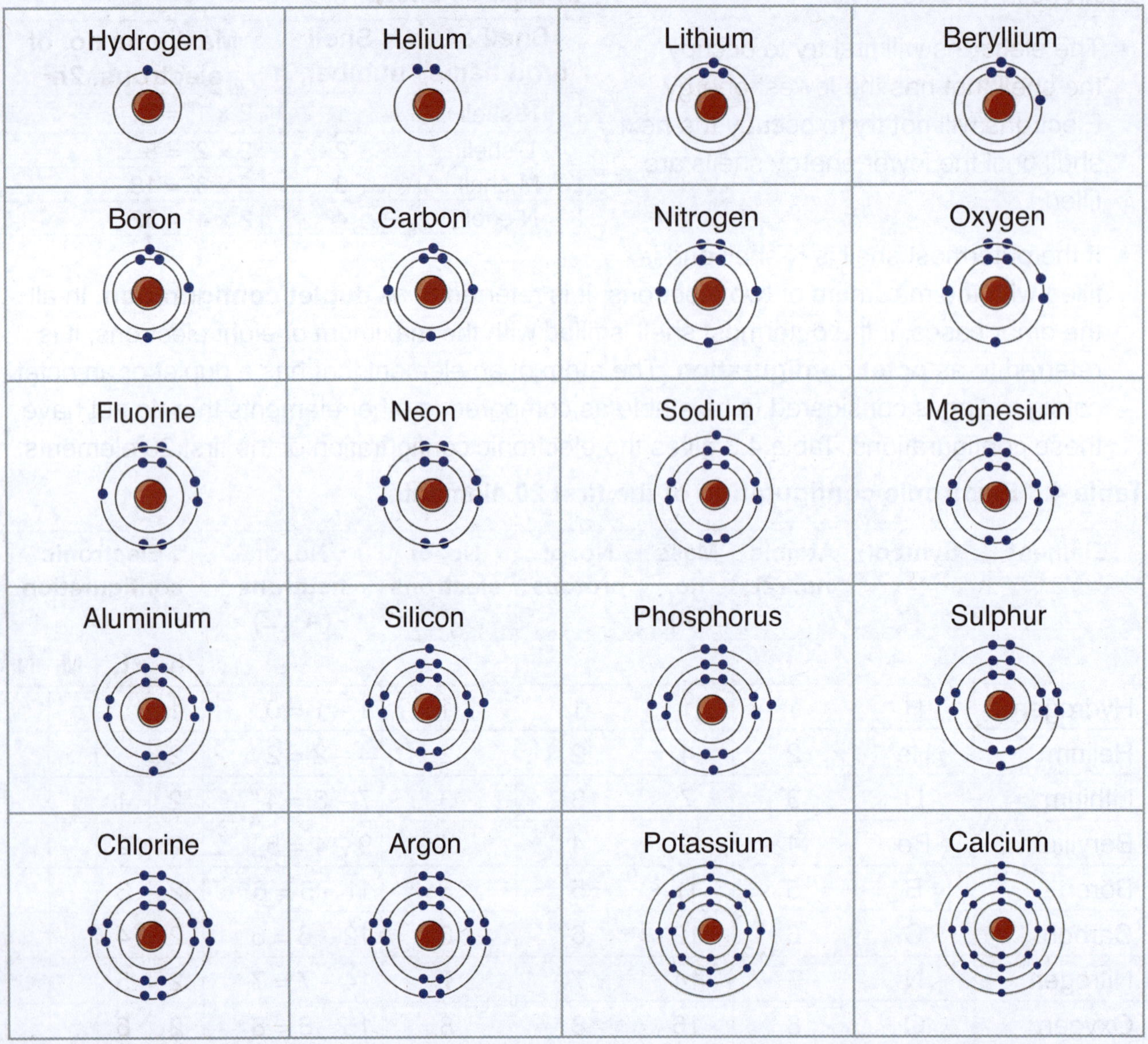

VALENCY

The combining capacity of the atom of an element with other atoms is known as its **valency**. It can also be defined as the number of electrons an atom can donate or accept in order to combine chemically with other atoms and form compounds.

Every atom tries to achieve an octet (or duplet) configuration by either accepting/losing or sharing valence electrons (electrons in the valence shell) to become stable. Valence electrons are the ones that take part in chemical reactions and result in the formation of different compounds.

DO YOU KNOW?

Elements that have eight electrons in their outermost shell or orbit are inactive and do not mostly take part in chemical reactions. These elements are called **inert gases** or **noble gases**, for example, neon and argon.

Valency of an element is always a whole number. We can determine the valency of an element by knowing its electronic configuration. Let us find out.

- Elements of metals have 1, 2 or 3 valence electrons in their valence shell. Thus, they tend to donate or lose electrons in order to achieve a complete octet. So, the valency of a metal is calculated as the number of valence electrons in the valence shell of its atom.
  For example, the electronic configuration of sodium is 2, 8, 1. It has one valence electron and hence its valency is 1.
- Elements of non-metals have 5, 6 or 7 valence electrons. Thus, they tend to accept or gain electrons in order to achieve a complete octet. So, the valency of a non-metal is 8 – the number of valence electrons. For example, the electronic configuration of chlorine is 2, 8, 7. It has 7 valence electrons and requires only one electron to complete its octet. Hence, its valency is 1 (8 – 7 = 1).
- Elements of noble or inert gases have a valency of 0 as their valence shells are already complete with 8 electrons. For example, helium has 2 valence electrons (duplet) and neon has eight valence electrons (octet).

Refer to Table 4.4 to learn about the valencies of some common elements.

Table 4.4 Valencies of some elements

Element	Valency	Element	Valency	Element	Valency
Sodium	1 (monovalent)	Magnesium	2 (divalent)	Chlorine	1 (monovalent)
Potassium	1 (monovalent)	Calcium	2 (divalent)	Carbon	4 (tetravalent)
Silver	1 (monovalent)	Aluminium	3 (trivalent)	Oxygen	2 (divalent)
Zinc	2 (divalent)	Hydrogen	1 (monovalent)	Iodine	1 (monovalent)

The valency of an element can also be defined as the number of hydrogen atoms that can combine or replace either indirectly or directly with one atom of the element. The valency of hydrogen is 1 (monovalent).

Variable Valency

Some elements exhibit more than one valency as their atoms have different combining capacities while forming molecules or compounds. That is, atoms of such elements can donate or accept different number of electrons depending upon the conditions. Hence, they are said to have **variable valency**. For example, iron can have valencies 2 and 3. In ferrous chloride ($FeCl_2$), the valency of iron is 2, whereas in ferric chloride ($FeCl_3$), its valency is 3.

Elements with variable valency are represented by writing the symbol of the element followed by its valency in Roman numerals within brackets. For example, Fe(II), Fe(III), Ca(I) and Ca(II). Refer to Table 4.5 to learn about some elements with variable valencies.

Table 4.5 Variable valencies of some elements

Element	Variable valencies	Representation
Copper	1, 2	Cu(I), Cu(II)
Iron	2, 3	Fe(II), Fe(III)
Silver	1, 2	Ag(I), Ag(II)
Mercury	1, 2	Hg(I), Hg(II)
Nickel	2, 3, 4	Ni(II), Ni(III), Ni(IV)

IONS

We have learnt that atoms are neutral (that is, they do not carry any charge) as the number of protons present inside the nucleus is equal to the number of electrons that revolve around the nucleus. However, when an atom donates or accepts one or more electrons, this equality or balance is lost and the atom acquires a positive or negative charge. For example, when a sodium atom loses an electron, it acquires a positive charge (Na^{+}) as the number of protons in it becomes more than the number of electrons. Similarly, when a chlorine atom accepts an electron, it acquires a negative charge (Cl^{-}) as the number of electrons in it becomes more than the number of protons.

An atom that attains a positive or a negative charge as a result of loss or gain of electrons is called an **ion**. The atom that donates or loses electrons attains a positive charge and is called a **cation** or positive ion. Examples of cations are potassium (K^{+}), calcium (Ca^{2+}) and zinc (Zn^{2+}). The atom that accepts or gains electrons attains a negative charge and is called an **anion** or negative ion. Examples of anions are bromide (Br^{-}), oxide (O^{2-}) and sulphide (S^{2-}). Ions can be classified as **simple** or **compound**. Ions that contain only one atom are called simple ions, such as chloride ion (Cl^{-}) and sodium ion (Na^{+}). Ions that contain group of atoms are called compound ions, such as ammonium ion (NH_4^{+}) and carbonate ion (CO_3^{2-}).

Table 4.6 shows chemical symbols of a few ions.

Ions cannot exist independently and thus always combine with other ions or elements. For example, carbonate is a compound ion with the formula CO_3^{2-}. It cannot exist independently and thus combines with other ions such as Ca^{2+} ion to form a compound calcium carbonate ($CaCO_3$). Thus, the calcium carbonate ($CaCO_3$) contains two ions: one is the positively charged Ca^{2+} ion and the other is the negatively charged CO_3^{2-} ion, where both ions have the valency 2.

Table 4.6 Some ions and their chemical symbols

Name of the ion	Chemical symbol	Name of the ion	Chemical symbol
Hydrogen	H^{+}	Hydride	H^{-}
Iron(II)	Fe^{2+}	Oxide	O^{2-}
Aluminium	Al^{3+}	Nitrate	NO_3^{-}
Magnesium	Mg^{2+}	Hydroxide	OH^{-}
Copper	Cu^{2+}	Hydrogen carbonate	HCO_3^{-}
Ammonium	NH_4^{+}	Phosphate	PO_4^{3-}

QUICK REVISION

Match the elements with their valencies.

1.	Aluminium	a.	Monovalent
2.	Magnesium	b.	Tetravalent
3.	Chlorine	c.	Divalent
4.	Carbon	d.	Trivalent

Previously, ions were also called radicals. Nowadays, the term "radical" is used for atoms, molecules or ions that have one or more unpaired electrons.

CONCEPT MAP

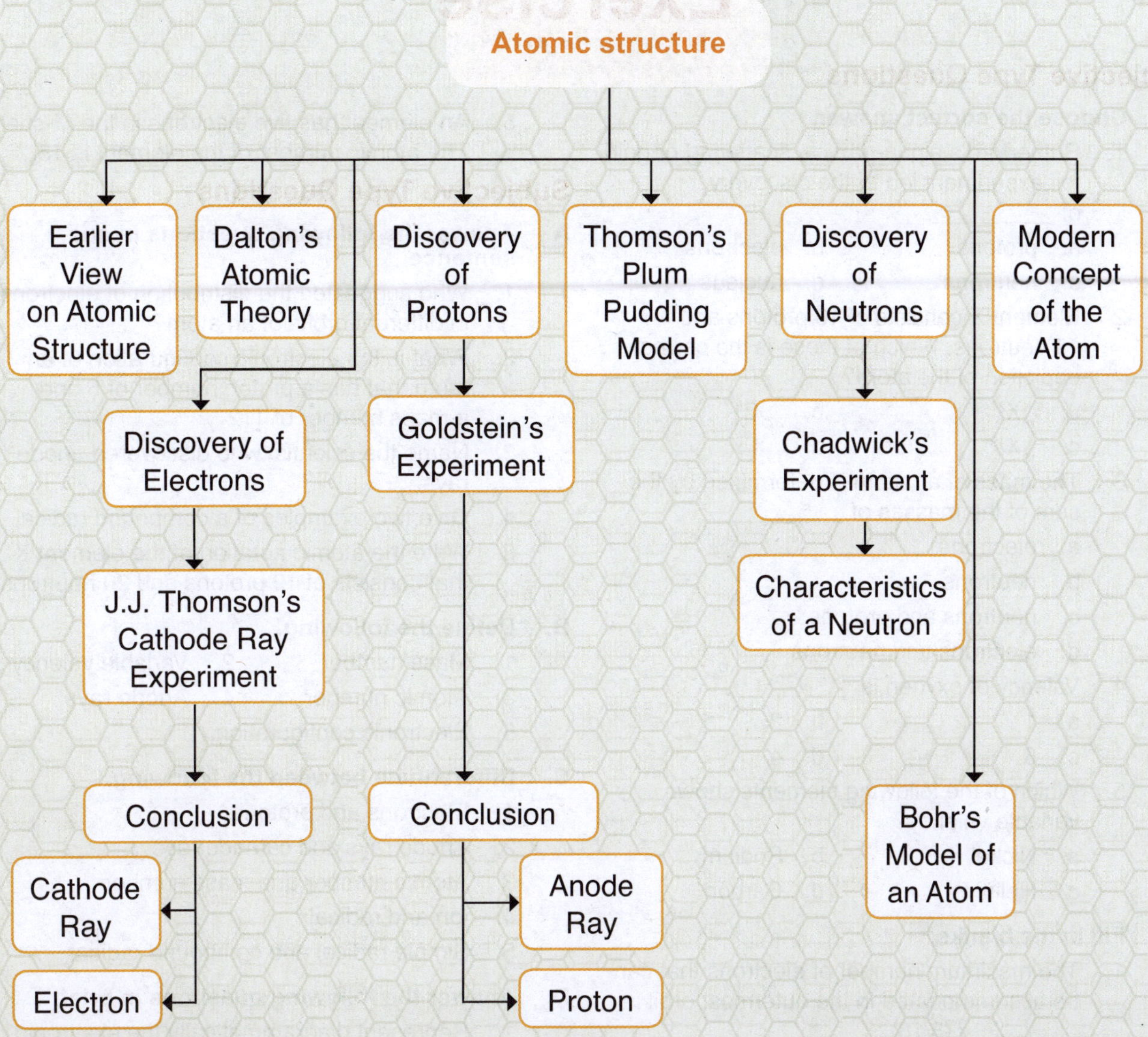

KEYWORDS

Paramanu: a particle that cannot be further divided

Protons: the subatomic particles present in the nucleus of an atom with a unit positive charge and mass equal to that of a hydrogen atom

Electrons: the subatomic particles that revolve around the nucleus of an atom with a unit negative charge and mass equal to 1/1837 times that of a hydrogen atom

Neutrons: the subatomic particles present in the nucleus of an atom that do not have any charge and have mass nearly equal to that of a proton

Atomic number: the number protons present in the nucleus of an atom of an element

Mass number: the sum of the number of protons and neutrons in the nucleus of an atom of an element

Electronic configuration: the systematic distribution or arrangement of electrons in various orbits or shells around the nucleus of an atom

Valency: the combining capacity of the atom of an element with other atoms

Exercise

Objective Type Questions

A. Choose the correct answer.

1. Rutherford's alpha-particle scattering or gold foil experiment led to the discovery of ________.
   a. protons b. electrons
   c. neutrons d. nucleus
2. Element X consists of 18 protons and 19 neutrons. Which of these is the correct depiction of the atom?
   a. $_{18}X^{37}$ b. $_{37}X^{18}$
   c. $_{18}X^{19}$ d. $_{19}X^{18}$
3. The mass of an atom is determined by the sum of the masses of ________.
   a. electrons
   b. neutrons
   c. neutrons and protons
   d. electrons and neutrons
4. Valency of oxygen is ________.
   a. 1 b. 2
   c. 3 d. 4
5. Which of the following elements shows variable valency?
   a. Nickel b. Sodium
   c. Helium d. Carbon

B. Fill in the blanks.

1. The maximum number of electrons that can be accommodated in the outermost orbit is ________ (8/18).
2. The total number of protons present in the nucleus of an atom is referred to as the ________ (atomic number/ mass number).
3. Electrons were discovered by ________ (Bohr/Thomson).
4. The positively charged centre of an atom is called the ________ (nucleus/proton).
5. The electrons present in the outermost shell of an atom are known as ________ (charged electrons/valence electrons).

C. Write T for True and F for False.

1. In the gold foil experiment, cathode rays produced a green glow at the other end of the tube.
2. The mass of an electron is about 1/2000 times that of a hydrogen atom.
3. The number of protons and electrons is always same in a neutral atom.
4. The fixed circular paths around the nucleus are called orbits.
5. An element has five electrons in the M-shell. The atomic number of the element is 15.

Subjective Type Questions

A. Answer the following questions in one sentence.

1. Who suggested the distribution of electrons in different orbits of an atom?
2. What is the electronic configuration of an atom that has a proton number of 5 and a mass number of 11?
3. Name the scientist who discovered anode rays.
4. Give two examples of a compound radical.
5. Write the atomic notation of the element X that consists of 19 protons and 20 neutrons.

B. Define the following.

1. Mass number 2. Variable valency
3. Atomic number 4. Anode rays
5. Electronic configuration

C. Differentiate between the following.

1. Electrons and protons
2. Anode rays and cathode rays
3. Atomic number and mass number
4. Ion and radical
5. Simple radical and compound radical

D. Answer the following questions in brief.

1. Represent diagrammatically the electronic configuration of magnesium.
2. An element consists of 15 protons and 16 neutrons. Mention the number of electrons, atomic number and mass number of this element.
3. Mention any four postulates of Dalton's atomic theory.
4. What is Thomson's plum pudding model?
5. What is valency? Explain with the help of an example.

E. Answer the following questions in detail.

1. Explain the discovery of electrons.
2. Explain Rutherford's alpha-scattering experiment and the conclusions drawn from it.
3. Explain the discovery of protons by Eugen Goldstein.
4. Explain the arrangement of electrons in an atom by Bohr and Bury.
5. Explain the discovery of neutrons.

Application-based Question

What happens to the flow (number and speed) of electrons if we introduce two anodes at one end of the cathode? (Hint: Recall the concept of J.J. Thomson cathode ray experiment.)

Picture-based Question

Bankei made a Bohr's model for calcium using three rings of different sizes for the various energy levels, 20 tennis balls to represent electrons and a cricket ball to represent the nucleus. He arranged all the items as shown in the first picture. Before showing this model to the teacher, he showed it to his friend Jenny. Jenny gave him one more ring that she had with her and asked him to arrange the tennis balls as shown in the second image.

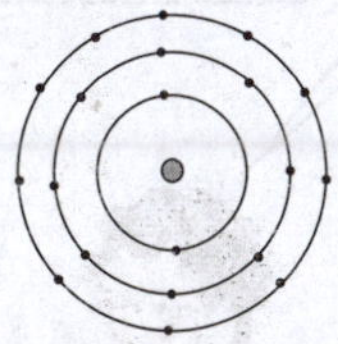
Bankei's model

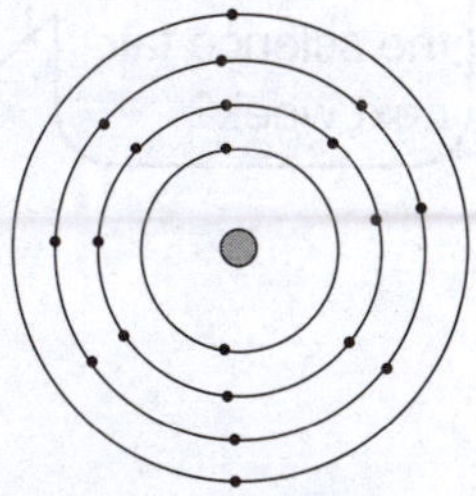
Jenny's model

1. What was wrong with the model made by Bankei?
2. How did Jenny help Bankei?
3. What life skill is associated with this?

Skill Booster

A. **21CS:** Information Literacy, Technology Literacy | **CC:** Computer Science | **BT:** Cognitive

Draw a timeline to show how the atomic theory has developed over the past several hundred years. Take help of the Internet.

B. **21CS:** Critical Thinking, Life Skills | **BT:** Cognitive, Affective

Shourya knows that the number of electrons in an atom X is 8 but does not know how to deduce the atomic number and valency of the atom from this information. His mother explained to him atomic number and mass number as well as the relation between the two.

1. Can Shourya now predict the valency of the atom?
2. What would be the atomic number of this atom?
3. What is the mass number of the atom if its nucleus contains eight neutrons?

Worksheet 4

My SEE Journal

A. What quality is shown by the children here?

____

____

B. Why is it better to discuss the ideas before starting the actual work?

____

____

C. Make Bohr's atomic model with your friends. How did each member contribute to completing this group activity?

____

____

____

____

My SDG Journal

17 PARTNERSHIPS FOR THE GOALS

A. What is the significance of the discovery of subatomic particle?

____

____

B. Make a chart highlighting all the major events that happened in the discovery of the three subatomic particles.

5 Language of Chemistry

Prior Knowledge

- Importance of matter in our daily life
- Classification of substances
- Chemical symbols
- Types of changes with examples
- Definition of chemical reactions with examples

Learning Objectives

- Representation of elements
- Representation of compounds
- Writing chemical equation of a reaction
- Balancing chemical equations

LET'S GET STARTED

In Class 7, we learned about a few terms that we use in chemistry. Let us see how many of those terms you still remember.

1. The shorthand representation of an element ____________
2. The combining capacity of an element ____________
3. Symbolic representation of a compound ____________
4. The symbolic representation of a chemical reaction ____________
5. Reactions that absorb heat ____________
6. The insoluble solid that forms in a chemical reaction ____________

We use a variety of substances in our daily life. Each substance around us is made of matter. From the food we eat to the water we drink to the air, we breathe and all the non-living objects are all made of matter. We know that each substance has a unique composition. We also know that chemical changes are caused by the chemical reactions that take place during a chemical change. In this chapter, we will revise and learn more about chemical reactions.

ELEMENTS

A substance that consists of only one kind of atoms is called an **element**. The smallest unit of an element is an atom. For example, the element gold contains only one kind of atoms, that is, gold atoms. Other examples of elements are carbon, sodium and oxygen. We know that all the atoms that make up an element are of the same kind, but two different elements cannot have the same kind of atoms. For instance, atoms of oxygen and atoms of hydrogen are different from each other. So, every element has its own unique properties.

So far, nearly 118 elements have been discovered. Of these, 90 elements are found naturally on Earth and the remaining 28 elements have been prepared artificially.

Characteristics of Elements

- Elements are pure substances that consist of only one kind of atoms.
- Each element has its own unique properties.
- The atoms of an element exhibit the same properties as the element.
- Elements cannot be separated or broken down into simpler components by physical or simple chemical methods.

REPRESENTATION OF ELEMENTS

Elements or atoms of an element are represented by symbols. The representation of an element using the short form or abbreviation of its name is known as its **chemical symbol**.

In earlier times, the elements were represented pictorially. Later, the elements were named after the name of the place where they were first found. For example, the name copper and its symbol Cu come from the Latin word *cuprum,* which means 'from the island of Cyprus'. In the modern method of representing elements, letters representing the names of the elements are used as symbols.

Features of the modern method of representation are as follows.

- The first letter of the name of the element is used as the symbol. The first letter is written as a capital letter. For example, H for hydrogen, O for oxygen and C for carbon.
- If two or more elements have their English names starting with the same letter, then a two-letter symbol is used. The first letter of the name is the first letter of the symbol and the next non-repeating letter of the name is the second letter of the symbol. The first letter is written as a capital letter and the second letter is written as a small letter. For example, Ca for calcium, Cd for cadmium, Cl for chlorine and Co for cobalt.
- For some elements, the symbols are derived from their Latin names. For example, the Latin name of potassium is *kalium* and its symbol is K. Similarly, the Latin name of gold is *aurum* and its symbol is Au.

Table 5.1 shows the English names of some elements and their chemical symbols. Table 5.2 shows the Latin names of some elements and their chemical symbols.

Table 5.1 Some elements and their chemical symbols

Element	Chemical symbol	Element	Chemical symbol
Helium	He	Phosphorus	P
Nitrogen	N	Magnesium	Mg
Iodine	I	Manganese	Mn
Aluminium	Al	Argon	Ar
Zinc	Zn	Platinum	Pt

Table 5.2 Some elements with their Latin names and chemical symbols

Element	Latin name	Chemical symbol
Sodium	*Natrium*	Na
Iron	*Ferrum*	Fe
Copper	*Cuprum*	Cu
Silver	*Argentum*	Ag
Mercury	*Hydrargyrum*	Hg

COMPOUNDS

The chemical substance formed when two or more atoms of different elements combine chemically in a fixed proportion is called a **compound**. A compound is made up of molecules of the same kind. For example, water contains only one kind of molecules, that is, water molecules. Other examples of compounds are carbon dioxide, salt and sugar.

Characteristics of Compounds

- Compounds are pure substances formed when two or more atoms of different elements combine together chemically in a fixed proportion.
- The properties of compounds are different from the properties of their constituent elements.
- Compounds exhibit their own physical and chemical properties.
- Compounds can be separated into their individual components by chemical methods.

REPRESENTATION OF COMPOUNDS

Just as we represent elements by their chemical symbols, compounds can be represented by chemical formulae. A chemical formula is the representation of a compound using the symbols of its constituent elements. In other words, the symbolic representation of the composition of a chemical compound is known as its **chemical formula**.

A chemical formula exhibits the different elements present in a molecule of a compound and the number of atoms of each combining or constituent element it contains. For example, the chemical formula of carbon dioxide is CO_2. This indicates that a molecule of carbon dioxide consists of one atom of carbon and two atoms of oxygen.

We can easily write the chemical formula of a compound if we know the symbols and valencies of atoms of the different elements forming the compound.

Follow the steps given below to write the chemical formula of a compound.

1. Write the symbols of the elements or radicals/ions that form the compound.
2. The metallic part (positive ion) of the compound should always be written first followed by the non-metallic part (negative ion).

3. Write the valencies of elements/ions on top of their symbols as superscripts.
4. If the valencies are identical, cancel the valencies. If the valencies are different, then interchange the valencies with respect to the symbols by making arrows and write them as subscripts.
5. Simplify the formula by dividing the valencies by a common factor, if divisible.
6. If the compound contains compound radicals, then the radicals are enclosed in brackets and the number is written outside the brackets as subscript. For instance, the valency of magnesium (Mg^{2+}) is two and that of nitrate (NO_3^-) is one. Thus, the chemical formula of magnesium nitrate is written as $Mg(NO_3)_2$.
7. The valency 1 need not be written in the final formula.

Keeping in mind the above steps, let us write the chemical formulae of some compounds.

Writing the Formulae of Chlorides

Calcium chloride

Step 1: Ca Cl (Write the symbols of the constituent elements, here calcium and chlorine.)

Step 2: Ca^2 Cl^1 (Write the valency of each element as superscript.)

Step 3: Ca^2 Cl^1 (Interchange the valencies and write them as subscripts.)

Ca_1 Cl_2

Step 4: Ca_1 Cl_2 (Divide the valencies by a common factor, if divisible)

Chemical formula of calcium chloride: $CaCl_2$ (Valency 1 need not be written)

Table 5.3 shows the chemical formulae of some common chlorides.

Table 5.3 Some metallic chlorides and their chemical formulae

Compound	Chemical Formula
Sodium chloride	NaCl
Potassium chloride	KCl
Magnesium chloride	$MgCl_2$
Copper chloride	$CuCl_2$
Zinc chloride	$ZnCl_2$

Writing the Formulae of Oxides

Magnesium oxide

Step 1: Mg O

Step 2: Mg^2 O^2

Step 3: Mg^2 O^2

Mg^2 O^2

Step 4: Mg_2 O_2 (Divide the valencies by a common factor, here 2)

Mg_1 O_1

Chemical formula of magnesium oxide: MgO

Table 5.4 shows the chemical formulae of some common metallic oxides.

Table 5.4 Some metallic oxides and their chemical formulae

Compound	Chemical Formula
Sodium oxide	Na_2O
Calcium oxide	CaO
Zinc oxide	ZnO
Copper oxide	CuO
Potassium oxide	K_2O

Writing the Formulae of Sulphides

Sodium sulphide

Step 1:	Na	S
Step 2:	Na^1	S^2
Step 3:	Na^1	S^2
	Na^2	S^1
Step 4:	Na_2	S_1

Chemical formula of sodium sulphide: Na_2S

Table 5.5 Some metallic sulphides and their chemical formulae

Compound	Chemical Formula
Zinc sulphide	ZnS
Ferric sulphide	Fe_2S_3
Hydrogen sulphide	H_2S
Calcium sulphide	CaS
Copper sulphide	Cu_2S

Refer to Table 5.5 to learn about chemical formulae of some sulphides.

In a chemical formula, the subscript denotes the number of atoms of the element present in one molecule of the compound. For example, in Fe_2S_3, there are 2 atoms of iron and 3 atoms of sulphur.

Refer to Table 5.6 to learn about the constituent elements present in some compounds and their chemical formulae.

Table 5.6 Some compounds with their constituent elements and chemical formulae

Compound	Constituent Elements	Chemical Formula	Compound	Constituent Elements	Chemical Formula
Methane	Carbon (C) Hydrogen(H)	CH_4	Sulphur dioxide	Sulphur (S) Oxygen (O)	SO_2
Sodium hydroxide	Sodium (Na) Oxygen (O) Hydrogen (H)	NaOH	Sulphuric acid	Hydrogen (H) Sulphur (S) Oxygen (O)	H_2SO_4
Calcium hydroxide	Calcium (Ca) Oxygen (O) Hydrogen (H)	$Ca(OH)_2$	Copper sulphate	Copper (Cu) Sulphur (S) Oxygen (O)	$CuSO_4$
Potassium nitrate	Potassium (K) Nitrogen (N) Oxygen (O)	KNO_3	Calcium carbonate	Calcium (Ca) Carbon (C) Oxygen (O)	$CaCO_3$

QUICK REVISION

Match the compounds with their chemical formulae.

1. Copper chloride	a. CaS
2. Zinc oxide	b. $CuCl_2$
3. Sodium oxide	c. ZnO
4. Calcium sulphide	d. Na_2O

FIND OUT

Why is it important to know the valencies to write a chemical formula?

Law of Conservation of Mass

The law of conservation of mass states that in an isolated system, mass can neither be created nor be destroyed by chemical reactions or physical transformations. Hence, during a chemical reaction, the atoms are only rearranged to provide new products. The rearrangement of atoms happens in such a way that the total mass of the reactants is equal to the total mass of the products, provided masses are measured under similar conditions. In other words, the number of atoms of each element in the reactants and the products remains the same.

For example, if A and B react to form C and D, then according to the law of conservation of mass:

Mass of A + Mass of B = Mass of C + Mass of D

That is, the total mass of the reactants should be equal to the total mass of the products formed in the reaction.

Molecular Mass

Molecular mass is expressed in the unit u. It is the total of atomic masses of all the atoms present in a molecule. Table 5.7 shows some elements with their atomic masses.

Table 5.7 Atomic masses of some elements

Element	Atomic mass	Element	Atomic mass	Element	Atomic mass
Lithium	6.9	Neon	20.2	Chlorine	35.4
Beryllium	9.0	Sodium	23.0	Potassium	39.1
Boron	10.8	Magnesium	24.3	Argon	39.9
Carbon	12.0	Aluminium	27.0	Calcium	40.0
Nitrogen	14.0	Silicon	28.1	Bromine	79.9
Oxygen	16.0	Phosphorus	31.0	Strontium	87.6
Fluorine	19.0	Sulphur	32.1	Iodine	126.9

Calculation of molecular mass of MgO (magnesium oxide)

Atomic mass of magnesium = 24.3 u

Atomic mass of oxygen = 16 u

So, the molecular mass of magnesium oxide (MgO) = 1 × 24.3 + 1 × 16 = 40.3 u.

Calculation of molecular mass of $CaCO_3$ (calcium carbonate)

Atomic mass of calcium = 40 u

Atomic mass of carbon = 12 u

Atomic mass of oxygen = 16 u

So, the molecular mass of calcium carbonate ($CaCO_3$) = 1 × 40 + 1 × 12 + 3 × 16 = 100 u.

CHEMICAL EQUATIONS

A **chemical equation** is the symbolic representation of a chemical reaction using chemical symbols and chemical formulae of the substances involved in it. The substances that react together in a chemical reaction are known as **reactants**. The new substances formed during a chemical reaction are known as **products**.

For example, carbon burns in the presence of oxygen to produce carbon dioxide. In this reaction, carbon and oxygen are the reactants, and carbon dioxide is the product. The simplest way to represent this reaction is in the form of a **word equation** as follows.

$$\text{Carbon} + \text{Oxygen} \longrightarrow \text{Carbon dioxide}$$

The word equation indicates the change of reactants to products through an arrow placed between them. The reactants are written on the left-hand side, and the combination is shown with a plus sign (+) between them. The products are written on the right-hand side. If there is more than one product, then a plus sign is written between the products. The head of the arrow points towards the products, which conveys the direction of the reaction.

The above chemical equation can also be represented using chemical symbols and chemical formulae for the reactants and products as given below.

$$C + O_2 \longrightarrow CO_2$$

Hence, we can say that a chemical equation is a short hand description of a chemical reaction. Representing a chemical reaction by a chemical equation saves space, time and energy.

Now consider the following equation,

$$Mg + O_2 \longrightarrow MgO$$

In the above equation, you will notice that the number of magnesium atoms on both sides of the arrow is the same, but the numbers of oxygen atoms on the left and right sides of the arrow are not equal. These types of chemical equations are called **unbalanced equations** or **skeletal equations**. As per the law of conservation of mass, the atoms themselves can neither be created nor destroyed during a simple chemical reaction. Hence, in a chemical equation, the number of atoms of each element on both sides of the arrow should always be equal. Such equations are called **balanced equations**.

QUICK REVISION

Write the word equations and skeletal equations for the following chemical changes.

1. Sodium reacts with water, forming sodium hydroxide and hydrogen.
2. Sulphur reacts with oxygen, forming sulphur dioxide.
3. Hydrogen reacts with chlorine, forming hydrogen chloride.
4. Nitrogen reacts with hydrogen, forming ammonia.

BALANCING A CHEMICAL EQUATION

Consider the reaction of magnesium with oxygen.

$$Mg + O_2 \longrightarrow MgO$$

1. Count the number of atoms of each element in reactants and products.

Element	Number of atoms in reactants (LHS)	Number of atoms in products (RHS)
Mg (Magnesium)	1	1
O (Oxygen)	2	1

From the above table, we can see that the number of magnesium atoms on both sides is the same but the number of oxygen atoms is different. Thus, this equation in unbalanced. So, we balance the equation to show the correct number of atoms participating in the reaction. How do we do that?

2. To balance the oxygen atoms on both sides of the equation, multiply the product (RHS) by 2.

Element	Number of atoms in reactants (LHS)	Number of atoms in products (RHS)
Mg (Magnesium)	1	$1 \times 2 = 2$
O (Oxygen)	2	$1 \times 2 = 2$

$$Mg + O_2 \longrightarrow 2MgO$$

Now, in the equation, the number of oxygen atoms is balanced but the number of magnesium atoms on both the sides is not balanced.

3. To balance the magnesium atoms on both sides of the equation, multiply the magnesium in the reactants (LHS) by 2.

Element	Number of atoms in reactants (LHS)	Number of atoms in products (RHS)
Mg (Magnesium)	$1 \times 2 = 2$	$1 \times 2 = 2$
O (Oxygen)	2	$1 \times 2 = 2$

$$2Mg + O_2 \longrightarrow 2MgO$$

The chemical equation, thus obtained, is said to be balanced.

What do Balanced Chemical Equations Convey?

We can get the following information by looking at a balanced chemical equation:

- The reactants that take part in the reaction and the products that are formed along with their symbols and formulae
- The physical state of the reactants and products along with the conditions required for the chemical reaction
- The number of atoms of each element of the reactants and the products that take part in the reaction
- Help in determining the mass of the reactants and the products involved in the chemical reaction

Limitations of Chemical Equations

- A chemical equation does not reveal if the reaction is complete or incomplete.
- It does not mention the speed of the reaction.
- It does not give the concentration of the reactants and products.
- It does not give the conditions of temperature, pressure and catalyst.
- It does not give any indication regarding the release or absorption of heat.
- It does not provide any information on the nature of a chemical reaction whether it is reversible or irreversible.

Making a Chemical Equation More Informative

A chemical equation can be made more informative in the following ways.

1. Physical states of the reactants and products are indicated by using the following notations.
   - (g) or (↑) for gaseous substances
   - (s) for solids
   - (l) for liquids
   - (aq) if the reactant or product is present as a solution in water
   - (↓) if the product is a precipitate
2. Evolution or absorption of heat during a chemical reaction can be indicated by adding or subtracting the term 'heat' or Δ on the product side.
3. The reaction conditions such as temperature, pressure and catalyst can be indicated above or below the arrow separating the reactants and products.
4. Concentrations of reactants can be indicated by adding the words dil. or conc. before their chemical formulae.
5. The reversibility of some of the reactions can be mentioned with a double-headed arrow.

Let us consider a few chemical equations and understand what extra information they provide. Look at the chemical equation representing the burning of carbon in the presence of oxygen.

$$\underset{\text{Carbon}}{C(s)} + \underset{\text{Oxygen}}{O_2(g)} \longrightarrow \underset{\text{Carbon dioxide}}{CO_2(g)} + \Delta$$

The above equation provides the following information.

- Carbon is present in solid state.
- Oxygen and carbon dioxide are in gaseous form.
- Δ sign shows that energy is released in the form of heat.

Let us consider one more chemical equation.

$$N_2(g) + 3H_2(g) \underset{\text{Fe (catalyst), Mo (promoter)}}{\overset{400-500\ ^\circ C,\ 200 \text{ atmosphere}}{\rightleftharpoons}} 2NH_3(g) + \text{heat}$$

Nitrogen Hydrogen Ammonia

The above equation provides the following information.

- The reactants nitrogen and hydrogen, as well as the product ammonia, are all in the gaseous form.
- Heat is released during the reaction.
- The reaction occurs at a temperature of 400–500 °C and a pressure of 200 atmospheres.
- Iron is used as a **catalyst**, and molybdenum acts as a **promoter**.
- The reaction is reversible.

WORD TO KNOW

catalyst: a substance that increases the rate of a chemical reaction without itself undergoing any chemical change

promoter: a substance that increases the efficiency of a catalyst

SOLVED PROBLEMS

1. Calculate the amount of oxygen gas required and magnesium oxide formed when 60 g of magnesium is burned completely with oxygen.

Solution:

- The balanced chemical equation for the reaction of magnesium and oxygen is

$$2Mg + O_2 \longrightarrow 2MgO$$

- The total mass of the products and reactants should be calculated.

Atomic mass of magnesium = 24 u; Atomic mass of oxygen = 16 u

So, the mass equation can be written as

$$2 \times 24.3 \quad + \quad 2 \times 16 \longrightarrow 2 \times (24.3 + 16)$$

$$48.6 \text{ g} \quad + \quad 32 \text{ g} \longrightarrow 80.6 \text{ g}$$

- Oxygen needed to burn 48.6 g of magnesium is 32 g.

Oxygen needed to burn 60 g of magnesium = (32/48.6) × 60 = 39.5 g

- Magnesium oxide formed by burning 48.6 g of magnesium = 80.6 g

Magnesium oxide formed by burning 60 g of magnesium = (80.6/48.6) × 60 = 99.5 g

Thus, when 60 g of magnesium is burned completely in oxygen, 39.5 g of oxygen is required and 99.5 g of magnesium oxide is formed.

2. Calculate the amount of carbon dioxide and calcium oxide (quicklime) formed by the decomposition of 25 g of calcium carbonate (limestone).

Solution:

- The balanced chemical equation for the decomposition of calcium carbonate is

$$CaCO_3 \longrightarrow CaO + CO_2$$

- The total mass of the products and reactants should be calculated.

  Atomic mass of calcium = 40 u; Atomic mass of oxygen = 16 u;
  Atomic mass of carbon = 12 u

  So, the mass equation can be written as

$$40 + 12 + (16 \times 3) \longrightarrow 40 + 16 + 12 + (2 \times 16)$$

$$100 \text{ g} \longrightarrow 56 \text{ g} + 44 \text{ g}$$

- 100 g of $CaCO_3$ on decomposition forms 56 g of CaO

  25 g of $CaCO_3$ on decomposition will form $(56/100) \times 25$ g = 14 g CaO

- 100 g of $CaCO_3$ on decomposition forms 44 g of CO_2

  25 g of $CaCO_3$ on decomposition will form $(44/100) \times 25$ g = 11 g CO_2

Thus, on decomposition of 25 g of calcium carbonate, 11 g of carbon dioxide and 14 g of calcium oxide will be formed.

QUICK REVISION

A. Balance the given chemical equations.

1. $Hg + O_2 \longrightarrow HgO$
2. $Al + Cl_2 \longrightarrow AlCl_3$
3. $Na + O_2 \longrightarrow Na_2O$

B. What information do you get from the following chemical equations?

1. $Zn(s) + 2HCl(aq) \longrightarrow ZnCl_2(aq) + H_2(g)$
2. $2AgCl(s) \xrightarrow{\text{Sunlight}} 2Ag(s) + Cl_2(g)$
3. $CO(g) + 2H_2(g) \xrightarrow{\text{340 atm}} CH_3OH(l)$
4. $6CO_2(g) + 6H_2O(l) \xrightarrow{\text{Sunlight}} C_6H_{12}O_6(s) + 6O_2(g)$

CONCEPT MAP

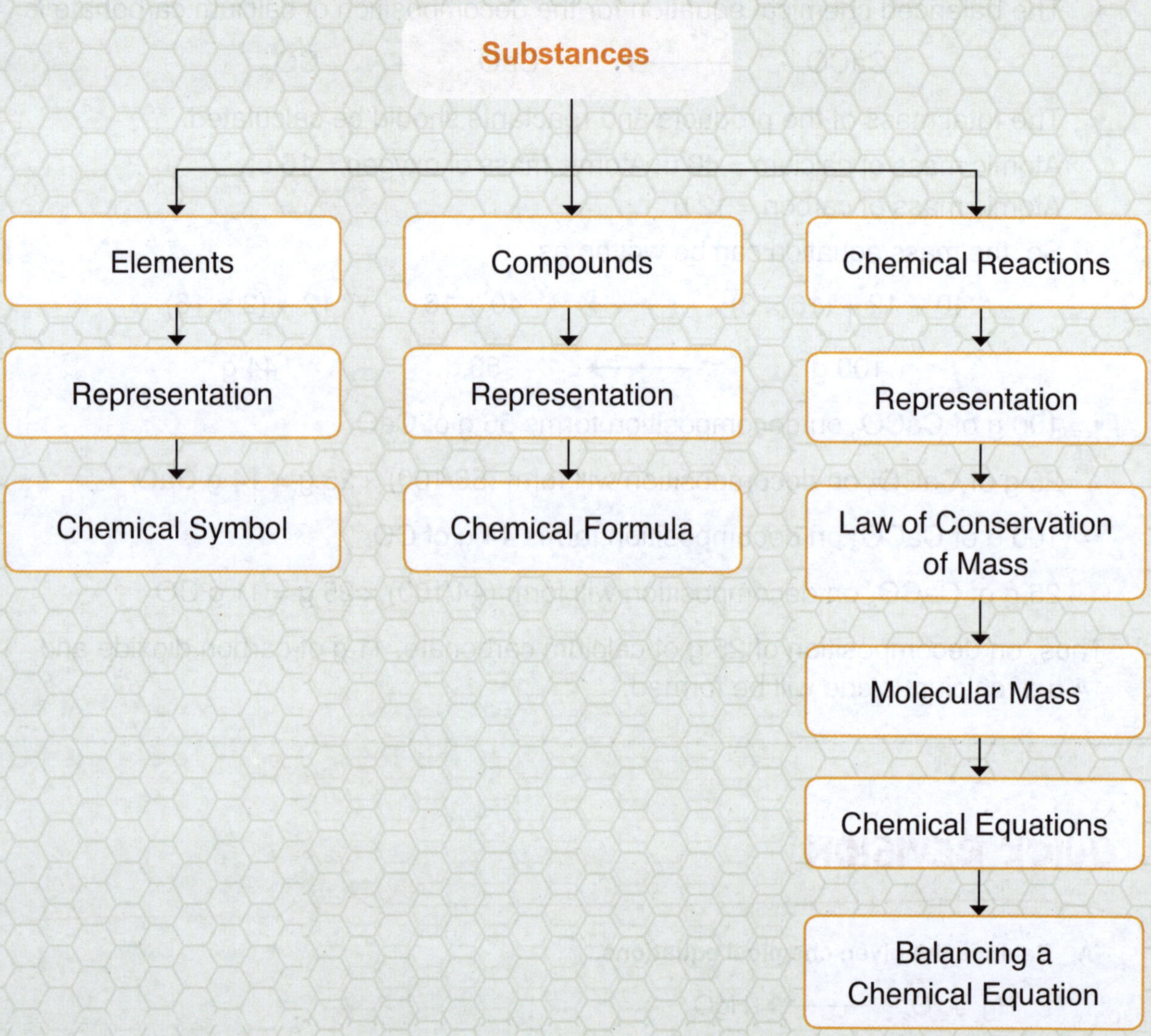

KEYWORDS

Chemical reaction: a chemical change resulting in the formation of one or more new substances

Chemical equation: the representation of a chemical reaction using symbols and formulae

Molecular mass: the total of atomic masses of all the atoms present in a molecule

Exercise

Objective Type Questions

A. Choose the correct answer.

1. The symbol of silver is
   a. Hb b. Sb
   c. Ag d. S
2. Identify the chemical formula of calcium hydroxide.
   a. CaOH b. $Ca(OH)_2$
   c. Ca_2OH d. $(Ca)_2OH$
3. Identify the correct balanced chemical equation from the following equations.
   a. $2BaCl_2 + Al_2(SO_4)_3 \longrightarrow 2BaSO_4 + AlCl_3$
   b. $3BaCl_2 + 2Al_2(SO_4)_3 \longrightarrow 3BaSO_4 + AlCl_3$
   c. $3BaCl_2 + Al_2(SO_4)_3 \longrightarrow 3BaSO_4 + 2AlCl_3$
   d. $BaCl_2 + Al_2(SO_4)_3 \longrightarrow BaSO_4 + 2AlCl_3$
4. Which of these is the correct molecular mass of $CaCO_3$?
   a. 100 u b. 200 u
   c. 300 u d. 400 u
5. According to the law of conservation of mass ____________.
   a. Mass of reactants = Mass of products
   b. Number of reactants = Number of products
   c. Mass of reactants > Mass of products
   d. Mass of reactants < Mass of products

B. Fill in the blanks.

1. A substance that contains only one kind of atoms is called ____________ (an element/a mixture).
2. The Latin name of sodium is____________ (*kalium*/*natrium*).
3. The chemical symbol of platinum is ____________ (P/Pt).
4. CaO is the chemical formula for ____________(copper oxide/calcium oxide).
5. The ____________ (physical/chemical) state of the reactants and products are mentioned along with the conditions required for the chemical reaction.

C. Write T for True and F for False.

1. The number of atoms of each element remains the same before and after a chemical reaction.
2. The chemical formula represents one molecule of the compound.
3. The chemical symbol of platinum is P.
4. The Latin name of potassium is *kalium*.
5. The name of copper and its symbol come from the Greek name *cuprum*.

Subjective Type Questions

A. Define the following.

1. Element
2. Compound
3. Chemical symbol
4. Chemical formula
5. Molecular mass

B. Differentiate between the following.

1. Elements and compounds
2. Chemical reaction and chemical equation
3. Reactants and products

C. Choose the odd one out. Give reasons for the choice.

1. Fe, Hg, Cu, Ar
2. Hydrogen, methane, nitrogen, oxygen
3. Cu, MgO, Al, He

D. Answer the following questions in brief.

1. What is an element? Give any two characteristics.
2. Write the characteristics of chemical changes.
3. Calculate the molecular mass of $MgCO_3$.
4. What is the law of conservation of mass?
5. What is the difference between atomic mass and molecular mass?

E. Answer the following questions in detail.

1. What are the steps involved in balancing a chemical equation? Explain with the help of an example.
2. Calculate the amount of oxygen and potassium chloride formed during the decomposition of 49 g of potassium chlorate. (Atomic mass of potassium = 39; oxygen = 16 and chlorine = 35.5)
3. Calculate the amount of calcium sulphate obtained by dissolving 112 g of calcium oxide (quicklime) in dilute sulphuric acid. (Atomic mass of calcium = 40; carbon = 12; hydrogen = 1; oxygen = 16 and sulphur = 32.1)

4. Calculate the mass of potassium nitrate obtained by neutralizing a solution containing 28 g of potassium hydroxide with nitric acid. (Atomic mass of nitrogen = 14; potassium = 39; oxygen = 16 and hydrogen = 1)
5. Explain how elements got their symbols.

Application-based Question

An element A has valency 1 and an element B has valency 3. What would be the formula of the compound formed by A and B if B is a metal?

Picture-based Question

Depict the molecular arrangement of the state of matter of the products formed in the following chemical reactions.

1. $Fe + CuSO_4 \longrightarrow FeSO_4 + Cu$
2. $CaCO_3 \longrightarrow CaO + CO_2$
3. $NaOH + HCl \longrightarrow NaCl + H_2O$

Skill Booster

A. **21CS:** Critical Thinking, Communication | **CC:** English | **BT:** Affective

Diki studies in class 8. She feels learning chemical formulae and writing chemical equations is a difficult task. She discusses with her classmate, Tashi, that chemistry would be fun without chemical formulae and equations. Tashi tells her that just like any other language, chemistry also has its own language. The way we cannot learn a new language in a few days, learning chemistry also takes some time. Chemical formulae and equations make the work of a chemist easier as they have a great significance. Do you agree with Tashi? Write a short note on the significance of chemical symbols, formulae and balanced chemical equations.

B. **21CS:** Collaboration, Communication | **BT:** Cognitive

A teacher asked her students to work in pairs and write a balanced chemical equation for the reaction between hydrogen and chlorine to produce hydrogen chloride. Adil and Bilal were twins who studied in the same class and sat together.

Adil's equation: $H + Cl \rightarrow HCl$

Bilal's equation: $H_2 + Cl_2 \rightarrow 2HCl$

Bilal told Adil that the equation written by him is incorrect and explained the reason. Adil listened carefully and made changes in his notebook.

What was wrong with Adil's equation? Why do you think Bilal's equation was correct?

Worksheet 5

Traditional Balancing Method

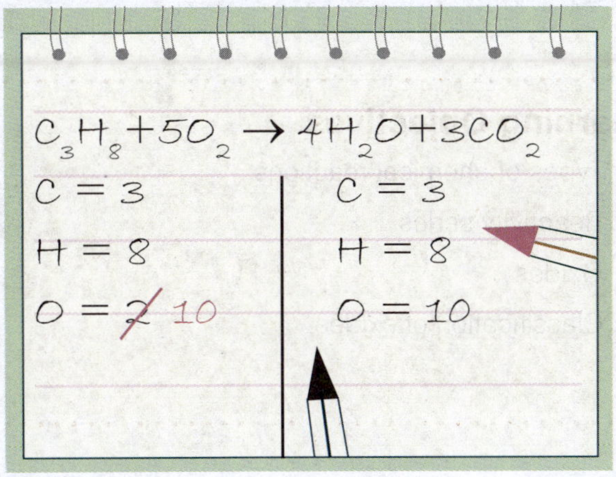

Algebraic Balancing Method

Algebraic method

- $C_4H_{10} + O_2 \longrightarrow CO_2 + H_2O$
- Put unknown coefficients in front of each molecular species in the equation:

$$xC_4H_{10} + yO_2 \longrightarrow zCO_2 + wH_2O$$

Write down the balance conditions for each element in terms of the variables (x, y, z, w).

- Balancing carbon

$$4x = z$$

- Balancing hydrogen

$$10x = 2w$$

- Balancing oxygen

$$2y = 2z + w$$

My SEE Journal

A. Which approach of balancing chemical equation do you think is easier to understand? Justify.

____

____

____

B. Do you think learning is more effective with the use of aids such as models? Substantiate.

____

____

____

C. Does a chemical equation tell whether the reaction is complete or incomplete?

____

____

My SDG Journal

4 QUALITY EDUCATION

A. In what way is balancing a chemical equation helpful to us?

____

____

B. What would have happened if standard symbols for elements were not used in a chemical equation?

____

____

C. Which element should be considered last when balancing chemical equations?

____

____

____

6 Chemical Reactions

Prior Knowledge

- Definition of chemical change with examples
- Chemical compounds and their formulas
- Definition of chemical reaction with examples

Learning Objectives

- Types of chemical reactions
- Reactivity series
- Oxides
- Classification of oxides

LET'S GET STARTED

A In the previous chapter, we learnt to balance chemical equations. Given below are a few word equations. Write the skeletal equations and balanced chemical equations for them.

1. Carbon + Oxygen ⟶ Carbon dioxide + Heat

   Skeletal equation: ____________________

   Balanced chemical equation: ____________________

2. Hydrogen + Oxygen ⟶ Water

   Skeletal equation: ____________________

   Balanced chemical equation: ____________________

3. Iron + Copper sulphate ⟶ Iron sulphate + Copper

   Skeletal equation: ____________________

   Balanced chemical equation: ____________________

4. Sodium + Water ⟶ Sodium hydroxide + Hydrogen

   Skeletal equation: ____________________

   Balanced chemical equation: ____________________

B Which law does the balancing of chemical reactions conform to?

____

____

A CHEMICAL REACTION

A chemical change in which one or more substances react or combine to form one or more new substances is called a **chemical reaction**. In a chemical reaction, atoms or ions (group of atoms having positive or negative charges) of the original substance(s) rearrange themselves to form new substances.

In this rearrangement process, either two or more substances combine with each other to form new substances or a substance may separate into two or more new substances. In other words, a chemical reaction is a process in which chemical bonds between the combining substances are broken down and new bonds are formed by rearranging atoms or ions in order to produce new substances. As shown in Fig. 6.1, when Compound 1 (made of ions A and B) reacts with Compound 2 (made of ions C and D), the ions A, B, C and D rearrange themselves to form Compound 3 (made of ions A and D) and Compound 4 (made of ions C and B).

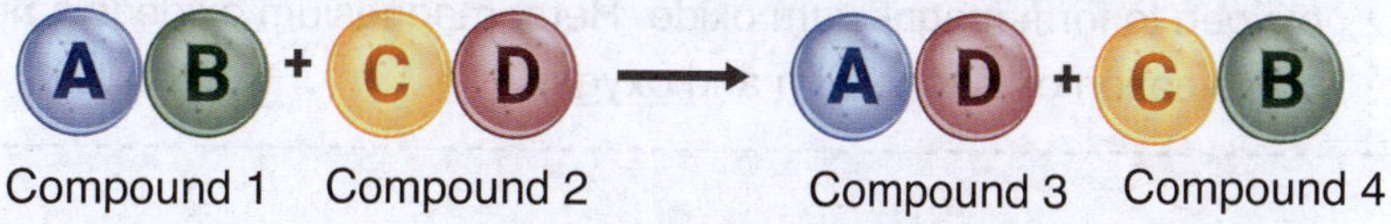

Fig. 6.1 Symbolic chemical reaction

During the course of a chemical reaction, change of energy occurs. Here, energy is either absorbed or released in the form of heat and light. In a few cases, sound is also produced.

Some real-life examples where energy is released or absorbed are as follows.

> **DO YOU KNOW?**
>
> The chemical reactions in which the reactants and products obtained have the same physical state are called **homogeneous reactions**.
>
> The chemical reactions in which the reactants and products obtained do not have the same physical state are called **heterogeneous reactions**.

- When a fuel is burned, it releases a lot of energy in the form of heat. Fuels such as petrol, diesel and kerosene are mainly made of compounds of carbon and hydrogen. These burn to form carbon dioxide, water and release heat.

$$\underset{\text{Methane}}{CH_4} + \underset{\text{Oxygen}}{2O_2} \longrightarrow \underset{\text{Carbon dioxide}}{CO_2} + \underset{\text{Water}}{2H_2O} + \text{Heat}$$

- During photosynthesis, energy from sunlight is absorbed by plants and used for preparing food.

$$\underset{\text{Carbon dioxide}}{6CO_2} + \underset{\text{Water}}{12H_2O} \xrightarrow[\text{Sunlight (light energy)}]{\text{Chlorophyll}} \underset{\text{Glucose}}{C_6H_{12}O_6} + \underset{\text{Oxygen}}{6O_2} + \underset{\text{Water}}{6H_2O}$$

- Bursting of crackers (Fig. 6.2) releases a lot of energy in the form of heat, light and sound.
- During cooking of food, heat is absorbed.

Fig. 6.2 Bursting of firecrackers (Exothermic reaction)

ACTIVITY 1

Aim: To observe that new substances are formed during chemical reactions

Materials required: Magnesium ribbon, Bunsen burner, tongs and china dish

Procedure:

1. Take a clean piece of magnesium ribbon (3–4 cm long).
2. With the help of tongs, heat the magnesium ribbon over the flame of the Bunsen burner.
3. You will observe that the magnesium ribbon burns with a dazzling white light and forms white-coloured powder (magnesium oxide).
4. Collect the powder in the china dish.

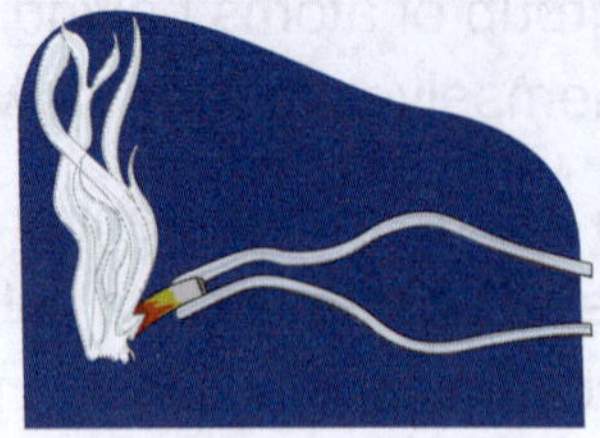

Burning of magnesium ribbon

Conclusion: We can observe that magnesium burns in the presence of oxygen to form magnesium oxide. Here, magnesium oxide is a new compound and it is formed by the combination of magnesium and oxygen.

TYPES OF CHEMICAL REACTIONS

Depending upon the nature of chemical changes occurring, chemical reactions can be categorized as combination, decomposition and displacement reactions. Let us learn more about these reactions.

Combination Reactions

Chemical reactions in which two or more reactants (elements or compounds) combine to form a single product are known as **combination reactions**. Combination reactions are also called **synthesis reactions**. A combination or synthesis reaction can be represented by the following general equation.

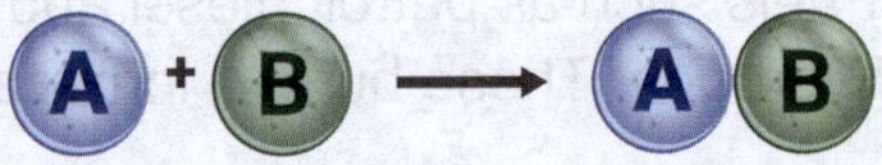

- Calcium oxide (lime) reacts with water to form slaked lime or calcium hydroxide.

$$\underset{\text{Calcium oxide}}{CaO} + \underset{\text{Water}}{H_2O} \longrightarrow \underset{\text{Calcium hydroxide}}{Ca(OH)_2}$$

- Carbon burns in the presence of oxygen to form carbon dioxide gas.

$$\underset{\text{Carbon}}{C} + \underset{\text{Oxygen}}{O_2} \xrightarrow{\text{Heat}} \underset{\text{Carbon dioxide}}{CO_2(g)}$$

- Calcium hydroxide reacts with carbon dioxide to form calcium carbonate and water.

$$\underset{\text{Calcium hydroxide}}{Ca(OH)_2} + \underset{\text{Carbon dioxide}}{CO_2} \longrightarrow \underset{\text{Calcium carbonate}}{CaCO_3(s)} + \underset{\text{Water}}{H_2O}$$

Decomposition Reactions

Chemical reactions in which a single reactant (compound) splits or breaks down to give two or more simpler products (constituent elements or other compounds) are known as **decomposition reactions**. A decomposition reaction can be represented by the following general equation:

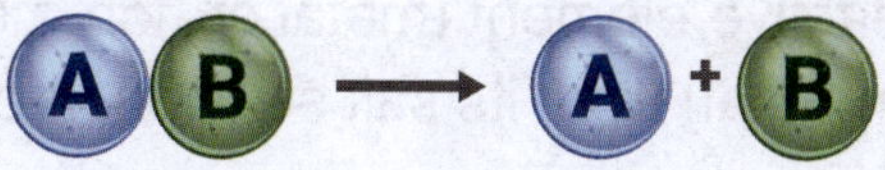

For decomposition reactions to occur, energy in the forms such as electricity, heat and light is required. For example, when lead(IV) oxide is heated, it splits to form lead(II) oxide and oxygen.

$$\underset{\text{Lead(IV) oxide}}{2PbO_2} \xrightarrow{\text{Heat}} \underset{\text{Lead(II) oxide}}{2PbO} + \underset{\text{Oxygen}}{O_2}$$

- Decomposition reactions that require energy in the form of heat are known as **thermal decomposition reactions**. These reactions are also known as thermolysis (*thermo* means 'heat' and *lysis* means 'breaking'). For example, calcium carbonate on heating decomposes into calcium oxide and carbon dioxide.

$$\underset{\text{Calcium carbonate}}{CaCO_3(s)} \xrightarrow{\text{Heat}} \underset{\text{Calcium oxide}}{CaO(s)} + \underset{\text{Carbon dioxide}}{CO_2(g)}$$

- Decomposition reactions that require energy in the form of light are known as **photochemical** or **photolytic decomposition reactions**. These reactions are also known as photolysis (*photo* means 'light' and *lysis* means 'breaking'). For example, silver chloride in the presence of light decomposes into silver and chlorine.

$$\underset{\text{Silver chloride}}{2AgCl} \xrightarrow{\text{Light}} \underset{\text{Silver}}{2Ag(s)} + \underset{\text{Chlorine}}{Cl_2(g)}$$

- Decomposition reactions that require energy in the form of electricity are known as **electrolytic decomposition reactions**. These reactions are also known as **electrolysis**. For example, when electric current is passed through water, it decomposes into hydrogen and oxygen.

$$\underset{\text{Water}}{2H_2O(l)} \xrightarrow{\text{Electric current}} \underset{\text{Hydrogen}}{2H_2(g)} + \underset{\text{Oxygen}}{O_2(g)}$$

Simple Displacement Reactions

Chemical reactions in which one element replaces or displaces the other element from its compound and forms a new compound are known as **displacement reactions**. These reactions are also known as **substitution reactions**.

In these reactions, the more reactive element (metal or non-metal) replaces the less reactive element (metal or non-metal) from its salt solution. A displacement reaction can be represented by the following general equation.

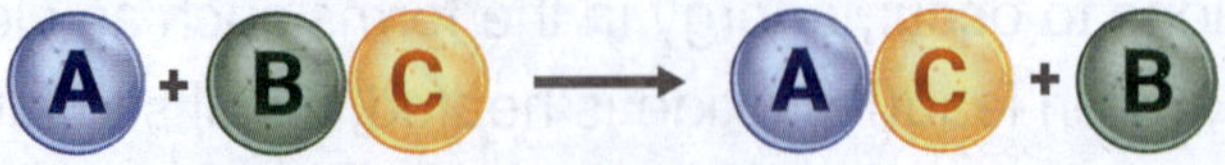

Examples of displacement reactions are as follows.

- Zinc reacts with copper sulphate solution to form zinc sulphate and copper.

$$Zn(s) + CuSO_4(aq) \longrightarrow ZnSO_4(aq) + Cu(s)$$

Zinc + Copper sulphate → Zinc sulphate + Copper

- Zinc is more reactive than copper. So, it displaces copper from its salt solution. The reverse reaction will not take place as copper is less reactive than zinc.

$$Cu + ZnSO_4 \longrightarrow \text{no reaction}$$

Copper + Zinc sulphate

- Sodium reacts with hydrochloric acid to form sodium chloride and hydrogen gas. Sodium is more reactive than hydrogen, and thus, it displaces hydrogen from hydrochloric acid.

$$2Na(s) + 2HCl(aq) \longrightarrow 2NaCl(aq) + H_2(g)$$

Sodium + Hydrochloric acid → Sodium chloride + Hydrogen

Double Displacement Reactions

Chemical reactions in which an exchange of ions takes place between two reactants (compounds in their aqueous solution) to form new compounds are called **double displacement reactions**. A double displacement reaction can be represented by the following general equation.

A double displacement reaction is of two types: precipitation reaction and neutralization reaction.

1. **Precipitation Reaction:** A type of double displacement reaction in which two compounds, in their aqueous states, react to form an insoluble solid (called precipitate) as one of the products is known as a **precipitation reaction**. For example:
   - When potassium sulphate solution reacts with barium chloride solution, barium sulphate (an insoluble white precipitate) and potassium chloride are formed.

$$K_2SO_4(aq) + BaCl_2(aq) \longrightarrow 2KCl(aq) + BaSO_4\downarrow$$

Potassium sulphate + Barium chloride → Potassium chloride + Barium sulphate

- When sodium chloride solution reacts with silver nitrate solution, silver chloride (an insoluble white precipitate) and sodium nitrate are formed.

$$\underset{\text{Sodium chloride}}{NaCl(aq)} + \underset{\text{Silver nitrate}}{AgNO_3(aq)} \longrightarrow \underset{\text{Sodium nitrate}}{NaNO_3(aq)} + \underset{\text{Silver chloride}}{AgCl\downarrow}$$

2. **Neutralization Reaction:** A type of double displacement reaction in which an acid reacts with a base resulting in the formation of salt and water is called a **neutralization reaction**. The salt formed contains the cation from the base and the anion from the acid. The hydrogen ion (H^+) of the acid combines with the hydroxide ion (OH^-) of the base to form water. For example:

- When sodium hydroxide solution (base) reacts with dilute hydrochloric acid, sodium chloride (salt) and water are formed.

$$\underset{\text{Sodium hydroxide}}{NaOH(aq)} + \underset{\text{Hydrochloric acid}}{HCl(aq)} \longrightarrow \underset{\text{Sodium chloride}}{NaCl} + \underset{\text{Water}}{H_2O}$$

- When zinc oxide (base) reacts with nitric acid, zinc nitrate (salt) and water are formed.

$$\underset{\text{Zinc oxide}}{ZnO} + \underset{\text{Nitric acid}}{2HNO_3} \longrightarrow \underset{\text{Zinc nitrate}}{Zn(NO_3)_2} + \underset{\text{Water}}{H_2O}$$

Importance of neutralization reactions in daily life

Neutralization reactions play an important role in our day-to-day life. Some of the examples of neutralization reactions from everyday life as discussed here.

- **Indigestion:** Indigestion may be caused by too much hydrochloric acid in the stomach. Antacids such as Milk of Magnesia (magnesium hydroxide) and baking soda (sodium bicarbonate) are used to neutralize the excess acid, relieving the symptoms of indigestion.
- **Ant bites:** The bite of an ant injects formic acid into the skin, which can be painful and cause the affected area to turn itchy, red and inflamed (Fig. 6.3). The acid is neutralized by rubbing moist baking soda (sodium bicarbonate), calamine solution (containing zinc carbonate) or even toothpaste on the affected area.

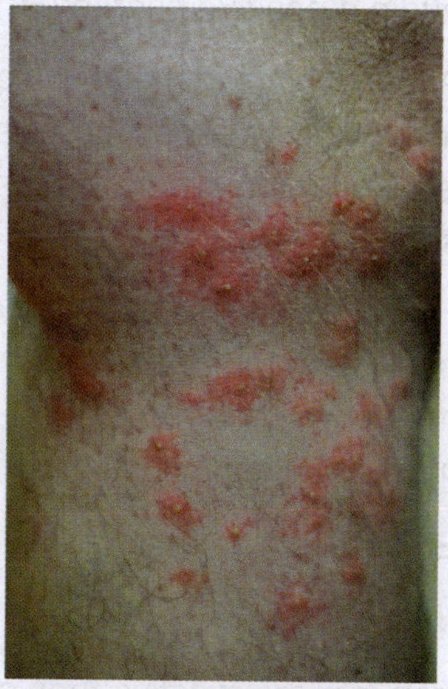

Fig. 6.3 Red inflamed skin due to ant bite

- **Treatment of soil:** Soil that is too basic or too alkaline is not good for growing crops. Using excessive fertilizers can make soil turn acidic. Acidic soil can be neutralized using slaked lime or quicklime, which is a base. If the soil is too basic, organic matter is added to it. Acids released during the decay of organic matter neutralize the excess of basic substances in the soil.
- **Treatment of wastewater:** Effluents released from factories often contain acidic substances and can change the nature of soil and water, thereby affecting living organisms. Slaked lime or calcium hydroxide is often used to neutralize the acidic substances in the effluent.

QUICK REVISION

Match the following.

Column 1	Column 2
$A + Y \longrightarrow AY$	Displacement reaction
$AB + XY \longrightarrow AY + XB$	Decomposition reaction
$AY \longrightarrow A + Y$	Double displacement reaction
$A + BY \longrightarrow AY + B$	Combination reaction

Reactivity Series

The arrangement of metals in the decreasing order of their reactivity is called the **reactivity series** of metals (Fig. 6.4). The metals placed higher in the reactivity series are more reactive than those placed below them.

Being a non-metal, hydrogen is also placed in the reactivity series because just like metals, it can also lose one electron and attain a positive charge (H^+) during chemical reactions.

A more reactive metal, which is placed at a higher position in the reactivity series, can displace a less reactive metal, which is placed at a lower position in the reactivity series from its salt solution.

However, a less reactive metal, which is placed at a lower position in the reactivity series, cannot displace a more reactive metal, which is placed at a higher position in the reactivity series from its salt solution.

Potassium	K	Most reactive
Sodium	Na	
Calcium	Ca	
Magnesium	Mg	
Aluminium	Al	
Zinc	Zn	
Iron	Fe	
Tin	Sn	
Lead	Pb	
Hydrogen	H	
Copper	Cu	
Mercury	Hg	
Silver	Ag	
Gold	Au	
Platinum	Pt	Least reactive

Fig. 6.4 Reactivity series of metals

Example: Iron reacts with copper sulphate to form iron sulphate and copper.

$$Fe + CuSO_4 \longrightarrow FeSO_4 + Cu$$

Iron is more reactive than copper and is placed higher than copper in the reactivity series. So, it can displace copper from its salt solution. The reverse reaction will not take place as copper is less reactive than iron.

$$Cu + FeSO_4 \longrightarrow \text{no reaction}$$

You can see the positions of copper and iron in the reactivity series. Thus, the reactivity series indicates which metals are more reactive as compared to others. Also, by looking at the reactivity series, we can predict whether a displacement reaction will take place or not.

ACTIVITY 2

Note: *This activity needs to be performed carefully in the presence and with the assistance of a teacher.*

Aim: To examine that a more reactive metal can displace a less reactive metal from its salt solution

Materials required: Three 250 mℓ glass beakers, 100 mℓ of copper sulphate solution, 100 mℓ of silver nitrate solution, 100 mℓ of iron sulphate solution, zinc granules and two small pieces of copper turnings

Procedure:

1. Take three clean 250 mℓ glass beakers and label them as A, B and C.
2. Take about 100 mℓ of copper sulphate solution in beaker A, 100 mℓ of silver nitrate solution in beaker B and 100 mℓ of iron sulphate solution in beaker C.
3. Add some zinc granules to beaker A. Add small pieces of copper turnings to beakers B and C.
4. Leave the beakers undisturbed for a few minutes and record your observations.

Observation:

Beaker	Reactants	Observation	Reaction	Inference
A	(Copper sulphate + Zinc)	The solution becomes colourless and a reddish-brown substance is deposited on the surface of the zinc granules.	$Zn + CuSO_4 \rightarrow ZnSO_4 + Cu$	The solution becomes colourless due to the displacement of copper from copper sulphate by zinc and formation of zinc sulphate. The displaced copper is deposited on zinc.
B	(Silver nitrate + Copper)	The solution becomes blue.	$Cu + 2AgNO_3 \rightarrow Cu(NO_3)_2 + 2Ag$	The solution becomes blue due to the formation of copper sulphate.
C	(Iron sulphate + Copper)	No change occurs in colour of the solution.	$Cu + FeSO_4 \rightarrow$ No reaction	The colour of the solution remains the same as no new substance is formed.

Conclusion: A more reactive metal can displace a less reactive metal from its salt solution.

Endothermic and Exothermic Reactions

Chemical reactions generally involve a change in energy during the course of the reaction. Energy is either absorbed or liberated during a chemical reaction and it mostly occurs in the form of heat and light. In some cases, sound is also produced. Based on whether heat energy is absorbed or liberated, chemical reactions are classified into two types.

- **Exothermic reactions:** Chemical reactions in which heat energy is liberated are called **exothermic reactions**. For example, when carbon burns in the presence of oxygen, carbon dioxide is formed along with the generation of heat.

$$\underset{\text{Carbon}}{C} + \underset{\text{Oxygen}}{O_2} \longrightarrow \underset{\text{Carbon dioxide}}{CO_2} + \text{Heat}$$

  Other examples of exothermic reactions are respiration, burning of fuels such as coal, petrol and kerosene, and rusting.

- **Endothermic reactions:** Chemical reactions in which heat energy is absorbed from the surroundings are called **endothermic reactions**. For example, when carbon and sulphur are heated together, carbon disulphide is formed.

$$\underset{\text{Carbon}}{C} + \underset{\text{Sulphur}}{2S} + \text{Heat} \longrightarrow \underset{\text{Carbon disulphide}}{CS_2}$$

DO YOU KNOW?

When we apply nail polish remover, we get a cooling effect on our finger nails and toe nails. This is because the acetone present in the nail polish remover absorbs heat from our body while evaporating.

When calcium carbonate is heated to a high temperature, calcium oxide and carbon dioxide are produced.

$$\underset{\text{Calcium carbonate}}{CaCO_3} \xrightarrow{\text{Heat}} \underset{\text{Calcium oxide}}{CaO} + \underset{\text{Carbon dioxide}}{CO_2}$$

ACTIVITY 3

Note: *This activity needs to be demonstrated by the teacher.*

Aim: To infer that the reaction of an acid with a base is an exothermic reaction

Materials required: Beaker, 10 mℓ dilute hydrochloric acid, 10 mℓ sodium hydroxide solution, thermometer, droppers and glass rod

Procedure:

1. Take a clean beaker and add 10 mℓ of dilute hydrochloric acid using a clean dropper to it.
2. With a fresh dropper, gradually add sodium hydroxide solution to the beaker.
3. Stir the solution with the help of a glass rod.
4. Place a thermometer in the solution and observe the reading.

Observation: When the thermometer is placed in the solution, a rise in temperature is noted.

Conclusion: During the reaction of an acid with a base, heat is released. This results in an increase in temperature. Hence, this reaction is an exothermic reaction.

ACTIVITY 4

Note: *This activity needs to be demonstrated by the teacher.*

Aim: To infer that dissolution of ammonium chloride in water is an endothermic reaction

Materials required: Beaker, ammonium chloride, 50 mℓ distilled water, spatula and glass rod

Procedure:

1. Take a clean beaker and add 50 mℓ of distilled water to it.
2. With the help of a spatula, add ammonium chloride to the water.
3. Stir the solution with the help of a glass rod.
4. Place a thermometer in the solution and observe the reading.

Observation: When the thermometer is placed in the solution, a decrease in temperature is noted.

Conclusion: During dissolution of ammonium chloride, energy is absorbed. This results in a decrease in temperature. Hence, dissolution of ammonium chloride in water is an endothermic reaction.

OXIDES

Decomposition reactions to form oxides: Decomposition is a chemical reaction where reactants split or break down to form simpler products. When compounds such as metal carbonates, nitrates and sulphates are heated to high temperature, they decompose to form respective metal oxides. Some of the examples are as follows.

- When a metal carbonate is heated, it decomposes to form respective metal oxide and carbon dioxide.

$$\underset{\text{Calcium carbonate}}{CaCO_3(s)} \xrightarrow{\text{Heat}} \underset{\text{Calcium oxide}}{CaO(s)} + \underset{\text{Carbon dioxide}}{CO_2(g)}$$

- When a metal nitrate is heated, it decomposes to form respective metal oxide, nitrogen dioxide and oxygen.

$$\underset{\text{Magnesium nitrate}}{2Mg(NO_3)_2} \xrightarrow{\text{Heat}} \underset{\text{Magnesium oxide}}{2MgO} + \underset{\text{Nitrogen dioxide}}{4NO_2} + \underset{\text{Oxygen}}{O_2}$$

- When a metal sulphate is heated, it decomposes to form respective metal oxide, sulphur dioxide and sulphur trioxide.

$$\underset{\text{Iron sulphate}}{2FeSO_4} \xrightarrow{\text{Heat}} \underset{\text{Iron oxide}}{Fe_2O_3} + \underset{\text{Sulphur dioxide}}{SO_2} + \underset{\text{Sulphur trioxide}}{SO_3}$$

ACTIVITY 5

Note: *This activity needs to be performed carefully in the presence and with the assistance of a teacher.*

Aim: To infer heating of calcium carbonate yields calcium oxide

Materials required: Bunsen burner, calcium carbonate (limestone), wire gauze, tripod stand, limewater, delivery tube, test tubes and clamp stand

Procedure:

1. Take a few lumps of limestone in a test tube. Close the mouth of the test tube with a cork.
2. Fit a delivery tube in the cork in such a way that the other end of the delivery tube dips into another test tube containing 3–4 mℓ limewater.
3. Heat the solid gently over a Bunsen burner. (**Note:** *If the room is dark, then glowing of lumps can be seen.*)
4. Observe and note down all the changes.

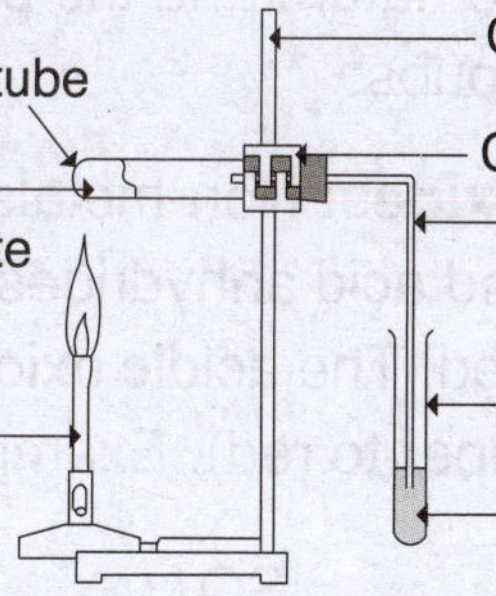

Observations:

1. The limewater turns milky. This proves the formation of CO_2 and hence the thermal decomposition of limestone.
2. A white solid is left behind in the test tube.

Conclusion: On heating, calcium carbonate ($CaCO_3$) yields a white solid, calcium oxide (CaO), and carbon dioxide (CO_2).

Equation:
$$\underset{\text{Calcium carbonate}}{CaCO_3} \xrightarrow{\text{Heat}} \underset{\text{Calcium oxide}}{CaO} + \underset{\text{Carbon dioxide}}{CO_2}$$

Note: *As calcium carbonate and calcium oxide are white in colour, one cannot distinguish the formation of calcium oxide.*

ACTIVITY 6

Note: *This activity needs to be performed carefully in the presence and with the assistance of a teacher.*

Aim: To infer heating of lead carbonate yields lead oxide

Materials required: Bunsen burner, test tubes, test tube holder, delivery tube, limewater

Procedure:

1. Take about 2 spatulas full of lead carbonate in a test tube. Close the mouth of the test tube with a cork.
2. Fit a delivery tube in the cork in such a way that the other end of the delivery tube dips into another test tube containing 3–4 mℓ limewater.
3. Heat the solid gently over a Bunsen burner.
4. Observe and note down all the changes.

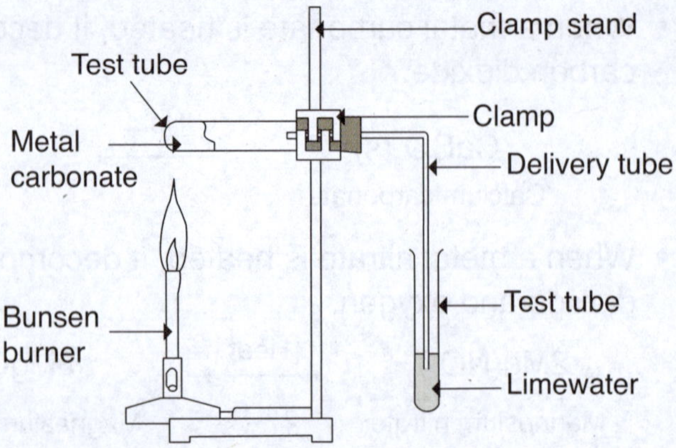

Observations:

1. The limewater turns milky. This proves the formation of CO_2 and hence the thermal decomposition of lead carbonate.
2. A yellow solid forms in the horizontal test tube. Colour change proves that a new compound is formed.

Conclusion: On heating, lead carbonate ($PbCO_3$) yields a yellow solid, lead oxide (PbO), and carbon dioxide (CO_2).

Equation:

$$\underset{\text{Lead carbonate}}{PbCO_3} \xrightarrow{\text{Heat}} \underset{\text{Lead oxide}}{PbO} + \underset{\text{Carbon dioxide}}{CO_2}$$

Classification of Oxides

Oxides are compounds that are formed by the reaction of oxygen with other elements. Oxygen reacts with both metals and non-metals to form respective oxides. Oxygen is highly reactive in nature.

Based on the nature and the properties exhibited by compounds, oxides are classified into four main groups:

- **Acidic oxides:** Non-metals react with oxygen to form acidic compounds of oxygen, also called acid anhydrides or acidic oxides, and when these combine with bases, salts are formed. The acidic oxides can be tested with litmus paper (these oxides turn a blue litmus paper to red). Examples: CO_2, SO_3 and SO_2.

$$\underset{\text{Sulphur trioxide}}{SO_3} + \underset{\text{Water}}{H_2O} \longrightarrow \underset{\text{Sulphuric acid}}{H_2SO_4}$$

$$\underset{\text{Sulphur dioxide}}{SO_2} + \underset{\text{Sodium hydroxide}}{2NaOH} \longrightarrow \underset{\text{Sodium sulphite (salt)}}{Na_2SO_3} + \underset{\text{Water}}{H_2O}$$

- **Basic oxides:** Metals react with oxygen to give basic compounds of oxygen, also called base anhydrides or basic oxides, and when these combine with acids, salts are formed. The basic oxides can be tested with litmus paper (these oxides turn a red litmus paper to blue). Examples: CaO, MgO, Na_2O and K_2O.

$$\underset{\text{Sodium oxide}}{Na_2O} + \underset{\text{Water}}{H_2O} \longrightarrow \underset{\text{Sodium hydroxide}}{2NaOH}$$

$$\underset{\text{Sodium oxide}}{Na_2O} + \underset{\text{Sulphuric acid}}{H_2SO_4} \longrightarrow \underset{\text{Sodium sulphate (salt)}}{Na_2SO_4} + \underset{\text{Water}}{H_2O}$$

- **Amphoteric oxides:** These are compounds of oxygen that exhibit both acidic and basic characteristics. These oxides on reaction with acid undergo neutralization reaction to form salt and water, thus exhibiting the basic property of the compound. Similarly, on reaction with base, they form salt and water, thus exhibiting the acidic property of the compound. Amphoteric oxides do not show any colour change neither with blue litmus nor with red litmus paper. Examples: Al_2O_3, ZnO, PbO and SnO.

$$\underset{\text{Zinc oxide}}{ZnO} + \underset{\text{Hydrochloric acid}}{2HCl} \longrightarrow \underset{\text{Zinc chloride}}{ZnCl_2} + \underset{\text{Water}}{H_2O} \quad \text{(basic nature)}$$

$$\underset{\text{Zinc oxide}}{ZnO} + \underset{\text{Sodium hydroxide}}{2NaOH} \longrightarrow \underset{\text{Sodium zincate}}{Na_2ZnO_2} + \underset{\text{Water}}{H_2O} \quad \text{(acidic nature)}$$

- **Neutral oxides:** Some compounds on reaction with oxygen form oxides which neither exhibit acidic nor basic characteristics. Hence, they do not form salts on reaction with acids or bases. Such compounds are called neutral compounds of oxygen. Examples: NO, CO and N_2O.

ACTIVITY 7

Aim: To test whether the given oxide is acidic, basic or neutral

Materials required: Test tube, glass rod, magnesium oxide (MgO), litmus paper and water

Procedure:

1. Take a test tube and add water to it.
2. Add magnesium oxide to the test tube and stir with a glass rod.
3. Test the solution with a litmus paper and record your observation.

Observation and Conclusion:

Sample	Observation	Conclusion
Magnesium oxide + water	Red litmus paper turns blue	Magnesium oxide is a basic oxide.

CONCEPT MAP

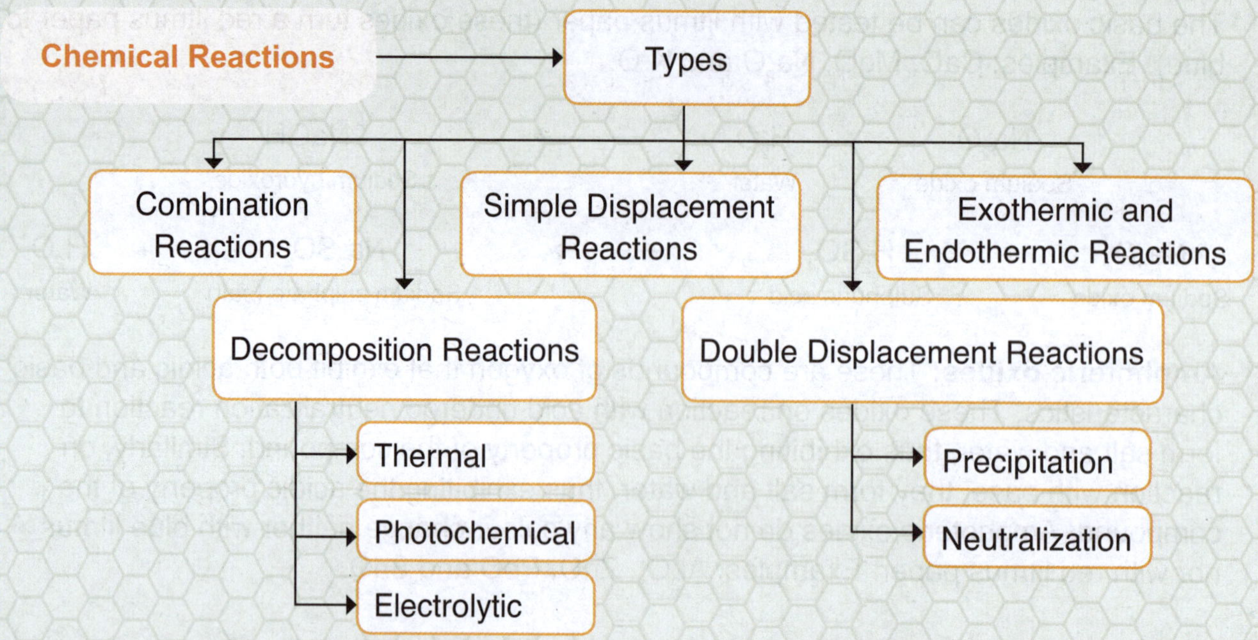

KEYWORDS

Chemical reaction: a chemical change resulting in the formation of one or more new substances

Combination reactions: chemical reactions in which two or more reactants (elements or compounds) combine to form a single product

Decomposition reactions: chemical reactions in which a single reactant splits or breaks down to give two or more products

Exothermic reactions: chemical reactions in which heat is evolved

Endothermic reactions: chemical reactions in which heat is absorbed

Double displacement reactions: chemical reactions in which an exchange of ions takes place between two reactants (aqueous solution) to form new compounds

Reactivity series: the arrangement of metals in the decreasing order of their reactivity

Neutralization reaction: a type of chemical reaction in which an acid reacts with a base to form salt and water

Exercise

Objective Type Questions

A. Choose the correct answer.

1. The following reaction is an example of ________.
   $Fe_2O_3 + 2Al \longrightarrow Al_2O_3 + 2Fe$
   a. combination reaction
   b. displacement reaction
   c. decomposition reaction
   d. double displacement reaction
2. The following reaction is an example of ________.
   $NH_3 + HCl \longrightarrow NH_4Cl$
   a. double displacement reaction
   b. displacement reaction
   c. combination reaction
   d. decomposition reaction
3. Which among the following is the most reactive metal?
   a. Sodium
   b. Potassium
   c. Gold
   d. Silver
4. Which of the following is an example of endothermic reaction?
   a. Burning of fuels
   b. Dissolution of ammonium chloride in water
   c. Rusting
   d. Respiration
5. Which of the following statements is true about basic oxides?
   a. They form salts with bases.
   b. They turn blue litmus to red.
   c. Carbon dioxide is an example of basic oxide.
   d. They turn red litmus to blue.

B. Fill in the blanks.

1. The reaction in which heat energy is released is known as ____________ (exothermic/endothermic) reaction.
2. A reaction in which a single substance splits to give two or more substances is called ____________(decomposition/ displacement) reaction.
3. The oxides that exhibit both acidic and basic characteristics are called ____________. (neutral oxides/amphoteric oxides)
4. The decomposition reaction that occurs in the presence of light is known as ____________ (photolysis/thermolysis).
5. Displacement reactions are also called ____________ reactions. (substitution/ synthesis)

C. Write T for True and F for False

1. Precipitation reactions produce insoluble salts.
2. Reaction of sodium chloride solution with silver nitrate solution is an example of a decomposition reaction.
3. Al_2O_3 is an example of neutral oxide.
4. Magnesium oxide is obtained from the thermal decomposition of magnesium sulphate.
5. The products of a neutralization reaction are salt and water.

Subjective Type Questions

A. Define the following.

1. Electrolysis
2. Neutralization reactions
3. Reactivity series
4. Amphoteric oxides
5. Endothermic reactions

B. Identify the type of chemical reaction.

1. $Fe + CuSO_4 \longrightarrow FeSO_4 + Cu$
2. $2Na + Cl_2 \longrightarrow 2NaCl$
3. $CaCO_3 \longrightarrow CaO + CO_2$
4. $BaCl_2 + Na_2SO_4 \longrightarrow BaSO_4 + 2NaCl$

C. Answer the following questions in brief.

1. What are the general chemical equations for single displacement and double displacement reactions?
2. Write a short note on decomposition reaction and its types.
3. List the properties of amphoteric oxides.
4. Explain neutralization reaction with the help of an example.
5. Explain the reaction of zinc and copper sulphate with the help of appropriate chemical equations.

D. Answer the following questions in detail.

1. Explain the various types of chemical reactions.
2. Explain the arrangement of metals in the reactivity series in detail.
3. Explain the formation of oxides from decomposition of metal carbonates, nitrates and sulphates.
4. What are the different types of oxides? Explain with examples.
5. Explain endothermic and exothermic reactions with examples.

Application-based Question

Sample A can displace sample B from its salt solution and sample B can displace sample C, but sample C cannot displace samples A and B. Sample A is less reactive than aluminium and Sample B is more reactive than tin, whereas sample C is situated in between mercury and gold.

Mention the names of these samples and arrange them in the decreasing order of their reactivity.

Picture-based Question

Rohit performed the experiment shown in the picture for the school Science Fair. He mixed a few drops of red food-colouring agent in vinegar and poured it into his model of rock that he made from old newspaper and clay. He then made a solution of baking powder in water. When the examiners visited his stall, he gently poured the baking soda solution into the opening of the rock. As soon as he poured the baking soda mixture, red-coloured froath erupted from the opening of the rock. Now, answer the following question.

1. Name the natural phenomenon demonstrated by Rohit in this experiment.
2. Name and write the reaction that takes place in this experiment.
3. The froath came out of the opening of the rock model due to the release of a gas. Can you name that gas? How can you test this gas?

Skill Booster

A. **21CS:** Collaboration, Communication | **EL** | **BT:** Cognitive, Psychomotor

Form pairs and perform an activity to test whether nitric oxide and sulphur dioxide are acidic, basic, amphoteric or neutral oxides.

B. **21CS:** Critical Thinking, Life Skills | **BT:** Cognitive, Affective

Prajwal and his friends were playing in their society park. There was a beehive on a tree. Some of the bees were moving near the ground under the tree. Unfortunately, when one of the children went near the tree, a bee stung his hand.

1. Prajwal rushed to his house immediately and got a white paste. He then applied the paste on the stung area of his friend's hand. What was the white paste made up of?
2. Do you think the white paste gave Prajwal's friend some relief? If so, how?

Worksheet 6

A small village was situated at 4,300 metres above sea level. The village had a mining centre, which was renowned for gold extraction. Undoubtedly, mining offered employment opportunities to the villagers, raising their living standards. But soon, the negative impact of mining started to appear on the lives of local people. Many people lost their land. Many adults and children got heart and lung diseases due to the pollution caused by various mining processes. Looking at all the side effects, all the villagers decided to protest. They asked the athourities to stop mining in their village.

My SEE Journal

Was the decision of protest to tackle the situation a small step towards the improvement of global environment development? What would be your suggestion to overcome this situation?

How mining is affecting the global environment?

My SDG Journal

17 PARTNERSHIPS FOR THE GOALS

Design an awareness poster depicting the impact of mining on human health.

7 Hydrogen

Prior Knowledge

- Reaction between metals and acids
- Reaction of hydrogen gas with oxygen
- Reducing agents

Learning Objectives

- Occurrence of hydrogen
- Preparation of hydrogen
- Properties of hydrogen
- Uses of hydrogen

LET'S GET STARTED

Carefully observe the given picture and answer the following questions.

1. What is the name of the gas that is released during the reaction?

____

2. In the reaction, how can we prove that the gas formed is hydrogen gas?

____

3. Mention any two physical properties of the hydrogen gas.

____

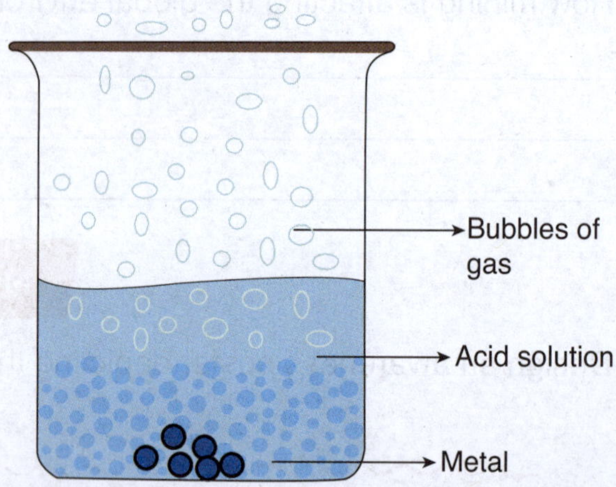

We have learned in the previous classes that hydrogen gas puts off a burning splinter with a 'pop' sound.

In 1766, British scientist Henry Cavendish discovered hydrogen by adding zinc to dilute sulphuric acid. He initially named the gas 'inflammable air'. In 1783, French scientist Antoine Lavoisier named the gas 'hydrogen'.

The word hydrogen comes from the Greek words *hydro* meaning 'water' and *genes* meaning 'formed' based on the finding that water is produced when hydrogen is burned.

Let us learn in detail about the occurrence, properties and uses of hydrogen in this chapter.

OCCURRENCE OF HYDROGEN

Hydrogen is one of the most abundant elements on Earth. The free state of hydrogen exists in the sun (Fig. 7.1), stars and in volcanic gases. Due to nuclear reactions that involve hydrogen gas, a large amount of heat and light is released in the Sun and stars.

Fig. 7.1 Hydrogen exists in the sun in huge amounts

Hydrogen occurs abundantly on Earth in combined states by forming compounds such as water (Fig. 7.2), hydrocarbons, acids and oils. It occurs as a constituent of animal and plant tissues in the form of proteins, fats and carbohydrates.

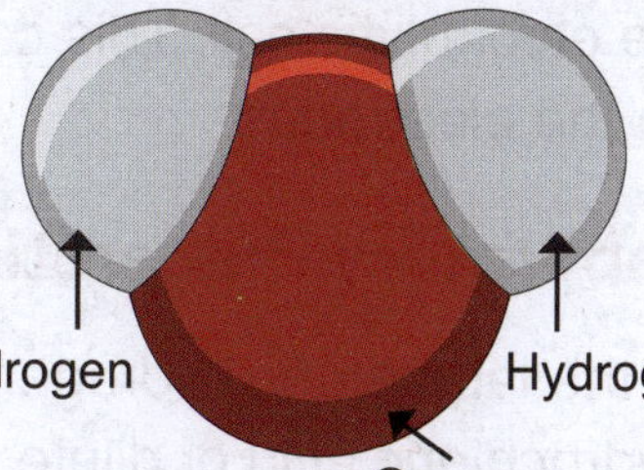

Fig. 7.2 Molecular structure of water (a combined form of hydrogen)

PREPARATION OF HYDROGEN

Let us look at the methods to prepare hydrogen.

Preparation of Hydrogen from Water by Electrolysis

Hydrogen is prepared by passing an electric current through water that contains a small quantity of acid, such as, dilute sulphuric acid. This method is called **electrolysis of water** and is widely used in the industrial preparation of hydrogen.

$$\underset{\text{Water}}{2H_2O} \xrightarrow{\text{Electric current}} \underset{\text{Hydrogen}}{2H_2\uparrow} + \underset{\text{Oxygen}}{O_2\uparrow}$$

The process of passing electric current through a chemical substance or compound in its aqueous solution or molten state to bring about its decomposition is known as **electrolysis**.

FIND OUT Why is a small quantity of dilute H_2SO_4 added to water for electrolysis?

In an electrolysis set-up, the important components are electrolytic cell, electrolyte, electrodes and battery.

Electrolytic cell: The process of electrolysis takes place in a container called the electrolytic cell (Fig. 7.3). It is a device that converts electrical energy into chemical energy or vice versa. It contains electrodes dipped in the electrolyte.

Electrolyte: Electrolyte is the molten or an aqueous solution of a chemical compound through which current passes to carry out the chemical reaction. In the solution or molten state, the compounds dissociate into ions. The ions flow towards the oppositely-charged electrodes, which causes the flow of current.

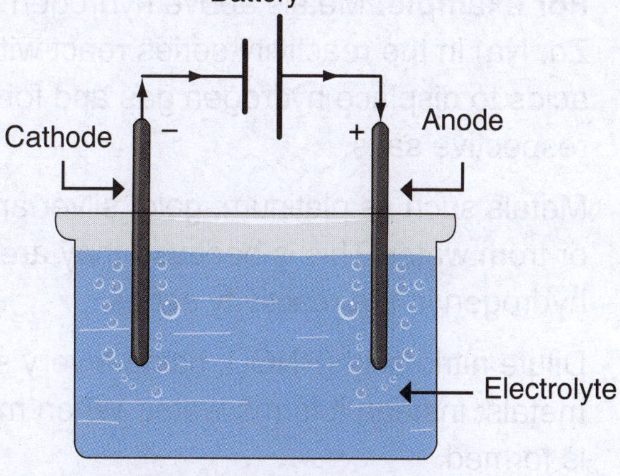

Fig. 7.3 Electrolytic cell

Electrodes: Electrodes are the two conducting terminals or rods dipped in the electrolytic solution. Electric current enters or leaves an electrolyte through these conducting rods. Electrodes are made up of metals or graphite.

The electrode that is connected to the positive terminal of the battery is called the **anode** (positive electrode) and the electrode that is connected to the negative terminal of the battery is called the **cathode** (negative electrode).

Battery: The electrodes are connected to a battery which provides electric current.

When an electric current is passed through the electrodes of an electrolytic cell, the ions in the electrolyte move towards the oppositely charged electrodes. Cations (positive charges) move towards the cathode, whereas anions (negative charges) move towards the anode of the electrolytic cell. This causes the constituents of the electrolyte to gradually get deposited on the electrodes.

Laboratory Preparation of Hydrogen

In the laboratory, hydrogen is prepared by the reaction of zinc granules with dilute hydrochloric acid or dilute sulphuric acid.

$$\underset{\text{Zinc}}{Zn} + \underset{\text{Dil. hydrochloric acid}}{2HCl} \longrightarrow \underset{\text{Zinc chloride}}{ZnCl_2} + \underset{\text{Hydrogen}}{H_2\uparrow}$$

$$\underset{\text{Zinc}}{Zn} + \underset{\text{Dil. sulphuric acid}}{H_2SO_4} \longrightarrow \underset{\text{Zinc sulphate}}{ZnSO_4} + \underset{\text{Hydrogen}}{H_2\uparrow}$$

In this process, zinc granules are preferred over pure zinc because pure zinc is non-porous and its reaction with dilute acids is very slow. Also, zinc is preferred to other metals because the reaction of zinc with either dilute HCl or dilute H_2SO_4 can be easily controlled in the laboratory.

Note: Metals such as sodium (Na) and potassium (K) are not preferred for the preparation of hydrogen, though they produce hydrogen, as they react with mineral acids very violently.

The choice of a metal to react with a dilute mineral acid for the synthesis of hydrogen depends on the position of the metal in the reactivity series.

For example: Metals above hydrogen (Ca, Mg, Zn, Na) in the reactivity series react with dilute acids to displace hydrogen gas and form their respective salts.

DO YOU KNOW?

Hydrogen that is just formed after a chemical reaction is referred to as 'nascent hydrogen' or 'newly born hydrogen'.

Metals such as platinum, gold, silver and copper do not displace hydrogen either from acids or from water. This is because they are less reactive than hydrogen and are placed below hydrogen in the reactivity series.

Dilute nitric acid (HNO_3), being a very strong oxidizing agent, will not liberate hydrogen with metals; instead it forms water. When magnesium reacts with dilute nitric acid, hydrogen is formed.

Choice of Dilute Acids (other than dil. nitric acid) in the Preparation of Hydrogen

An active metal usually displaces hydrogen gas. Dilute nitric acid (HNO_3) is a very strong oxidizing agent which can oxidize the free hydrogen and convert into water. On the other hand, the use of concentrated nitric acid results in the formation of a mixture of oxides of nitrogen. Therefore, dilute HNO_3 is not used for hydrogen preparation.

Other mineral acids such as dilute hydrochloric acid and dilute sulphuric acid are extensively used in the preparation of hydrogen. However, concentrated sulphuric acid is not used in the preparation of hydrogen for reacting with zinc as it will produce sulphur dioxide (SO_2) instead of H_2 gas.

ACTIVITY 1

Aim: To prepare hydrogen gas in the laboratory using dilute hydrochloric acid and zinc granules

Materials required: Thistle funnel, dilute hydrochloric acid, delivery tube, two-holed rubber cork, zinc granules, Woulfe bottle, gas jar, trough, water and beehive shelf

Note: This activity needs to be performed very carefully as a teacher demonstration.

Precautions:

- Make sure the entire set-up is airtight.
- The end of the thistle funnel must be dipped in the dilute hydrochloric acid.
- The entire set-up should be kept away from fire.

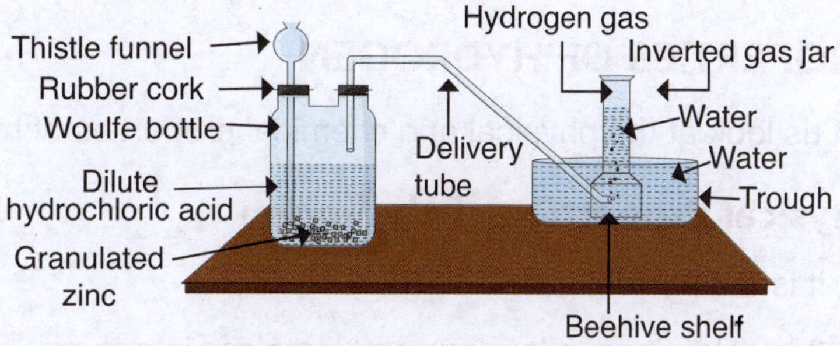

- The collection of hydrogen gas should be done only after the entire volume of air inside the apparatus is expelled out.

Procedure:

1. Set up the apparatus as shown in the figure.
2. Take a few zinc granules in a Woulfe bottle and close its mouth with a two-holed rubber cork.
3. Fix the thistle funnel in one hole and the delivery tube in the other hole of the rubber cork.
4. Connect the other end of the delivery tube to the beehive shelf that is immersed under the water in the trough.
5. Gently pour the dilute hydrochloric acid through the thistle funnel until the zinc granules are completely immersed.

Observation: The level of water in an inverted gas jar reduces indicating the formation of hydrogen gas.

Collection of the gas: Allow some hydrogen gas to escape from the jar as it is mixed with the air within the apparatus. Place an inverted gas jar filled with water on the beehive shelf. Collect the hydrogen gas by the downward displacement of water. It is collected by the downward displacement of water as it is lighter than air. When the bubbles stop forming, it indicates that the reaction is complete. Remove the gas jar from the trough that is filled with colourless hydrogen gas and keep it in the inverted position. Similarly, several jars can be used to collect more amount of hydrogen gas.

Bosch's Process

Bosch's process is used to prepare hydrogen industrially.

During this process, steam is passed at a temperature of 1200°C over carbon (red-hot coke) producing hydrogen gas and carbon monoxide.

$$\underset{\text{Carbon}}{C} + \underset{\text{Steam}}{H_2O(g)} \longrightarrow \underset{\text{Carbon monoxide}}{CO} + \underset{\text{Hydrogen gas}}{H_2}$$

The excess steam in the reaction again reacts with the water gas (that is, a mixture of CO and H_2) at a temperature of nearly 450 °C in the presence of catalysts (chromium oxide or iron oxide) resulting in the further formation of hydrogen gas and carbon dioxide.

$$\underset{\text{Water gas}}{CO + H_2} + H_2O(g) \longrightarrow CO_2 + 2H_2$$

The carbon dioxide produced during this reaction is further dissolved in cold water or caustic potash solution under pressure of about 20–25 atmosphere. The undissolved hydrogen can be removed.

PROPERTIES OF HYDROGEN

Let us look at the physical and chemical properties of hydrogen.

Physical Properties of Hydrogen

- It is the lightest gas.
- It is colourless, odourless and tasteless in nature.
- It can conduct heat better than other gases.
- It is insoluble in water.

Hydrogen can burn itself (combustible gas) but does not support the process of combustion.

Chemical Properties of Hydrogen

Let us look at how hydrogen reacts with various substances.

GREENATHON

Instead of hydrocarbon fuels such as petrol and diesel, hydrogen could be used as fuel, which is more eco-friendly.

Reaction with Oxygen

Hydrogen reacts with oxygen to produce a pale blue flame and produces water vapour and heat.

$$\underset{\text{Hydrogen}}{2H_2} + \underset{\text{Oxygen}}{O_2} \longrightarrow \underset{\text{Water}}{2H_2O} + \text{Heat}$$

As heat energy is released in this reaction, this reaction is a combustion reaction and also an exothermic reaction.

Reaction with Chlorine

In the presence of diffused sunlight, hydrogen reacts with chlorine to form hydrogen chloride.

$$\underset{\text{Hydrogen}}{H_2} + \underset{\text{Chlorine}}{Cl_2} \longrightarrow \underset{\text{Hydrogen chloride}}{2HCl}$$

In the presence of direct sunlight, the reaction of hydrogen with chlorine takes place with an explosion.

Reaction with Nitrogen

Hydrogen reacts with nitrogen under specific conditions such as high pressure (200 atm), high temperature (450°C), presence of a catalyst (iron) and a promoter (molybdenum) to form ammonia.

$$\underset{\text{Hydrogen}}{3H_2} + \underset{\text{Nitrogen}}{N_2} \longrightarrow \underset{\text{Ammonia}}{2NH_3}$$

The above reaction is referred to as **Haber's process**.

Reaction with Sulphur

Hydrogen reacts with boiling sulphur to form hydrogen sulphide.

$$\underset{\text{Hydrogen}}{H_2} + \underset{\text{Sulphur}}{S} \longrightarrow \underset{\text{Hydrogen sulphide}}{H_2S}$$

Reaction with Litmus

Hydrogen, being neutral (neither acidic nor basic), does not change the colour of either blue litmus or red litmus.

Reaction with Metals

Hydrogen reacts with highly reactive metals at high temperatures to form respective metal hydrides.

$$\underset{\text{Hydrogen}}{H_2} + \underset{\text{Potassium}}{2K} \longrightarrow \underset{\text{Potassium hydride}}{2KH}$$

$$\underset{\text{Hydrogen}}{H_2} + \underset{\text{Sodium}}{2Na} \longrightarrow \underset{\text{Sodium hydride}}{2NaH}$$

$$\underset{\text{Hydrogen}}{H_2} + \underset{\text{Calcium}}{Ca} \longrightarrow \underset{\text{Calcium hydride}}{CaH_2}$$

Reducing Property of Hydrogen: Oxidation–Reduction Reactions

Oxidation: The process of removal of hydrogen or addition of oxygen to a substance is known as **oxidation** and the substance that removes hydrogen or adds oxygen to another substance is called an **oxidizing agent**.

$$\underset{\text{Zinc}}{2Zn} + \underset{\substack{\text{Oxygen}\\ \text{(Oxidizing agent)}}}{O_2} \longrightarrow \underset{\text{Zinc oxide}}{2ZnO}$$

In the above reaction, oxygen reacts with zinc to form zinc oxide (oxygen gets added to zinc here). So, oxygen acts as an oxidizing agent here.

$$\underset{\substack{\text{Hydrogen}\\ \text{sulphide}}}{H_2S} + \underset{\substack{\text{Chlorine (Oxidizing}\\ \text{agent)}}}{Cl_2} \longrightarrow \underset{\text{Hydrogen chloride}}{2HCl} + \underset{\text{Sulphur}}{S}$$

In the above reaction, chlorine reacts with hydrogen sulphide to remove hydrogen from hydrogen sulphide and thus oxidizes sulphur. So, chlorine acts as an oxidizing agent here.

Reduction: The process of removal of oxygen or addition of hydrogen to a substance is known as **reduction** and the substance that removes oxygen or adds hydrogen to another substance is called a **reducing agent**.

$$\underset{\text{Copper oxide}}{CuO} + \underset{\substack{\text{Hydrogen}\\ \text{(Reducing agent)}}}{H_2} \longrightarrow \underset{\text{Copper}}{Cu} + \underset{\text{Water}}{H_2O}$$

In the above reaction, when hydrogen gas is passed over heated metal oxides, the oxides are reduced to the corresponding metals. So, hydrogen acts as a reducing agent here.

$$\underset{\text{Bromine}}{Br_2} + \underset{\substack{\text{Hydrogen sulphide}\\ \text{(Reducing agent)}}}{H_2S} \longrightarrow \underset{\text{Hydrogen bromide}}{2HBr} + \underset{\text{Sulphur}}{S}$$

In the above reaction, hydrogen sulphide reacts with bromine to add hydrogen to bromine. So, hydrogen sulphide acts as a reducing agent here.

The reactions in which both oxidation and reduction take place simultaneously are referred to as **redox reactions**.

- In the reaction between lead oxide and hydrogen, hydrogen is oxidized to water and lead oxide is reduced to lead.

Oxidation ($H_2 \rightarrow H_2O$)

$$\underset{\text{Lead oxide}}{PbO} + \underset{\text{Hydrogen}}{H_2} \longrightarrow \underset{\text{Lead}}{Pb} + \underset{\text{Water}}{H_2O}$$

Reduction ($PbO \rightarrow Pb$)

- In the reaction between copper oxide and hydrogen, hydrogen is oxidized to water and copper oxide is reduced to copper.

Oxidation ($H_2 \rightarrow H_2O$)

$$\underset{\text{Copper oxide}}{CuO} + \underset{\text{Hydrogen}}{H_2} \longrightarrow \underset{\text{Copper}}{Cu} + \underset{\text{Water}}{H_2O}$$

Reduction ($CuO \rightarrow Cu$)

USES OF HYDROGEN

Common uses of hydrogen are as follows.

- The liquid form of hydrogen is widely used as a rocket fuel.
- It is used in cutting and welding of metals as **oxy-hydrogen flame** (Fig. 7.4).

Fig. 7.4 Oxy-hydrogen flame

- It is used in the preparation of ammonia through Haber's process. Ammonia produced by this method is used in the manufacture of explosives and fertilizers such as urea (Fig. 7.5).

Fig. 7.5 Urea

- It is used as a reducing agent in the extraction of pure metals from their oxides.
- It is used in the **hydrogenation of oils** for the conversion of liquid vegetable oils into *vanaspati* and margarine in the presence of nickel as a catalyst.
- It is used in the manufacture of petrol, methanol and hydrochloric acid.
- It is used to fill balloons (Fig. 7.6), which help to study weather conditions, such as, air pressure, temperature and wind speed.

Fig. 7.6 Hydrogen-filled balloons

Use of hydrogen fuel (a non-polluting fuel) instead of fossil fuels can help in reducing pollution and also in conserving fossil fuels.

DO YOU KNOW?

Due to the highly inflammable nature of hydrogen, helium gas (a non-inflammable gas) is preferred over hydrogen to fill balloons.

QUICK REVISION

Write T for True and F for False.

1. Hydrogen is used as an oxidizing agent in the extraction of pure metals from their oxides.
2. Liquid hydrogen is used as a rocket fuel.
3. Zinc is used as a catalyst in the conversion of vegetable oils into *vanaspati*.
4. Hydrogen is used in the manufacture of methanol.
5. Hydrogen balloons are used to study the weather.

CONCEPT MAP

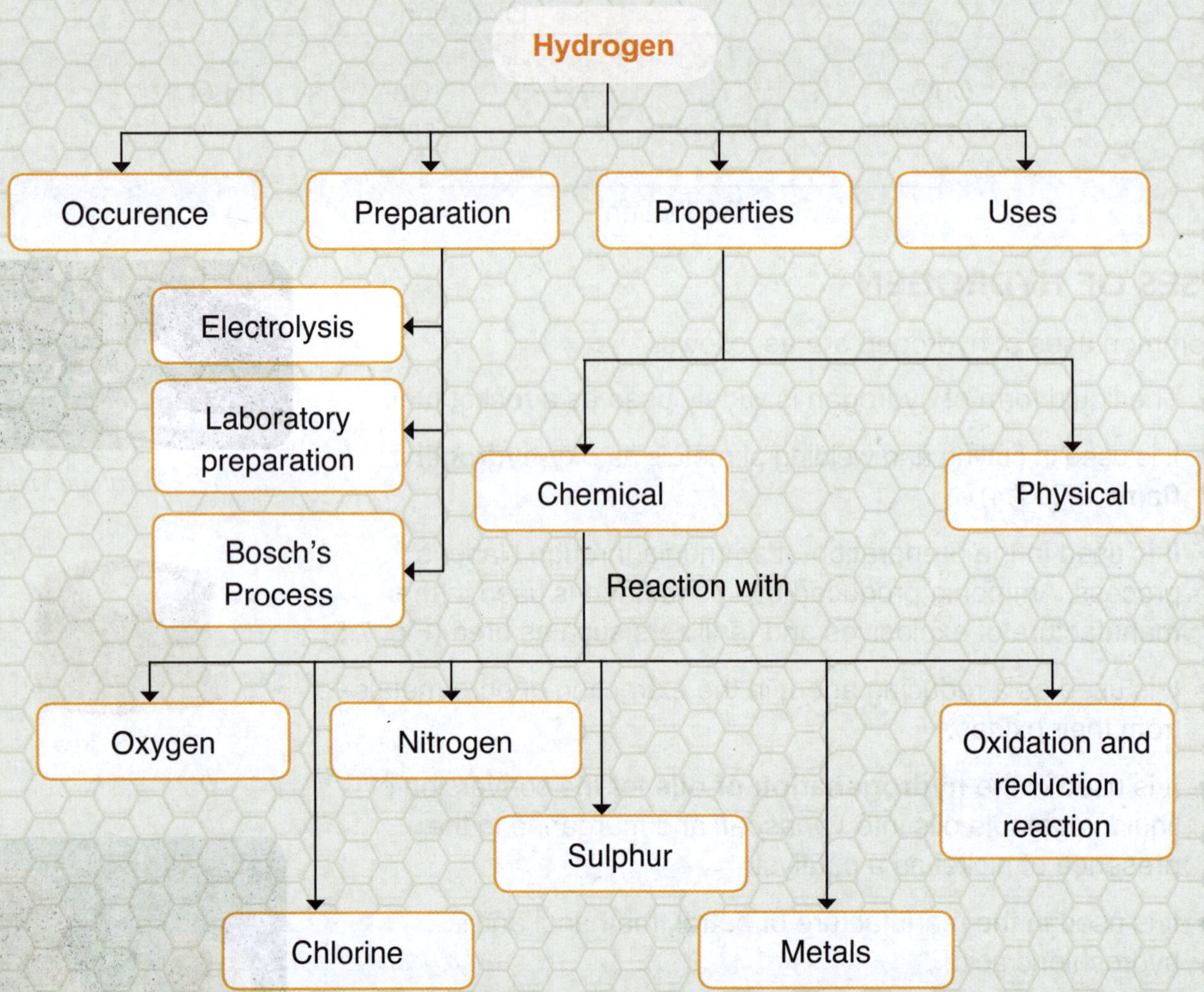

KEYWORDS

Electrolysis of water: the decomposition of water into oxygen and hydrogen due to the passage of electric current through water containing a small quantity of acid

Oxidation: the process of removal of hydrogen or addition of oxygen to a substance

Oxidizing agent: the substance that removes hydrogen or adds oxygen to another substance

Reduction: the process of removal of oxygen or addition of hydrogen to a substance

Reducing agent: the substance that removes oxygen or adds hydrogen to another substance

Redox reaction: a reaction in which both oxidation and reduction take place simultaneously

Hydrogenation of oils: the conversion of liquid vegetable oils into *vanaspati* using hydrogen in the presence of nickel as a catalyst

Exercise

Objective Type Questions

A. Choose the correct answer.

1. Complete the word equation given below:
   Metal + dilute acids ⟶ Salt + ____________
   a. Water
   b. Hydrogen gas
   c. Carbon dioxide
   d. Carbon monoxide
2. Which statement describes a test for hydrogen gas?
   a. It turns blue litmus paper red.
   b. It turns red litmus paper blue.
   c. It turns limewater cloudy.
   d. Lighted matchstick burns off with a 'pop' sound.
3. In the laboratory, hydrogen gas is prepared in large amounts by the reaction of ____________.
   a. zinc and dilute hydrochloric acid
   b. copper and dilute hydrochloric acid
   c. zinc and dilute nitric acid
   d. silver and dilute hydrochloric acid
4. Which of the following chemical reactions of hydrogen is also referred to as combustion?
   a. Reaction of hydrogen with metals
   b. Reaction of hydrogen with sulphur
   c. Reaction of hydrogen with chlorine
   d. Reaction of hydrogen with oxygen
5. Hydrogen on reaction with sodium at high temperature forms ____________.
   a. NaH b. NaOH
   c. Na_2CO_3 c. NaO

B. Fill in the blanks.

1. The flame used in cutting and welding of metals is ____________ (oxy-hydrogen flame/hydro-oxy flame).
2. The process of addition of hydrogen to a substance is ____________ (oxidation/reduction).
3. The reactions in which both oxidation and reduction take place simultaneously are referred to as ____________ (redox reactions/displacement reactions).
4. Hydrogen reacts with metals at high temperatures to form respective ____________ (metal hydroxides/metal hydrides).
5. The catalyst used in the hydrogenation of oils is ____________ (iron/nickel).

C. Write T for True and F for False.

1. Hydrogen is a combustible gas but does not support the process of combustion.
2. Hydrogen exists abundantly on Earth in the combined form.
3. Nickel reacts with cold water to form nickel oxide and releases hydrogen gas.
4. Hydrogen acts as a reducing agent in all chemical reactions.
5. Hydrogen is neutral in nature.

Subjective Type Questions

A. Define the following.

1. Oxidizing agent
2. Electrolysis
3. Reducing agent
4. Redox reaction
5. Haber's process

B. Complete and balance the following equations.

1. $PbO + H_2 \longrightarrow$ ____________
2. $Ca + \text{dil. } HCl \longrightarrow$ ____________
3. $Zn + \text{dil. } H_2SO_4 \longrightarrow$ ____________
4. $Na + H_2O \text{ (cold)} \longrightarrow$ ____________
5. $Ca + H_2 \longrightarrow$ ____________

C. Name the following.

1. The method used for the conversion of liquid vegetable oils into *vanaspati*.
2. The catalyst used in Haber's process.
3. Any two compounds in which hydrogen exists in combined form.
4. Any two metals that react vigorously with cold water and displace hydrogen.
5. The reactant reduced in the reaction between lead oxide and hydrogen.

D. Answer the following questions in brief.

1. Define displacement reaction with the help of an example.
2. How is hydrogen prepared from water using the method of electrolysis?
3. State the physical properties of hydrogen.
4. Explain the preparation of ammonia using hydrogen.

5. Distinguish between oxidation and reduction.
6. Explain the formation of metal hydrides from hydrogen.

E. Answer the following questions in detail.

1. Explain the occurrence of hydrogen.
2. Explain the preparation of hydrogen in the laboratory.
3. Explain any four chemical properties of hydrogen with equations.
4. Mention the various uses of hydrogen.
5. Explain how hydrogen is prepared by the displacement of dilute acids by metals.
6. Explain the preparation of hydrogen on reaction of sodium with water.

Application-based Question

Is it possible to displace hydrogen from acids or water by metals such as platinum and gold? If not, why?

Picture-based Question

Look at the given picture and answer the following questions.

1. Name the process taking place.
2. What is the electrolyte used in this electrolytic cell?
3. Name two electrodes.
4. Why is the volume of hydrogen gas formed double than that of oxygen gas?

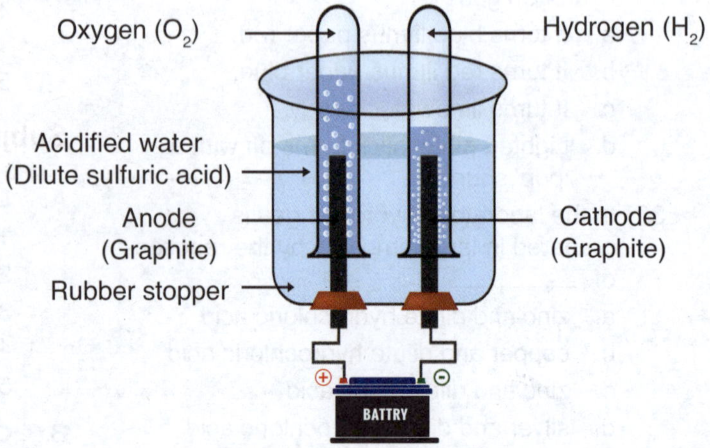

Skill Booster

A. **21CS:** Collaboration, Communication | **AL** | **BT:** Affective, Psychomotor

Pair up with one of your classmates. Refer library books to find out about the procedure of hydrogenation of oils. Share each other's ideas and make a chart and displaying the same on your school notice board.

B. **21CS:** Communication, Information Literacy | **BT:** Cognitive

Find out information about:

- Hydrogen fuel cells
- Disasters caused due to hydrogen gas explosions

Make a short report on your findings and share with your classmates.

Worksheet 7

Bidya was reading a journal when she came across an article on the hydrogen explosion. It reads as quoted below.

"Hydrogen is classified among the extremely flammable substances by its properties compared with methane and petrol. The main risk involved with hydrogen is that of fire or explosion (84% of recorded accidents) due to its very wide flammability range (from 4 to 75% in air, even more in atmospheres rich in oxygen or chlorine), as well as its very low ignition temperature. Accidentology has recorded several ignition sources for flammable clouds formed by hydrogen."

After looking into the statistics and reading about hydrogen as an explosive, Bidya feels it is her responsibility to create awareness among her friends about hydrogen as a highly flammable substance and inform them not to use hydrogen balloons for birthday parties.

My SEE Journal

A. What values do you get from Bidya?

B. If all of us stopped buying hydrogen balloons at once, what impact would it have on the lives of balloon sellers? Can you think of another way to reduce the amount of hydrogen used in balloons without having an adverse effect on the lives of balloon vendors?

My SDG Journal

13 CLIMATE ACTION

On combustion, hydrogen produces water as a by-product. How can this property of hydrogen be used to fight global warming? What are all the hazards associated with it and how can those be minimized?

8 Water

Prior Knowledge

- Importance of water
- Why water is known as a universal solvent
- Solubility of water

Learning Objectives

- Water cycle
- Properties of water
- Solutions, suspensions and colloids
- Unsaturated, saturated and supersaturated solutions
- Water of crystallization
- Hydrated, anhydrous and hygroscopic substances
- Reactivity of metals with cold water, hot water and steam
- Hard and soft water

LET'S GET STARTED

In previous classes, you learned about water and its properties. Read the following statements and write T for true and F for false.

1. The oceans are the main source of freshwater on Earth.
2. The amount of water on Earth is maintained by the water cycle.
3. The rate of evaporation of water is higher on a humid day.
4. Water can dissolve everything in it.
5. Oceans have an infinite supply of water for the future. So, there is no requirement to save it for the future.

Water is one of the most essential components of life. It covers nearly 71% of the Earth's surface. Around 97% of the water on Earth is present in seas and oceans, but it is not suitable for drinking and other uses as it has high salt content. The freshwater constitutes about 3% of the Earth's total water. The major part of freshwater is frozen in glaciers and polar ice caps. Hence, only about 0.01% of the total water on Earth is available for human consumption, irrigation and other uses.

Due to the increase in population and environmental pollution, there is a considerable decrease in the availability of freshwater on Earth. Pure drinking water has become a precious resource, which needs to be saved for future generations.

WATER CYCLE

The natural process in which there is a continuous circulation of water from the Earth's surface to the atmosphere and back to the Earth's surface is known as the **water cycle** (Fig. 8.1). This happens repeatedly and in a particular order to form a cycle.

In this process, water gets converted into all the three states of matter (solid, liquid and gas) but in different stages. The various steps involved in water cycle are shown in the following figure.

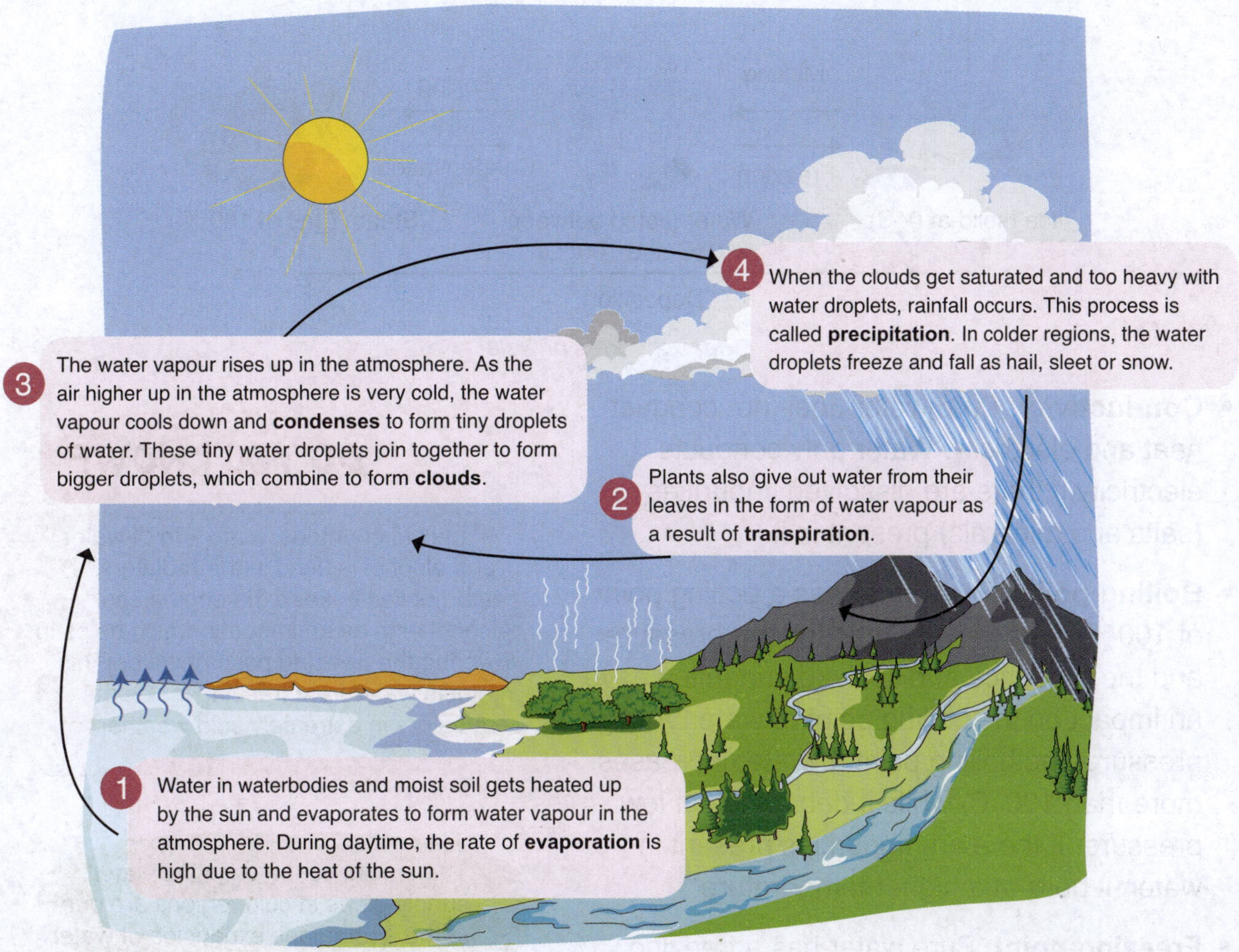

Fig. 8.1 Water cycle

PROPERTIES OF WATER

Water is made up of two elements: hydrogen and oxygen. These elements combine chemically in a fixed proportion (in the ratio of 2 : 1) to form a water molecule. Therefore, the chemical formula of water is H_2O.

The properties of water are different from those of its constituents (hydrogen and oxygen). The constituents of water cannot be separated by physical methods. However, on passing electric current, water decomposes into hydrogen and oxygen. This is called **electrolysis of water**.

Let us learn about some more properties of water.

- **Nature:** Water is colourless, tasteless, odourless and transparent in its pure form.
- **Forms of water:** We know that water exists in three different states in nature: solid, liquid and gas. The three states of water are interchangeable, that is, water can be changed from one form to another by changing the temperature. Fig. 8.2 shows the three states of water and their interchangeability by heating or cooling.

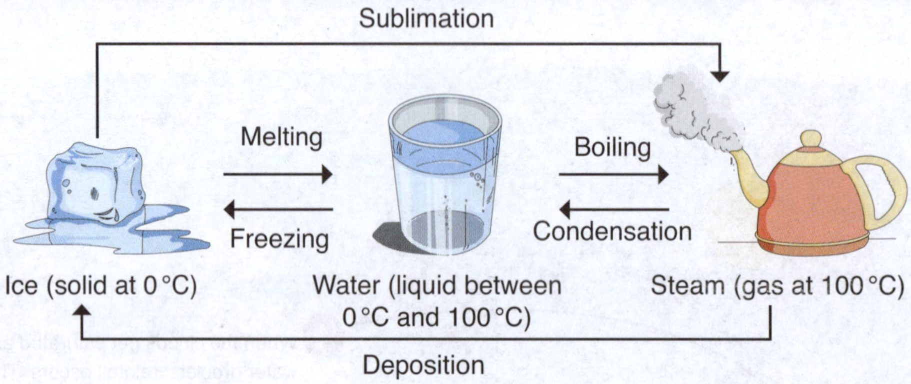

Fig. 8.2 Forms of water

- **Conductivity:** Pure water does not conduct heat and electricity. Water only conducts electricity if there are dissolved impurities (salts and minerals) present in it.
- **Boiling point:** Pure water has a boiling point of 100 °C at sea level. Atmospheric pressure and the presence of dissolved impurities have an impact on the boiling point of water. At high pressure, the boiling point of water increases more than 100 °C, while it decreases at low pressure. If there are impurities present in water, it boils at a higher temperature.
- **Freezing point:** Pure water has a freezing point of 0 °C at sea level. If there are impurities present in water, the freezing point becomes lower than 0 °C. Also, as the pressure increases, the freezing point of water decreases.

DO YOU KNOW?

In cold countries, a mixture of water and alcohol is used in the radiators of automobiles to keep the engine cool. Alcohol acts as an impurity, which helps in lowering the freezing point of water. This restricts water from freezing inside the radiators in extremely cold weather.

The cracks observed in the water supply pipes in cold regions are due to the anomalous expansion of water when it freezes at 0 °C. On freezing, water expands and occupies more space than liquid water. This results in cracking of water pipes.

- **Density and anomalous expansion of water:** The density of water is 1 g/cm^3 at 4 °C. Normally, substances expand on heating and contract on cooling. Water also contracts on cooling until the temperature reaches 4 °C.However, on cooling below 4 °C, water expands instead of contracting up to 0 °C. At 0 °C, water has the maximum volume in the form of ice. This unusual and unique property of water is known as **anomalous expansion** of water.

$$\text{Density} = \frac{\text{Mass}}{\text{Volume}}$$

As a result of this property, the density of water is maximum at 4 °C. When water is cooled below 4 °C, it expands instead of contracting and becomes less dense (or lighter). At 0 °C, water freezes to form ice. Due to expansion, the volume of ice at 0 °C is more than the volume of water at 4 °C. As we know, density is inversely proportional to volume; that is, density decreases when volume increases, hence the density of ice at 0 °C is less than the density of water. That is why, ice floats on the surface of water (Fig. 8.3).

Fig. 8.3 Ice floating on water

- **Effect of anomalous expansion of water:** In cold regions, where atmospheric temperature falls to 0 °C or below, water on the surface of ponds and lakes cools and freezes into ice. The frozen ice floats on the surface of the water as the density of ice is less than the density of water. As water is a bad conductor of heat, the ice layer prevents loss of heat from the lower layers of water. Thus, water below the layer of floating ice has temperatures greater than 0 °C, which helps in the survival of aquatic life present underneath.

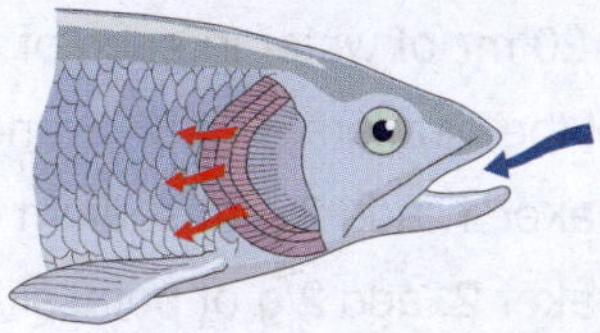

Fig. 8.4 Aquatic animals use dissolved oxygen

- **Gases dissolved in water and their importance:** Atmospheric gases such as oxygen and carbon dioxide can dissolve in water. Dissolved oxygen, which is very important for the survival of many aquatic animals, is used for respiration (Fig. 8.4). Aquatic plants make use of dissolved carbon dioxide to prepare food and release oxygen which is used by fish.

Soft drinks contain carbon dioxide gas dissolved in water at high pressure, in which carbon dioxide is the solute and water is the solvent. Apart from oxygen and carbon dioxide, other gases such as ammonia, chlorine, methane and nitrogen can also dissolve in water.

- **Water contains dissolved solids:** Substances such as salts, minerals, metals or ions, which are called the Total Dissolved Solids (TDS), dissolve in water.
  - The nutrients present in the soil and the food prepared by the leaves of plants are transported to other parts of the plants in the form of their solution.
  - Water acts as a medium to dissolve nutrients and minerals present in the food that living things eat. This helps in the easy absorption of nutrients by the body. The absorbed food and nutrients are carried to various body parts through the blood.
  - Even the waste products in our body are soluble in water and are excreted out from the body through water (sweat and urine).

WATER—A UNIVERSAL SOLVENT

Water can dissolve a wider variety of substances than any other liquid. Hence, water is also called the **universal solvent**. However, all substances do not dissolve in water. For example, when salt is added to water and stirred, it dissolves completely in water, but sand does not dissolve in water.

Substances that dissolve completely in water are said to be **soluble** in water. Substances that do not dissolve in water are said to be **insoluble** in water.

Similarly, liquids that dissolve in water are said to be **miscible** with water, for example, vinegar and alcohol. Liquids that do not dissolve in water are called **immiscible** with water, for example, oil and petrol.

ACTIVITY 1

Aim: To test the dissolving capacity of water with various salts

Materials required: Four beakers, measuring cylinder, weighing balance, four glass rods, spatula, sodium chloride, potassium chloride, sodium carbonate, calcium carbonate and water

Procedure:

1. Take 20 mℓ of water in each of the four beakers.
2. Label the beakers as 1, 2, 3 and 4.
3. In beaker 1, add 2 g of sodium chloride (weighed using a weighing balance).
4. In beaker 2, add 2 g of potassium chloride.
5. In beaker 3, add 2 g of sodium carbonate.
6. In beaker 4, add 2 g of calcium carbonate.
7. Mix the contents of the glass beakers with the help of a glass rod. Use separate glass rods for each beaker and observe.

Observation:

- Sodium chloride, potassium chloride and sodium carbonate salts dissolve in water, whereas calcium carbonate does not dissolve in water but gets settled at the bottom of the beaker.
- Potassium chloride dissolves in water completely faster than sodium chloride, followed by sodium carbonate.

Conclusion: From this activity, we can conclude that different salts have different solubility in water.

SOLUTIONS

A **solution** is a homogeneous mixture of two or more substances. A solution contains two main components: solute and solvent. The major component of a solution is called the **solvent**. The component that dissolves in a solvent is called the **solute**.

Examples of solutions:

- Aerated drinks
- Tincture of iodine
- Glucose solution
- Copper sulphate solution
- Salt solution

Solubility is the ability of a substance to dissolve in a given solvent. Some solutes are only sparingly soluble in a given solvent, while some other solutes may dissolve to a greater extent in the same solvent. For example, turmeric is sparingly soluble in water while salt dissolves to a greater extent in water. Based on the amount of a solute present in a solvent at a given temperature, solutions can be classified as unsaturated, saturated or supersaturated.

Unsaturated, Saturated and Supersaturated Solutions

Table 8.1 shows differences between unsaturated, saturated and supersaturated solutions.

Table 8.1 Difference between unsaturated, saturated and supersaturated solutions

Unsaturated solution	Saturated solution	Supersaturated solution
A solution in which solute concentration is low and more solute can be dissolved in the solvent at a given temperature is called an **unsaturated solution**. An unsaturated solution contains less amount of dissolved solute than a saturated solution.	A solution in which no more solute can be dissolved in the solvent at a given temperature is called a **saturated solution**. A saturated solution contains the maximum amount of dissolved solute at the given temperature.	A solution in which there is more amount of solute in the solvent at a given temperature is called a **supersaturated solution**. A supersaturated solution contains more amount of dissolved solute than a saturated solution.

SUSPENSIONS

Suspensions are heterogeneous mixtures. The particles in a suspension are larger than those of a solution and can be separated by filtration. A suspension contains small, undissolved solid particles suspended in a fluid (a liquid or a gas). These particles can be seen distinctly. When the suspension is kept undisturbed, the particles settle down.

Examples of suspensions:

- Sand in water (Fig. 8.5)
- Powdered chalk in water
- Dust in air
- Soot in air
- Oil in water

Fig. 8.5 Sand particles settle at the bottom of the beaker

COLLOIDS

Colloids are heterogeneous mixtures. Every colloid contains two parts: dispersed phase and dispersion medium. The particles of colloids (solid or liquid) have intermediate size between those of suspension and solution particles.

The particles of colloids do not dissolve but get dispersed in the medium and cannot be separated by filtration. The particles can scatter light due to their large size. For instance, we are able to observe the light from car headlamps through fog.

Examples of colloids:

- Milk (dispersed phase: liquid; dispersion medium: liquid) (Fig. 8.6)
- Fog (dispersed phase: solid; dispersion medium: gas)
- Insecticide sprays (dispersed phase: solid; dispersion medium: gas) (Fig. 8.7)
- Soap lather (dispersed phase: gas; dispersed medium: liquid)

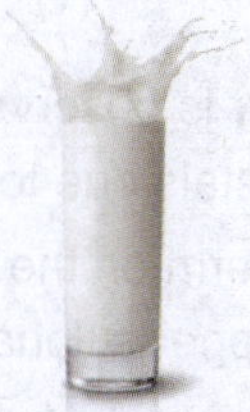

Fig. 8.6 Milk

Fig. 8.7 Fog

Refer to Table 8.2 to distinguish between suspensions and colloids.

Table 8.2 Differences between suspensions and colloids

Suspensions	Colloids
• The size of the suspended particles is large; thus these particles are visible to the naked eye.	• The size of the suspended particles is very small and hence, they are not visible to the naked eye.
• The particles get settled when kept undisturbed.	• The particles do not settle on standing.
• Suspensions can be separated by filtration.	• Colloids cannot be separated by filtration.
• Examples: Sand in water and oil in water	• Examples: Milk and fog

WATER OF CRYSTALLIZATION

Some of the salts contain water molecules trapped inside them. The fixed number of water molecules available in one formula unit of a salt is known as **water of crystallization.**

Examples: $CuSO_4 \cdot 5H_2O$, $CaSO_4 \cdot 2H_2O$, $Na_2CO_3 \cdot 10H_2O$, $Na_2SO_4 \cdot 10H_2O$, $FeSO_4 \cdot 7H_2O$

The water in these salts is responsible for the shape and colour of the crystals. When these crystals are heated, the water present in the salts is lost.

ACTIVITY 2

Aim: To observe the loss of water of crystallization in hydrated copper sulphate

Materials required: Copper sulphate crystals, Bunsen burner, test tube, test tube holder and spatula

Procedure:

1. Take some copper sulphate crystals in a test tube.
2. Heat the test tube on a Bunsen burner as shown in Fig. A.

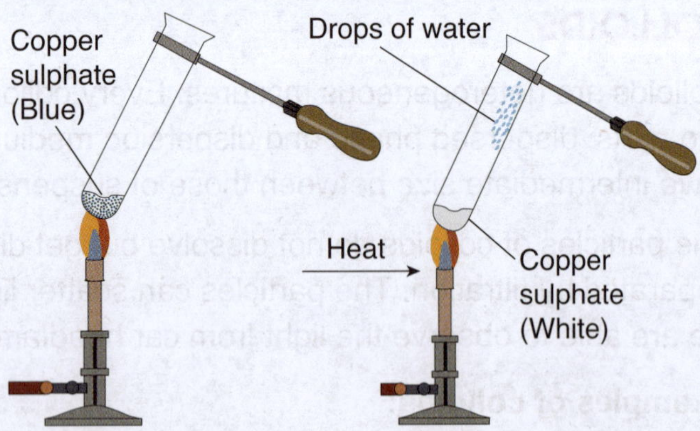

Fig. A *Fig. B*

Observation:

1. The blue colour of the copper sulphate crystals changes into white after heating.
2. Water droplets get collected on the upper sides of the test tube.

Conclusion:

1. The change in colour is observed due to dehydration (the removal of water molecules trapped in the copper sulphate crystals due to heating).
2. The water droplets form on the upper sides of the test tube due to the water of crystallization lost during heating of copper sulphate crystals.

HYDRATED, ANHYDROUS AND HYGROSCOPIC SUBSTANCES

Hydrated substances: Substances that contain water of crystallization are called **hydrated substances**.

Examples:

- Magnesium sulphate ($MgSO_4 \cdot 7H_2O$): Epsom salt
- Ferrous sulphate ($FeSO_4 \cdot 7H_2O$): Green vitriol
- Copper (II) sulphate ($CuSO_4 \cdot 5H_2O$): Blue vitriol
- Calcium sulphate ($CaSO_4 \cdot 2H_2O$): Gypsum

Anhydrous substances: Substances that do not contain water of crystallization are called **anhydrous substances**.

For instance, when we heat copper sulphate crystals ($CuSO_4 \cdot 5H_2O$), the water molecules evaporate.The remaining salt without water is referred to as the anhydrous salt, which is depicted by the chemical formula $CuSO_4$.

$$\underset{\text{Hydrated copper sulphate}}{CuSO_4 \cdot 5H_2O} \xrightarrow{\text{Heating}} \underset{\text{Anhydrous copper sulphate}}{CuSO_4} + 5H_2O$$

TALK TIME

During rainy season, common salt often becomes moist. Why?

Efflorescent substances: Substances that lose water of crystallization when exposed to air are called efflorescent substances. This phenomenon is called **efflorescence**.

Examples: Washing soda and Glauber's salt ($Na_2SO_4 \cdot 10H_2O$) are examples of efflorescent substances.

Deliquescent substances: Substances that absorb moisture when exposed to air, become moist and lose their crystalline form are called deliquescent substances and this phenomenon is called **deliquescence**.

DO YOU KNOW?

Have you ever seen small pouches, containing some crystals, kept in new bottles and shoes? The crystals present in these pouches are of silica gel. Being hygroscopic, silica gel absorbs moisture from the items and keeps them dry. These pouches can be reused.

Examples: Caustic soda (that is, sodium hydroxide), magnesium chloride, calcium chloride and iron(III) chloride are some examples of deliquescent substances.

Hygroscopic substances: Substances that are capable of absorbing water from their surroundings without changing their physical state (unlike deliquescent substances) are called **hygroscopic substances**.

Examples: Zinc chloride, anhydrous calcium chloride, potassium hydroxide, phosphorus pentoxide, sodium chloride, sodium hydroxide and silica gel crystals are a few examples of hygroscopic substances.

Hygroscopic substances are used as drying agents to remove moisture from other substances without undergoing any chemical reaction with them.

QUICK REVISION

Fill in the blanks with the correct words.

1. Solutions are ____________ (homogeneous/heterogeneous) mixtures.
2. Suspensions are ____________ (homogeneous/heterogeneous) mixtures.
3. In glucose solution, ____________ (glucose/water) is the solute and ____________ (glucose/water) is the solvent.
4. Milk is an example of ____________ (solution/colloid).
5. Sand in water is an example of ____________ (suspension/colloid).

REACTION OF METALS WITH WATER

Different metals react with water in different ways to form metal oxides or metal hydroxides and hydrogen gas.

$$\text{Metal} + \text{Water} \longrightarrow \text{Metal oxide or Metal hydroxide} + \text{Hydrogen gas}$$

Reaction with Cold Water

Metals such as sodium, potassium and calcium react vigorously with cold water to form their respective hydroxides and release hydrogen gas. A large amount of heat is also released. Reactions in which heat is released are called **exothermic reactions**.

$$\underset{\text{Sodium}}{2Na} + \underset{\text{Water}}{2H_2O} \longrightarrow \underset{\text{Sodium hydroxide}}{2NaOH} + \underset{\text{Hydrogen}}{H_2(g)}$$

$$\underset{\text{Potassium}}{2K} + \underset{\text{Water}}{2H_2O} \longrightarrow \underset{\text{Potassium hydroxide}}{2KOH} + \underset{\text{Hydrogen}}{H_2(g)}$$

$$\underset{\text{Calcium}}{Ca} + \underset{\text{Water}}{2H_2O} \longrightarrow \underset{\text{Calcium hydroxide}}{Ca(OH)_2} + \underset{\text{Hydrogen}}{H_2(g)}$$

Fig. 8.8 Reaction of sodium with water

In case of reaction of sodium and potassium with water, a large amount of heat is released that makes the hydrogen gas catch fire as shown in Fig. 8.8. Thus, sodium and potassium are stored in kerosene because they can react vigorously with the moisture present in the air.

Other metals do not react with cold water.

Reaction with Hot Water

Magnesium reacts slowly with hot water forming hydrogen gas and white magnesium hydroxide that is sparingly soluble in water.

$$\underset{\text{Magnesium}}{Mg} + \underset{\text{Water}}{2H_2O} \longrightarrow \underset{\text{Magnesium hydroxide}}{Mg(OH)_2} + \underset{\text{Hydrogen}}{H_2(g)}$$

Reaction with Steam

- Magnesium reacts vigorously with steam producing magnesium oxide and hydrogen gas.

$$\underset{\text{Magnesium}}{Mg} + \underset{\text{Steam}}{H_2O(g)} \longrightarrow \underset{\text{Magnesium oxide}}{MgO} + \underset{\text{Hydrogen}}{H_2(g)}$$

- Zinc and iron react only with steam to form their respective oxides and hydrogen. However, the reaction occurs less vigorously.

$$\underset{\text{Zinc}}{Zn} + \underset{\text{Steam}}{H_2O(g)} \longrightarrow \underset{\text{Zinc oxide}}{ZnO} + \underset{\text{Hydrogen}}{H_2(g)}$$

$$\underset{\text{Iron}}{3Fe} + \underset{\text{Steam}}{4H_2O(g)} \longrightarrow \underset{\text{Iron oxide}}{Fe_3O_4} + \underset{\text{Hydrogen}}{4H_2(g)}$$

- Aluminium also reacts with steam to produce aluminium oxide and hydrogen gas.

$$\underset{\text{Aluminium}}{2Al} + \underset{\text{Steam}}{3H_2O(g)} \longrightarrow \underset{\text{Aluminium oxide}}{Al_2O_3} + \underset{\text{Hydrogen}}{H_2(g)}$$

  The aluminium oxide formed during the reaction forms a strong sticky layer on the surface of aluminium metal. As a result, no more aluminium metal is exposed to react further with steam. Hence, the reaction stops after some time.

- Metals that are placed lower in the reactivity series such as platinum, gold, silver and copper do not react with water at all. Hence, they are extremely durable.

Generally non-metals do not react with water under any conditions.

Phosphorus, a very reactive non-metal that can catch fire when exposed to air, is actually stored in water as it does not react with water.

ACTIVITY 3

Note: *This activity needs to be performed as a teacher demonstration.*

Aim: To conclude that metals react with water whereas non-metals do not

Materials required: Two 250 mℓ glass beakers, cold water, small pieces of sodium and charcoal, knife, forceps

Procedure:

1. Take a clean 250 mℓ glass beaker and fill it with 100 mℓ of cold water.
2. Cut a small piece of sodium using a knife and dry it with a filter paper.
3. With the help of a tong or forceps, slowly drop the piece of sodium metal into the beaker.
4. Try to touch the beaker after the reaction is over. Ensure that the reaction is no longer taking place and touch it from a safe distance.
5. Repeat the above activity with charcoal in a separate beaker and record your observations.

Observation table:

S.No.	Sample	Observation
1.	Sodium piece	Release of heat, gas and light would be observed. When touched, we can feel the surface of the beaker to be hot.
2.	Charcoal piece	No reaction would be observed.

Conclusion: Sodium, being a metal, reacts with water, and charcoal, being a non-metal, does not react with water.

HARD WATER AND SOFT WATER

Soft water easily lathers with soaps and contains very little amount of calcium and magnesium salts. Rainwater is an example of soft water.

Hard water contains high amounts of calcium and magnesium salts and do not lather with soaps. Hard water forms a thick, curd-like, insoluble substance, known as **scum** when treated with soap. Hence, hard water cannot be used for laundry.

How Hardness is Caused

Hardness of water is caused due to the presence of salts of magnesium and calcium dissolved in it.

Hardness of water is of two types.

- **Temporary hardness:** Temporary hardness is due to the presence of dissolved bicarbonates of magnesium and calcium in water.
- **Permanent hardness:** Permanent hardness is due to the presence of dissolved sulphates and chlorides of magnesium and calcium in water.

ACTIVITY 4

Aim: To analyze water samples for their hardness

Materials required: Distilled water, hard water, soap solution and test tubes

Note: Hard water can be prepared by adding a pinch of magnesium chloride to distilled water.

Procedure:

1. Take two test tubes and label them as 1 and 2.
2. Take 10 mℓ of distilled water in test tube 1 and 10 mℓ of hard water in test tube 2.
3. Add 5–6 drops of soap solution into each of the test tubes and mix the contents of the test tubes gently.
4. Observe the contents of the test tubes and record your observations.

Conclusion: Test tube 1, which contains distilled water, forms lather. Test tube 2, containing hard water, does not show any lather formation and a layer of curd-like scum can be seen inside it.

Disadvantages of Hard Water

- Hard water is unfit for drinking and cooking purposes.
- It is also not suitable for washing clothes as it results in the wastage of soap. Further, the scum formed leaves stains on clothes.
- In industries that use hard water, the deposits of magnesium and calcium salts formed at high temperatures result in scale formation in machine parts. This may also lead to the explosion of boilers and minimize the heating efficiency of radiators.
- Scale formation may result in the blockage of water pipes that are used for the transportation of hard water.

Methods of Softening Hard Water

The process of removing dissolved salts of magnesium and calcium from hard water to get soft water is called the **softening of water**.

It can be done by the following methods.

By boiling: Temporary hardness of water can be easily removed by boiling.

On boiling, the magnesium and calcium bicarbonates are converted into their respective carbonates. These carbonates are insoluble in nature and can be removed by filtration to obtain soft water.

$$\underset{\text{Magnesium bicarbonate}}{Mg(HCO_3)_2} \xrightarrow{\text{Heat}} \underset{\text{Magnesium carbonate}}{MgCO_3} + \underset{\text{Water}}{H_2O} + \underset{\text{Carbon dioxide}}{CO_2}$$

$$\underset{\text{Calcium bicarbonate}}{Ca(HCO_3)_2} \xrightarrow{\text{Heat}} \underset{\text{Calcium carbonate}}{CaCO_3} + \underset{\text{Water}}{H_2O} + \underset{\text{Carbon dioxide}}{CO_2}$$

Permanent hardness of water cannot be removed by boiling because the salts (chlorides and sulphates of calcium and magnesium) are stable to heat.

By treating with chemicals such as washing soda (Na_2CO_3): Permanent hardness of water can be removed by adding washing soda or sodium carbonate.

During this process, the sulphates and chlorides of magnesium and calcium are converted into their respective carbonates. These carbonates are insoluble in nature and can be removed by the filtration to obtain soft water.

$$\underset{\text{Magnesium sulphate}}{MgSO_4} + \underset{\text{Sodium carbonate}}{Na_2CO_3} \longrightarrow \underset{\text{Magnesium carbonate}}{MgCO_3} + \underset{\text{Sodium sulphate}}{Na_2SO_4}$$

$$\underset{\text{Calcium chloride}}{CaCl_2} + \underset{\text{Sodium carbonate}}{Na_2CO_3} \longrightarrow \underset{\text{Calcium carbonate}}{CaCO_3} + \underset{\text{Sodium chloride}}{2NaCl}$$

The addition of washing soda to the bicarbonate of calcium can also remove temporary hardness of water to obtain soft water.

$$\underset{\text{Calcium bicarbonate}}{Ca(HCO_3)_2} + \underset{\text{Sodium carbonate}}{Na_2CO_3} \longrightarrow \underset{\text{Calcium carbonate}}{CaCO_3} + \underset{\text{Sodium bicarbonate}}{2NaHCO_3}$$

QUICK REVISION

Fill in the blanks.

1. ____________ (Sodium/Iron) reacts with cold water.
2. ____________(Soft/Hard) waster lathers with soap.
3. Boiling can remove ____________ (temporary/permanent) hardness of water.
4. Washing soda removes ____________(temporary/permanent) hardness of water.

CONCEPT MAP

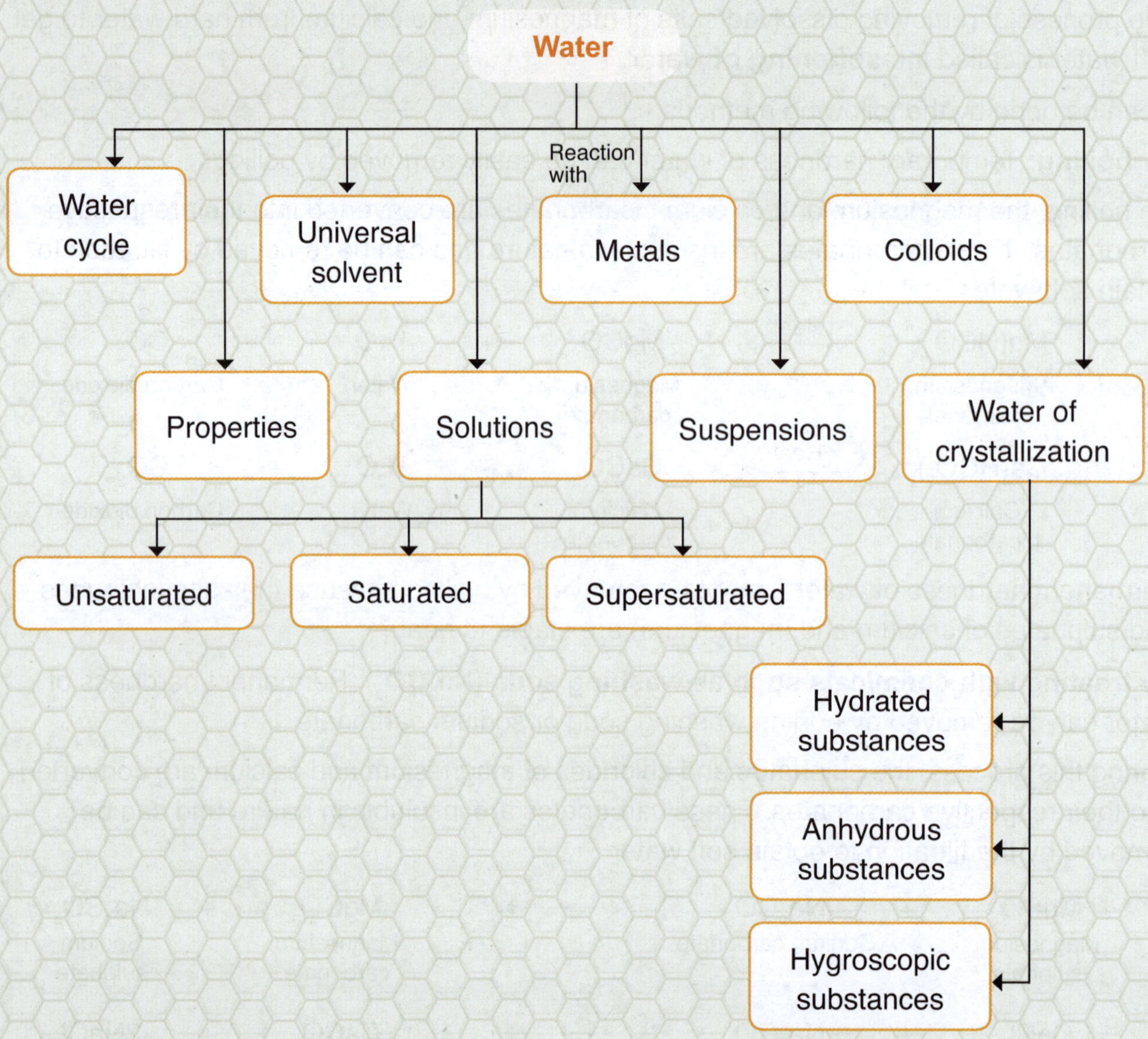

KEYWORDS

Solution: a solution is a uniform mixture of a solute in a solvent

Solubility: the property of a substance to dissolve in a given liquid

Hydrated substances: the substances that contain water molecules within them

Anhydrous substances: the substances that do not contain water molecules within them

Hygroscopic substances: the substances that are capable of attracting water from their surroundings

Water of crystallization: the fixed number of water molecules available in one formula unit of a salt

Soft water: water that easily lathers with soap and is free from salts of magnesium and calcium

Hard water: water that does not lather with soap due to the presence of magnesium and calcium salts

Exercise

Objective Type Questions

A. Choose the correct answer.

1. Which of these is not a property of water?
   a. Colourless
   b. Tasteless
   c. Opaque
   d. Universal solvent
2. Which of the following metals reacts vigorously with water?
   a. Gold b. Silver
   c. Potassium d. Platinum
3. Which of these is used to soften water?
   a. Bleaching powder
   b. Calcium carbonate
   c. Sodium chloride
   d. Washing soda
4. Which of the following is an example of a suspension?
   a. Milk b. Soda
   c. Oil in water d. Fog
5. Which of the following causes temporary hardness in water?
   a. Bicarbonates of magnesium
   b. Chlorides of calcium
   c. Sulphates of magnesium
   d. Nitrates of potassium

B. Fill in the blanks.

1. Water that does not give lather with soap is ____________ (hard water/soft water).
2. Colloid is a ____________ (homogeneous/heterogeneous) mixture.
3. Substances that contain water molecules within them are referred to as ____________ (hydrated/anhydrous) substances.
4. The substance present in larger component in the solution is known as ____________ (solute/solvent)
5. ____________ (Water filter/Boiling) is the easiest method to remove temporary hardness of water.

C. Write T for True and F for False.

1. Pure water is a good conductor of electricity.
2. The density of ice at 0 °C is less than the density of water.
3. Large amount of heat is released when potassium reacts with water.
4. Magnesium reacts with cold water to form magnesium oxide and hydrogen gas.
5. Nickel reacts with cold water to form nickel oxide and releases hydrogen gas.
6. Sulphates and chlorides of magnesium and calcium cause temporary hardness of water.

Subjective Type Questions

A. Define the following.

1. Universal solvent
2. Water cycle
3. Anomalous expansion of water
4. Suspensions
5. Colloids

B. Differentiate between the following.

1. Solutions and colloids
2. Soft water and hard water
3. Temporary hardness and permanent hardness
4. Boiling point of water and freezing point of water
5. Unsaturated and saturated solution

C. Choose the odd one out. Give reasons for the choice.

1. Magnesium sulphate, calcium sulphate, magnesium chloride, magnesium bicarbonate
2. Glacier, dew, snow, hail
3. Vinegar, alcohol, acetic acid, oil
4. Sand in water, powdered chalk in water, fog, dust in air
5. Soap lather, insecticide sprays, milk, oil in water

D. Answer the following questions in brief.

1. Why is water called the universal solvent? Explain with an example.
2. Write any two drawbacks of hard water.
3. Distinguish between suspensions and colloids.
4. Differentiate between hydrated, anhydrous and hygroscopic substances.

E. Answer the following questions in detail.

1. Explain how water is circulated in nature.
2. List the properties of water and briefly explain each.
3. Explain the importance of anomalous expansion of water.

4. What are the methods used for softening hard water?
5. Describe water of crystallization with the help of an example.
6. Explain the reaction of metals with cold water, hot water and steam with an example for each.

Application-based Question

You are given two unlabelled samples of water. One is soft water, the other is hard water. How will you determine which of the two samples is soft water and which is hard water?

Picture-based Questions

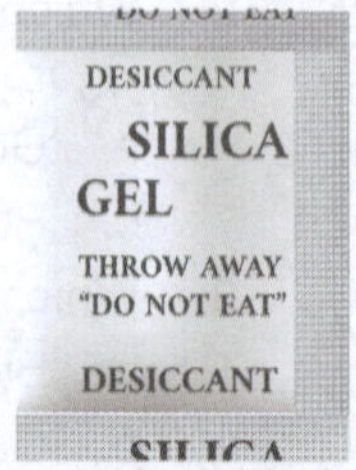

A. Look at the picture and answer the following questions.
   1. Where do you see these packets?
   2. What is their role?
   3. Which other chemicals can serve the same purpose as these silica gel crystals? Name any two.

B. Look at the picture and answer the following questions.
   1. Which element, when it comes in contact with water, burns like this?
   2. Why does this happen?
   3. Name another element that also reacts with water in a similar way.
   4. How are these elements stored?

Skill Booster

A. **21CS:** Communication, Information Literacy | **CC:** English | **BT:** Cognitive

Try to visit a nearby water treatment plant and collect information about the various processes that are followed in the purification of water. Prepare a report on your observations and submit it to your teacher.

B. **21CS:** Information Literacy, Media Literacy | **CC:** Computer Science | **BT:** Cognitive, Affective

Collect information from the Internet, newspapers and magazines about the Ganga Action Plan. Prepare a comprehensive report on the aim, plan of action, results and the conclusion to be drawn from them.

Worksheet 8

My SEE Journal

A. Who do you think is doing an environmentally friendly act? Why do you think so?

B. Will the act mentioned above affect you directly? Elaborate.

C. How would you suggest the boy doing a wrongful act to correct the mistake and do it rightfully?

My SDG Journal

12 RESPONSIBLE CONSUMPTION AND PRODUCTION

A. Is it essential for us to purchase a distilled water bottle each time we go out?

B. How can we reduce the use of certain substances that are harmful to the environment while manufacturing and post manufacturing also?

C. Draw different coloured bins and sort the waste generated at home in the specific bins.

9 Carbon and Its Compounds

Prior Knowledge

- Importance of carbon
- Uses of carbon

Learning Objectives

- Occurrence of carbon
- Crystalline forms of carbon
- Amorphous forms of carbon
- Carbon dioxide: Preparation, properties and uses
- Carbon monoxide: Properties, uses and harmful effects

LET'S GET STARTED

Look at the following pictures. What is common in all of these?

1

Diamond

2

Pencil lead

3

Coal

Carbon is the fourth most abundant element in the universe and the fifteenth most abundant element in the Earth's crust. The name carbon comes from the Latin word *carbo,* meaning coal. It is present in all living things such as human beings, plants, animals and even in non-living things such as wood, petroleum, coal, natural gas and plastics. Due to its chemical nature, carbon forms various compounds with other elements. It is a non-metal and is represented by the symbol C.

Majority of the things that we use in our everyday lives contain carbon, for example, food, clothes, fuels, medicines, paper and plastics.

In this chapter, we will learn about the occurrence, properties, various forms and uses of carbon.

OCCURRENCE OF CARBON

Carbon exists both in free state and combined state in nature. In the free state, carbon is mainly found in three forms: diamond, graphite and coal. In the combined state, carbon exists in the form of numerous organic and inorganic compounds. Table 9.1 lists a few organic and inorganic compounds of carbon.

DO YOU KNOW?

Carbon forms the largest number of compounds. The branch of chemistry that deals with the study of carbon compounds is referred to as organic chemistry.

Table 9.1 Few organic and inorganic compounds of carbon

Organic Compounds of Carbon	
Food nutrients	Carbohydrates, proteins, fats and vitamins are the important nutrients of food, which are present in both plants and animals. All these are organic compounds that mainly consist of carbon, hydrogen and oxygen atoms.
Carbohydrates	Glucose, cellulose, starch and other sugars are various forms of carbohydrates. All these are made up of carbon, hydrogen and oxygen atoms. Cellulose is the most abundant organic compound on Earth.
Hydrocarbons	These are organic compounds that contain only carbon and hydrogen atoms, for example, methane (CH_4) and ethane (C_2H_6). Petroleum and natural gas are the important hydrocarbons found in nature as fossil fuels. Many other fuels, such as petrol, diesel and kerosene, are obtained from petroleum. The main constituent of natural gas is methane.
Acids and alcohols	Carbon is an essential constituent of many acids and alcohols. For example, carbonic acid (H_2CO_3), acetic acid (CH_3COOH), methyl alcohol (CH_3OH) and ethyl alcohol (C_2H_5OH).
Inorganic Compounds of Carbon	
Carbon dioxide	It exists in the atmosphere (about 0.03% by volume) and is the major gaseous compound of carbon present in the air. It is soluble in water and is present as dissolved carbon dioxide in water bodies.
Carbon monoxide	It is another gaseous compound of carbon present in the air. It is formed during combustion of fuels in vehicles and factories.
Salts	Mineral salts such as carbonates and bicarbonates are important carbon compounds found in nature. For example, $CaCO_3$ (chalk, limestone, marble), $MgCO_3$ (magnesite), Na_2CO_3 (washing soda), $NaHCO_3$ (baking soda) and $Ca(HCO_3)_2$.

ALLOTROPY

The property of an element to exist in various physical forms with identical chemical properties but different physical properties is known as **allotropy**. Carbon, oxygen, sulphur and phosphorus are a few elements that exhibit allotropy. The different physical forms in which an element can exist are called **allotropes** or **allotropic forms** of that element.

Allotropes of carbon can be broadly grouped as: **crystalline** and **amorphous**. In crystalline form, the carbon atoms are arranged in a symmetrical pattern that repeats itself. Graphite, diamonds and fullerenes are examples of crystalline forms of carbon. In amorphous form, there is no symmetrical or regular arrangement of the carbon atoms. Coal and charcoal are examples of amorphous forms of carbon. Table 9.2 lists some differences between the crystalline and the amorphous forms of carbon.

Table 9.2 Differences between crystalline and amorphous forms of carbon

Crystalline Form	Amorphous Form
This form has a regular shape and size.	This form does not have a regular shape and size.
In this form, the carbon atoms are arranged in a definite repeating order or geometrical pattern. It also has sharp edges and plane surfaces and is thus known as a crystal.	In this form, the carbon atoms are not arranged in a definite order or geometrical pattern. It does not have sharp edges and plane surfaces. It is also known as the non-crystalline form of carbon.
It has fixed melting and boiling points.	It does not have any fixed melting and boiling points.
Examples: Diamond, graphite and fullerenes	Examples: Charcoal, lampblack, coke and coal

Crystals are solid substances that have definite geometrical forms and sharp edges in which constituent ions, atoms or molecules are arranged in a regular repeating pattern that extends in all directions. The study of crystals and their formation is known as **crystallography**.

CRYSTALLINE FORMS OF CARBON

Diamond, graphite and fullerene are the crystalline forms of carbon.

Diamond

Diamond (Fig. 9.1) is the purest form of carbon and is the hardest known naturally occurring substance. Due to its extreme hardness, diamond is used in cutting tools. As a result, only a diamond can cut another diamond.

Fig. 9.1 Diamond

Occurrence of Diamond

Diamond mines are found in various parts of the world such as South Africa, Brazil, Angola, Ghana and India. South Africa is the leading producer and supplier of about 70 per cent of the world's diamonds. In India, diamonds are widely found in the Kollur mines in Andhra Pradesh and the Panna mines in Madhya Pradesh.

DO YOU KNOW?

Kohinoor, the famous diamond, was mined from the Kollur mines in the Guntur district of Andhra Pradesh.

Naturally, diamonds are produced from carbon that has been subjected to very high pressure and temperature about 150 km below the Earth's surface. Through natural processes, these diamonds come to the surface of Earth, which are then mined. Diamonds are measured in **carats**, which is one-fifth of a gram.

Synthetic diamonds: They are prepared through artificial processes in which pure carbon is compressed under extremely high pressure and temperature conditions; hence, they are also known as artificial or cultivated diamonds. They are widely used in polishing, grinding and cutting tools.

Structure of Diamond

In a diamond, each carbon atom is connected to four other carbon atoms by strong chemical bonds. This forms a tetrahedral shape in which one carbon atom lies at the centre and the four surrounding carbon atoms lie at the four corners of the tetrahedron.

Each of the four carbon atoms at the corners is further attached to four other carbon atoms, thus extending the tetrahedral arrangement. Each carbon atom is at an equal distance from its neighbouring carbon atoms and is thus held firmly in its place.

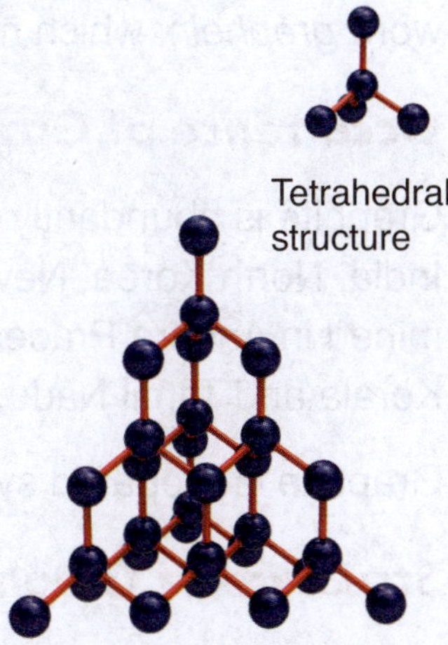

Fig. 9.2 Structure of diamond

Due to the closely-packed and rigid arrangement of these carbon atoms, diamond crystal has a rigid, three-dimensional structure (Fig. 9.2). That is why, a diamond is hard in nature and has a high density and a high melting point.

Properties of Diamond

- Diamond is the hardest known naturally occurring substance on Earth.
- Pure diamonds are colourless, lustrous and crystalline solids. They are transparent in appearance.
- It has a high refractive index, which gives a diamond its sparkling appearance.
- It has a high density (3.5 g/cm^3) and a high melting point (about 3550 °C).
- It is a poor conductor of electricity.
- When heated to about 800 °C in the presence of oxygen, diamonds form carbon dioxide.
- It is insoluble in all solvents and is chemically inactive.
- The beauty and shine of a diamond depends on the way it is cut and polished.

DO YOU KNOW?

Due to the presence of some metallic impurities, diamonds occur in various colours such as blue, green, yellow, red and grey.

Uses of Diamond

- Diamonds are widely used as precious gems in jewellery. Their powder is used to polish other diamonds and precious stones.
- They are used for drilling hard rocks and cutting glass.

- They are used as surgical tools by eye surgeons for removing cataract from eyes.
- Black or grey diamonds (called carbonado and bort) are used in the manufacture of high precision thermometers.
- They are used to manufacture radiation-proof windows in space satellites and spacecraft.

Graphite

Graphite, another crystalline form of carbon, is a dark grey or black, opaque solid. It is lighter than diamond and soft and slippery to touch. The word graphite is derived from the Greek word *gréphein*, which means 'to write or draw'.

Occurrence of Graphite

Graphite is abundantly found in various parts of the world such as Sri Lanka, Russia, China, India, North Korea, New York, Canada and Mexico. In India, large amounts of graphite are mined in Andhra Pradesh, Jammu and Kashmir, Uttar Pradesh, Rajasthan, Jharkhand, Kerala and Tamil Nadu.

Graphite is prepared synthetically by heating coke at a temperature of 3000 °C.

Structure of Graphite

In graphite, carbon atoms are arranged in the form of flat layers or sheets. In each layer, every carbon atom is attached to three other carbon atoms by strong chemical bonds which form flat hexagonal rings. Each hexagonal ring is made up of six carbon atoms.

The different layers of carbon atoms in graphite are linked to each other by weak forces of attraction (Fig. 9.3). As a result, these layers can slip over each other, giving graphite its soft and slippery texture.

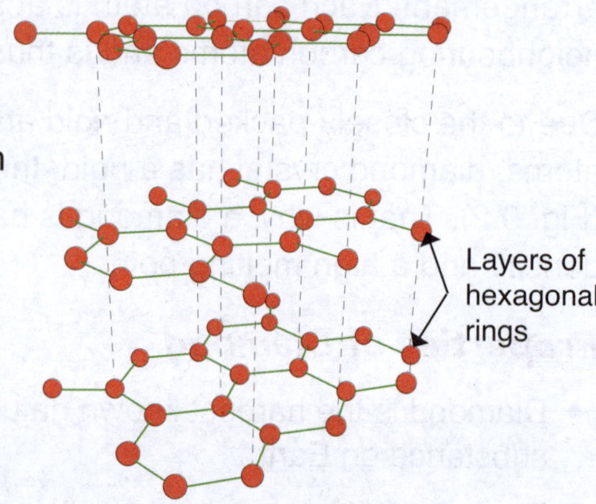

Fig. 9.3 Layered structure of graphite

A carbon atom has four valence electrons (atomic number = 6, valency = 4). This means it can form four bonds. In the crystal structure of graphite, each carbon atom is linked to only three other carbon atoms. This implies that the fourth valence electron of each carbon atom remains free to move around inside its crystal structure. The presence of these free electrons in graphite makes it a good conductor of electricity.

Properties of Graphite

- Graphite is dark grey or black in colour and has a metallic lustre.
- It is opaque, soft and slippery to touch.
- It has a density of about 2.2 g/cm^3.
- It has a melting point of around 3700 °C and hence, can withstand high temperatures.

DO IT YOURSELF

Using clay dough and toothpicks, make models of the geometrical structures of diamond and graphite.

- It is a good conductor of electricity and heat.
- When heated to about 700 °C in air, graphite forms carbon dioxide.
- It is insoluble in most solvents and is slightly more chemically active than diamond.

Uses of Graphite

- It is used as electrodes in electric furnaces and electric cells (Fig. 9.4).
- Due to its soft and slippery nature, graphite is widely used in machinery parts as a lubricant.
- It is used to make pencil leads.
- It is used to manufacture crucibles that are used to melt metals, as graphite is a good conductor of heat and has a high melting point.
- It is used as a moderator in nuclear reactors to slow down the speed of fast moving neutrons.
- It is used to make black paint and printer's ink because of its black colour and insoluble nature.

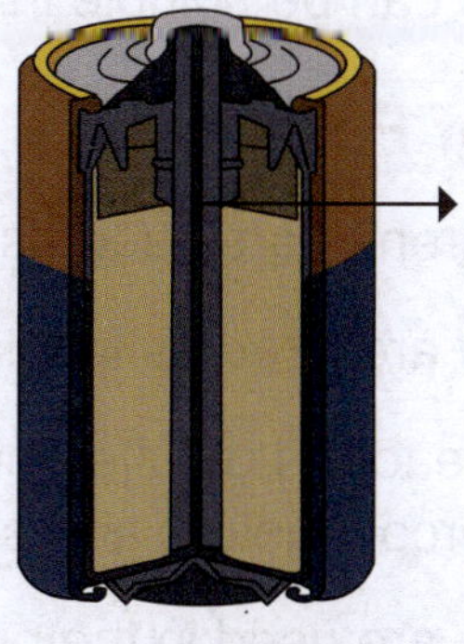

Fig. 9.4 Graphite rod as electrode in an electric cell

Fullerene

Fullerene is another crystalline allotrope of carbon, which has been discovered recently. The fullerene molecule, buckminsterfullerene (C_{60}), was discovered in 1985 collectively by the scientists Richard E. Smalley, Robert F. Curl, Sean O'Brien, James Heath and Harold Kroto.

The name 'buckminsterfullerene' was given to the fullerene molecule discovered as a homage to an American architect and scientist Buckminster Fuller. The geodesic dome buildings (Fig. 9.5) designed by him resemble the structure of buckminsterfullerene.

Fig. 9.5 Geodesic dome

Structure of Fullerene

Fullerene is the crystalline form of carbon with a large number of carbon atoms. The number of carbon atoms in the crystal structure of one molecule of fullerene can vary from 30 to 900. The arrangement of carbon atoms in fullerenes is in the form of hexagonal and pentagonal rings that are interlocked with each other.

Fullerenes can form a closed, cage-like structure (that is, a hollow sphere, known as **buckyballs**) or a cylindrical shape (known as carbon nanotubes or **buckytubes**).

The molecule of buckminsterfullerene is a spherical fullerene whose appearance is similar to a soccer ball (football) (Fig. 9.6). It consists of 60 carbon atoms and is represented with the molecular formula C_{60}.

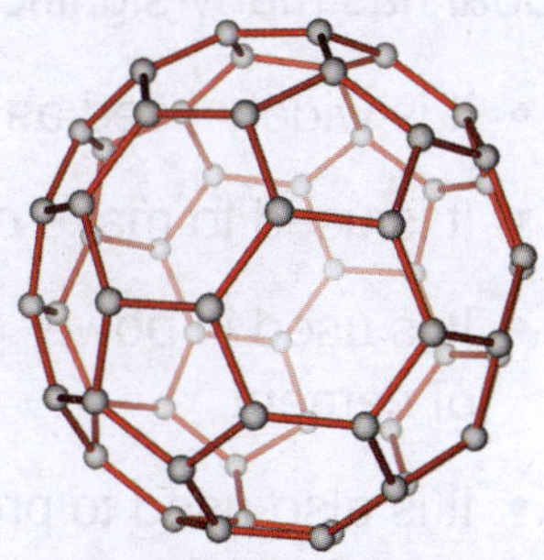

Fig. 9.6 Structure of spherical fullerene

Properties of Fullerenes

- Fullerenes are found in soot, interstellar dust (space between stars) and in carbon-rich rocks.
- They are bad conductors of electricity.
- They are magnetic in nature.
- They are odourless.
- They can be soluble in solvents such as chloroform, benzene or toluene.

Uses of Fullerenes

- Fullerenes are used as lubricants.
- They are used as insulators.
- Some forms of fullerenes can conduct heat and electricity. So, they are used as superconductors and semiconductors.
- They are used in the process of drug delivery.

AMORPHOUS FORMS OF CARBON

Coal, charcoal, lampblack, gas carbon and coke are the amorphous forms of carbon. Out of these, only coal is the naturally formed amorphous form of carbon while the rest are human-made amorphous forms.

Coal

Coal is a black, hard, solid fossil fuel (Fig. 9.7). It is formed when organic matter (mainly plants and trees) gets deposited deep inside the earth and gets decomposed under high pressure, high temperature and in the absence of air over a period of millions of years.

Fig. 9.7 Coal

There are different varieties of coal based on the carbon content. The different varieties of coal are anthracite, bituminous, sub-bituminous, lignite and peat. Anthracite is the best variety of coal having 92–98 percent carbon content.

Uses of Coal

Coal has many significant uses.

- It is widely used as a fuel in industries and homes.
- It is used to make coal gas, coal tar and coke.
- It is used in power generation, production of steel, extraction of ores and manufacturing of cement.
- It is also used to prepare organic compounds such as benzene and naphthalene, dyes, wax, fertilizers and shampoos.

Charcoal

Charcoal is a black, soft and porous solid. It is prepared by heating organic substances such as wood, bone and sugar at high temperatures in the absence of air or oxygen. Due to strong heating, the larger molecules of the organic substances break down into smaller molecules. The process of breaking down of organic substances by heating them at high temperatures in the absence of air is called **destructive distillation**. During this process, the gases and liquids that have low boiling points are released into the air, leaving behind only charcoal as the residue.

Different Types of Charcoal

Based on the source from which it is obtained, charcoal is of different types: activated charcoal, wood charcoal, bone or animal charcoal and sugar charcoal.

Activated charcoal

Activated charcoal is also known as **activated carbon**. It is obtained from charcoal by heating it in the presence of hot gases, resulting in the development of minute pores and internal spaces. This enhances its surface area, resulting in good adsorbing property.

Uses of activated charcoal

- It is widely used as a decolourizing agent.
- It is used in water purification systems to remove excess chlorine and odour from water.
- It is used in the purification of gold and extraction of metals.
- It is used in the medicinal field to treat poisoning.

Wood charcoal

Wood charcoal (Fig. 9.8) is prepared by the destructive distillation of wood in the absence of air (Fig. 9.9). Wood shavings or saw dust are used for this. In this process, wood charcoal is left behind as a black, porous solid residue and gases such as carbon dioxide, carbon monoxide, methane and hydrogen are produced. A mixture of these gases is combustible in nature and is called **wood gas**.

Fig. 9.8 Wood charcoal

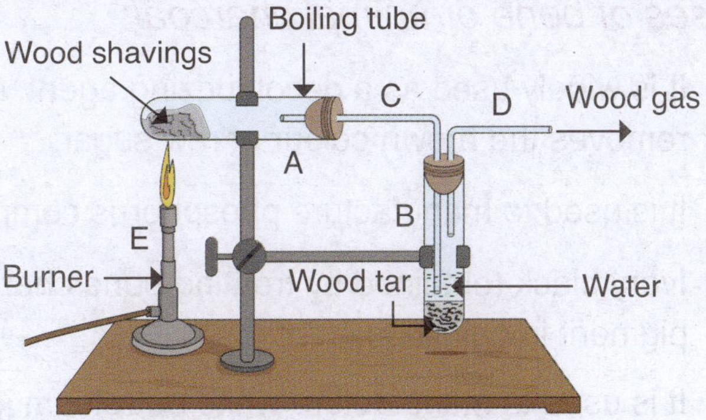

Fig. 9.9 Destructive distillation of wood

Properties of wood charcoal

- It is black in colour, porous and brittle in nature.
- Because of its porous nature, wood charcoal can float in water.
- The porous nature of wood charcoal gives it a large surface area with less volume. Thus, it acts as a good adsorbent. **Adsorption** is the property of a substance due to which it can hold the molecules of solids, liquids or gases as a thin film or layer on its surface. The substance on whose surface adsorption takes place is called an **adsorbent**.
- It is a bad conductor of electricity and heat.

Uses of wood charcoal

- It is widely used as a fuel. It is considered a better fuel than wood as it is less polluting and releases more heat.
- It is used as a decolourizing agent in sugar solutions, petroleum products and alcohols due to its adsorbing nature. It can adsorb coloured substances on its surface.
- It is one of the important ingredients of gunpowder that is used as an explosive.
- It is used to make deodorants as it adsorbs foul-smelling gases.
- It is used in making gas masks for military and industrial purposes to remove poisonous gases from the air that is breathed in.
- It is used in water purification. It is used as an adsorbent in water filters and in water treatment plants to adsorb impurities and foul smell from water.

Bone or animal charcoal

Bone or animal charcoal is prepared by the destructive distillation of animal bones. The bones are first boiled in water to remove any fatty substances present and then subjected to destructive distillation. It contains about 10–12 percent carbon and the remaining amount contains calcium phosphate and calcium carbonate. Bone charcoal has good decolourizing property.

Uses of bone or animal charcoal

- It is widely used as a decolourizing agent, especially to decolourize sugar solutions as it removes the brown colour of raw sugar.
- It is used to manufacture phosphorus compounds.
- Ivory black (obtained by treating bone charcoal with hydrochloric acid) is used as a black pigment in paintings.
- It is used to manufacture white petroleum jelly and bone ash.

Sugar charcoal

Sugar charcoal is considered to be the purest form of amorphous carbon. It is a grey or black-coloured residue prepared by dehydrating cane sugar using concentrated sulphuric acid. It is also prepared by the destructive distillation of cane sugar.

Uses of sugar charcoal

- It is used as a decolourizing agent.
- It is used in the extraction of metals from their oxides by acting as a reducing agent.

Example: $\underset{\text{Lead oxide}}{PbO} + \underset{\text{Sugar charcoal}}{C} \longrightarrow \underset{\text{Lead}}{Pb} + \underset{\text{Carbon monoxide}}{CO}$

- It is used to manufacture artificial diamonds.

Lampblack (Soot)

Lampblack is produced when hydrocarbons or carbon-rich substances such as oil, kerosene, petrol and wax are burned in a limited supply of air or oxygen (Fig. 9.10). These substances burn with a smoky flame that contains free carbon. The free carbon produced during this process deposits as a fine black powder, which is referred to as lampblack. It consists of almost 99% carbon. It is also called **carbon black** or **soot**.

Fig. 9.10 Lampblack

In kerosene lamps, the soot that is formed along the walls of chimney is nothing but lampblack.

Uses of Lampblack (Soot)

- Lampblack is used in the preparation of black paints, printer's ink, black carbon paper and shoe polish.
- It is used in the manufacture of tyres.
- It is used to make gunpowder and *kajal*.

ACTIVITY 1

Aim: To prepare *kajal* at home from cooking oil, mustard oil or castor oil

Materials required: Wick made of cotton, any cooking oil, such as mustard oil, earthen lamp (*diya*), matchbox, boxes and a copper plate

Procedure:

1. Take around 10 mℓ of cooking oil in an earthen lamp.
2. Place the wick that is made of cotton into the oil.
3. Light the lamp with the help of a matchstick.
4. By using a few boxes, place the copper plate at some height over the lamp.
5. The position of the copper plate should be in such a way that the flame touches the inner surface of the copper plate. Observe what happens after sometime.

Preparation of *kajal*

Observation and conclusion: A black soot deposit is observed on the inner surface of the copper plate. This black soot is lampblack, which is widely used as *kajal* at home.

Gas Carbon

Gas carbon is produced by the destructive distillation of coal. It is also prepared by heating hydrocarbons at high temperatures in a closed container. Gas carbon deposits as a greyish substance on the inner walls of the container. It is a good conductor of electricity.

Uses of Gas Carbon

- It is used in the manufacture of electrodes.
- It is used as the carbon rod in arc lamps.

Coke

Coke is a hard, porous and grey-coloured substance obtained as a residue from the destructive distillation of coal. It contains about 95% carbon and does not produce smoke on burning. It was first used by Chinese iron workers in the 9th century.

Uses of Coke

- Coke is used as a household and an industrial fuel. It is a non-polluting fuel.
- It is used in the extraction of metals by acting as a reducing agent.
- It is used to manufacture steel and iron.
- It is used to produce water gas (composed of CO and H_2) and producer gas (composed of CO and N_2). Both are used as gaseous fuels.

QUICK REVISION

Match the amorphous form of carbon to its relevant use.

1. Wood charcoal	a. Electrodes
2. Animal charcoal	b. Black paint
3. Lampblack	c. Water gas
4. Gas carbon	d. Phosphorus compounds
5. Coke	e. Deodorant

CARBON DIOXIDE

Air contains around 0.03% of carbon dioxide. It plays an important role as green plants prepare their food using carbon dioxide from air during photosynthesis.

Carbon dioxide was discovered by Von Helmont. He discovered the gas when he burned charcoal. The gas that was released did not support combustion. Later, in 1775, Joseph Black discovered carbon dioxide by treating calcium carbonate with dilute acids. Afterwards, Antoine Lavoisier named the gas carbon dioxide.

Occurrence of Carbon Dioxide

Carbon dioxide can occur in the free state as well as in the combined state. In the free state, carbon dioxide exists as a trace gas in the atmosphere. As carbon dioxide dissolves in water reasonably, it is present in the dissolved form in water bodies. It is also released during volcanic eruptions.

In the combined state, carbon dioxide is found in Earth's crust in the form of metallic bicarbonates and carbonates such as calcium carbonate ($CaCO_3$) and magnesium carbonate ($MgCO_3$). It also occurs in sea shells and coral reefs.

Preparation of Carbon Dioxide

Laboratory Preparation of Carbon Dioxide

In the laboratory, carbon dioxide is prepared by reacting marble chips with dilute hydrochloric acid. Marble chips are mainly made of calcium carbonate.

In this reaction, calcium carbonate reacts with dilute hydrochloric acid to form calcium chloride, water and carbon dioxide.

$$\underset{\text{Calcium carbonate}}{CaCO_3} + \underset{\text{Hydrochloric acid}}{2HCl} \longrightarrow \underset{\text{Calcium chloride}}{CaCl_2} + \underset{\text{Water}}{H_2O} + \underset{\text{Carbon dioxide}}{CO_2}$$

ACTIVITY 2

Aim: To demonstrate the preparation of carbon dioxide from marble chips (calcium carbonate)

Materials required: Marble chips, dilute hydrochloric acid, round-bottomed flask, thistle funnel, beehive shelf, two-holed rubber cork, delivery tube and gas jar

Procedure: The apparatus for the experiment is set up as shown in the figure.

1. Some marble chips are taken in a round-bottomed flask.
2. Using the thistle funnel, dilute hydrochloric acid is added into the flask.
3. No heating is needed for the reaction to occur.

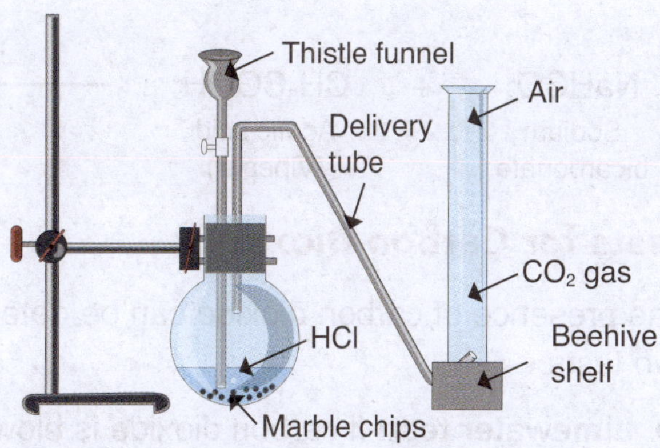

Observation: Calcium carbonate present in marble chips reacts with hydrochloric acid to form calcium chloride and water with the release of carbon dioxide gas. The gas released can be seen as bubbles in the flask. This gas passes through the delivery tube and gets collected in the inverted jar that is placed on the beehive shelf.

Conclusion: Carbon dioxide gas thus produced gets collected in the gas jar by the upward displacement of air as it is heavier than air.

Other Methods of Preparation of Carbon Dioxide

Carbon dioxide can also be prepared by the following methods.

> When preparing carbon dioxide from marble chips, hydrochloric acid is preferred over sulphuric acid. This is because calcium carbonate reacts with sulphuric acid to form insoluble calcium sulphate. This forms a layer over the marble chips and stops further reaction.

- **Combustion:** When any compound containing carbon or hydrocarbon is burned in the presence of oxygen, it releases carbon dioxide.

$$\underset{\text{Carbon}}{C} + \underset{\text{Oxygen}}{O_2} \longrightarrow \underset{\text{Carbon dioxide}}{CO_2}$$

$$\underset{\text{Methane}}{CH_4} + \underset{\text{Oxygen}}{2O_2} \longrightarrow \underset{\text{Carbon dioxide}}{CO_2} + \underset{\text{Water}}{2H_2O}$$

- **Action of heat on metal carbonates and bicarbonates:** When metal carbonates and bicarbonates are heated, carbon dioxide is produced.

$$\underset{\text{Copper carbonate}}{CuCO_3} \xrightarrow{\text{Heat}} \underset{\text{Copper oxide}}{CuO} + \underset{\text{Carbon dioxide}}{CO_2}$$

$$\underset{\text{Sodium bicarbonate}}{2NaHCO_3} \xrightarrow{\text{Heat}} \underset{\text{Sodium carbonate}}{Na_2CO_3} + \underset{\text{Carbon dioxide}}{CO_2} + \underset{\text{Water}}{H_2O}$$

- **Action of acids on metal carbonates and bicarbonates:** Acids such as hydrochloric acid, sulphuric acid and vinegar (acetic acid) react with metal carbonates and bicarbonates to release carbon dioxide.

$$\underset{\text{Calcium carbonate}}{CaCO_3} + \underset{\text{Hydrochloric acid}}{2HCl} \longrightarrow \underset{\text{Calcium chloride}}{CaCl_2} + \underset{\text{Carbon dioxide}}{CO_2} + \underset{\text{Water}}{H_2O}$$

$$\underset{\text{Sodium bicarbonate}}{NaHCO_3} + \underset{\text{Acetic acid (Vinegar)}}{CH_3COOH} \longrightarrow \underset{\text{Sodium acetate}}{CH_3COONa} + \underset{\text{Carbon dioxide}}{CO_2} + \underset{\text{Water}}{H_2O}$$

Tests for Carbon Dioxide

The presence of carbon dioxide can be detected by two tests.

- **Limewater test:** If carbon dioxide is blown into a test tube containing limewater, it turns the limewater milky. Limewater is the other name for a dilute solution of calcium hydroxide. Calcium hydroxide reacts with carbon dioxide to form white, insoluble calcium carbonate. Thus, the limewater turns milky (Fig. 9.11).

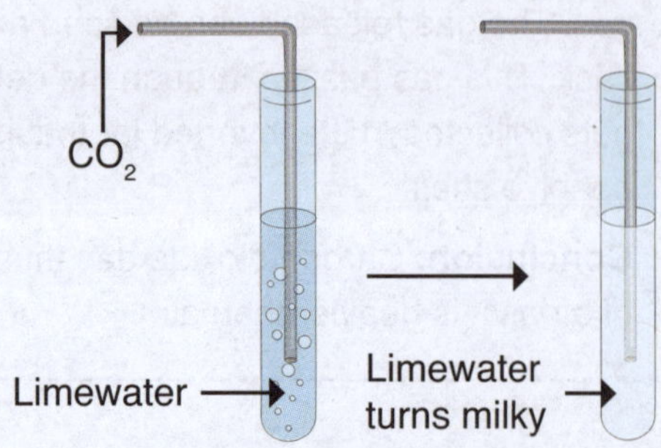

Fig. 9.11 Limewater test

- **Burning matchstick test:** If a burning matchstick is introduced into a jar containing carbon dioxide, the matchstick extinguishes. This is because carbon dioxide does not support combustion.

ACTIVITY 3

Aim: To show that carbon dioxide does not support combustion

Materials required: Gas jar containing CO_2 and matchstick

Procedure: Light the matchstick and introduce it into the jar containing CO_2.

Observation: The matchstick extinguishes.

Conclusion: Carbon dioxide does not support combustion. Hence, the matchstick extinguishes.

Properties of Carbon Dioxide

Physical Properties

- Carbon dioxide is a colourless and odourless gas. It has a sour taste because of its acidic nature.
- It is heavier than air. Hence, it can be poured from one container to another like liquids.
- It is reasonably soluble in water. At high pressure, it dissolves in high quantity in water. Hence, it is dissolved in aerated drinks at high pressure.
- Carbon dioxide solidifies upon cooling at −78 °C to form dry ice.

Chemical Properties

Carbon dioxide is also a chemically reactive gas. The following are its chemical properties.

- **Combustion:** Carbon dioxide does not support combustion and is itself a non-combustible gas. But metals such as sodium, potassium and magnesium burn in the presence of carbon dioxide to form respective oxides and black specks of carbon.

$$\underset{\text{Potassium}}{4K} + \underset{\text{Carbon dioxide}}{CO_2} \longrightarrow \underset{\text{Potassium oxide}}{2K_2O} + \underset{\text{Carbon (black specks)}}{C}$$

- **Reaction with limewater:** Carbon dioxide reacts with limewater and turns it milky. However, when more carbon dioxide is passed through the milky solution, the calcium carbonate formed further reacts with carbon dioxide to form calcium bicarbonate, which is soluble in water. Hence, the solution becomes clear.

$$\underset{\text{Calcium hydroxide}}{Ca(OH)_2} + \underset{\text{Carbon dioxide}}{CO_2} \longrightarrow \underset{\substack{\text{Calcium carbonate} \\ \text{(Insoluble milky suspension)}}}{CaCO_3} + \underset{\text{Water}}{H_2O}$$

$$\underset{\substack{\text{Calcium carbonate} \\ \text{(Insoluble)}}}{CaCO_3} + \underset{\text{Carbon dioxide}}{CO_2} + \underset{\text{Water}}{H_2O} \longrightarrow \underset{\substack{\text{Calcium bicarbonate} \\ \text{(Soluble)}}}{Ca(HCO_3)_2}$$

- **Reaction with basic oxides:** Carbon dioxide reacts with basic oxides such as magnesium and sodium oxides to form respective metal carbonates.

$$\underset{\text{Carbon dioxide}}{CO_2} + \underset{\text{Magnesium oxide}}{MgO} \longrightarrow \underset{\text{Magnesium carbonate}}{MgCO_3}$$

$$\underset{\text{Carbon dioxide}}{CO_2} + \underset{\text{Sodium oxide}}{Na_2O} \longrightarrow \underset{\text{Sodium carbonate}}{Na_2CO_3}$$

- **Reaction with bases:** Carbon dioxide reacts with bases to form corresponding salts (carbonates) and water. Upon further reaction with more carbon dioxide, the corresponding bicarbonates are formed.

$$\underset{\text{Potassium hydroxide}}{2KOH} + \underset{\text{Carbon dioxide}}{CO_2} \longrightarrow \underset{\text{Potassium carbonate}}{K_2CO_3} + \underset{\text{Water}}{H_2O}$$

$$\underset{\text{Potassium carbonate}}{K_2CO_3} + \underset{\text{Carbon dioxide}}{CO_2} + \underset{\text{Water}}{H_2O} \longrightarrow \underset{\text{Potassium bicarbonate}}{2KHCO_3}$$

- **Reaction with water:** When carbon dioxide dissolves in water, it forms carbonic acid (a weak acid).

$$\underset{\text{Water}}{H_2O} + \underset{\text{Carbon dioxide}}{CO_2} \longrightarrow \underset{\text{Carbonic acid}}{H_2CO_3}$$

- **Reaction of carbon dioxide with litmus solution/paper:** Place a piece of moist blue litmus paper/blue litmus solution into the container that contains carbon dioxide gas. The litmus paper/litmus solution will turn from blue to red due to the acidic nature of the carbon dioxide gas.

Uses of Carbon Dioxide in Everyday Life

Carbon dioxide is mainly used by plants in photosynthesis. It is also used in industries and bakeries. Some uses of carbon dioxide are as follows.

- **Photosynthesis:** Plants are the main source of food and oxygen for all living organisms on Earth. Green plants make use of carbon dioxide from the air to prepare their own food. In this process, carbon dioxide reacts with water in the presence of sunlight and chlorophyll to form glucose and oxygen. Hence, carbon dioxide is an essential gas for plants.

- **Baking industry:** In the preparation of bakery products such as breads, cakes and pastries (Fig. 9.12), baking soda (sodium bicarbonate) is added to the dough. Upon heating, it releases CO_2 within the dough in the form of bubbles, making the dough rise. As a result, cakes and breads become soft and fluffy in nature.

Fig. 9.12 Bakery product

- **Fire extinguishers:** Carbon dioxide does not support combustion and is heavier than air. Hence, it is used in fire extinguishers to put out fires. Carbon dioxide is stored in cylinders in liquefied form. When pressure is applied, the liquid form gets converted into the gaseous form. The carbon dioxide gas thus produced forms a layer over the fire and cuts off the supply of air (oxygen).
- **Aerated drinks:** In aerated drinks, CO_2 is dissolved in water under pressure. When the bottle is opened, CO_2 escapes from the drink with a fizz. At low temperatures, carbon dioxide dissolves in water at a higher rate.
- **Refrigeration and preservation of food items:** Solid carbon dioxide, called **dry ice** (Fig. 9.13), is used as a refrigerant to preserve food items such as fruits, vegetables and meat.

Fig. 9.13 Dry ice

- **Preparation of urea:** Urea is an important agricultural fertilizer. It is manufactured by the reaction of carbon dioxide with ammonia.
- **Medical uses:** A mixture of 5% carbon dioxide and 95% oxygen, called **carbogen**, is used in hospitals to support breathing in patients who have respiratory diseases such as asthma and pneumonia.

FIRE EXTINGUISHERS

Devices that are used to put out fire caused by accidents are called **fire extinguishers**. Different types of fire extinguishers are used to put out fires caused by different reasons. Some of the commonly used fire extinguishers are discussed here.

Soda-acid Fire Extinguisher

A soda-acid fire extinguisher (Fig. 9.14) consists of sodium bicarbonate and sulphuric acid solutions. It consists of a strong iron cylinder that is filled with sodium bicarbonate solution. In the upper part of the iron cylinder, a sealed glass bottle containing sulphuric acid is kept. In case of a fire, the cylinder is inverted, and the knob is struck hard on the ground. As a result, the glass bottle breaks and sulphuric acid mixes with sodium bicarbonate. The reaction that occurs between sodium bicarbonate and sulphuric acid solutions is given below.

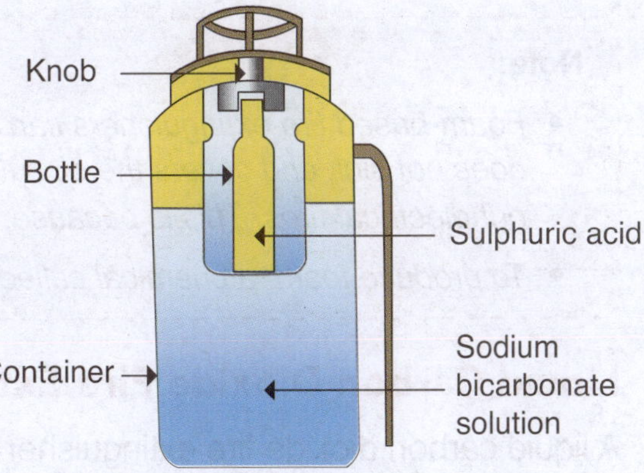

Fig. 9.14 Soda-acid fire extinguisher

$$\underset{\text{Sodium bicarbonate}}{2NaHCO_3} + \underset{\text{Sulphuric acid}}{H_2SO_4} \longrightarrow \underset{\text{Sodium sulphate}}{Na_2SO_4} + \underset{\text{Water}}{2H_2O} + \underset{\text{Carbon dioxide}}{2CO_2}$$

The mixture of water and carbon dioxide produced during the above reaction, releases from the nozzle with great pressure. This mixture spreads over the fire and cuts off air supply. As a result, the fire extinguishes.

Note: *Soda-acid fire extinguishers help to put out fires caused by wood, paper, coal and textiles but not in case of fires caused due to oils and electric faults due to the following reasons.*

- ***Oil fires:*** *The water and carbon dioxide mixture released by a soda-acid fire extinguisher is heavier than oil. So, this mixture sinks below oil exposing it to air.*
- ***Electrical fires:*** *The presence of water in the mixture released from the nozzle of the fire extinguisher makes a soda-acid fire extinguisher unfit to put out fires caused by electric faults. This is because water released is a conductor of electricity due to the presence of salts in it.*

Foam-based Fire Extinguisher

Like soda-acid fire extinguisher, a foam-based fire extinguisher (Fig. 9.15) also consists of an iron container filled with sodium bicarbonate. A sealed glass bottle containing aluminium sulphate (instead of sulphuric acid) is fixed in the upper part of the iron cylinder. In case of a fire, the cylinder is inverted and struck on the ground. This breaks the glass bottle allowing the aluminium sulphate to mix with sodium bicarbonate resulting in the following chemical reaction.

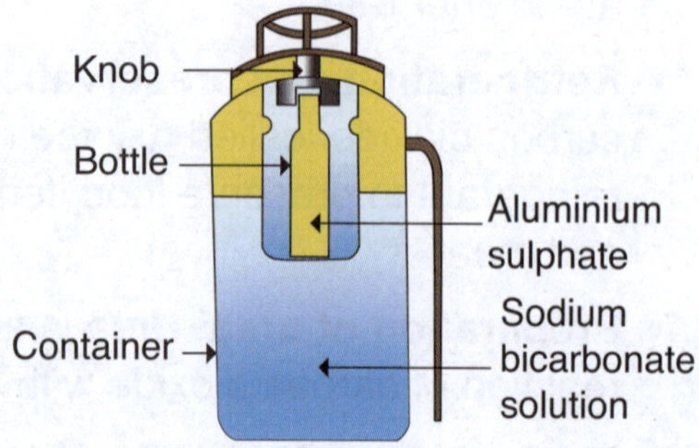

Fig. 9.15 Foam-based fire extinguisher

$$Al_2(SO_4)_3 + 6NaHCO_3 \longrightarrow 3Na_2SO_4 + 2Al(OH)_3 + 6CO_2$$

Aluminium sulphate + Sodium bicarbonate → Sodium sulphate + Aluminium hydroxide + Carbon dioxide

The carbon dioxide and aluminium hydroxide produced in the above reaction gush out as a foam from the nozzle of the fire extinguisher. When sprayed on fire, the foam cuts off the supply of air and produces a cooling effect.

Note:

- *Foam-based fire extinguishers can be used to put out oil-fed fires as the form being lighter does not sink and covers the oil cutting off the air supply. However, it cannot be used to put out electrical fires. This is because, the solutions are prepared in water.*
- *To produce foam, a chemical called* ***saponin*** *is used.*

Liquid Carbon Dioxide Fire Extinguisher

A liquid carbon dioxide fire extinguisher (Fig. 9.16) is an improvised fire extinguisher. It consists of liquid carbon dioxide stored in an iron cylinder under high pressure. When the valve is released, the pressure reduces. Under reduced pressure, the liquid carbon dioxide gets converted into its gaseous state and comes out of the nozzle as a white jet. When poured over a burning material, the carbon dioxide gas released cuts off the supply of oxygen and puts off fire.

Fig. 9.16 Liquid carbon dioxide fire extinguisher

Note: *A liquid carbon dioxide fire extinguisher can be used to put out both oil-fed and electrical fires.*

CARBON DIOXIDE CYCLE

The process by which the amount of carbon dioxide is maintained in the atmosphere is called carbon dioxide cycle (Fig. 9.17). We have already learnt that the amount of carbon dioxide gas in the atmosphere is about 0.03% which remains constant through various processes. Some of these processes take up the carbon dioxide, thereby reducing its amount. At the same time, some other processes produce carbon dioxide, thereby increasing its amount. Together these processes help in maintaining the amount of carbon dioxide in the atmosphere in a cyclic manner.

> **DO YOU KNOW?**
>
> In colder regions, plants of warmer climates are grown in a house made of glass walls. The glass allows heat rays to enter the house but does not allow them to move out of the house. Hence, the heat rays get trapped inside the glass house. This provides sufficient warmth to the plants to grow properly. The glass house is called greenhouse.

Addition of Carbon Dioxide to the Atmosphere

Here are some of the processes that release carbon dioxin in the atmosphere:

- Respiration in human beings, plants and animals
- Combustion of fuels
- Decaying of dead plants and animals
- Natural activities such as volcanic eruptions
- Emissions from factories and vehicles
- From seawater (when the amount of carbon dioxide increases in water)

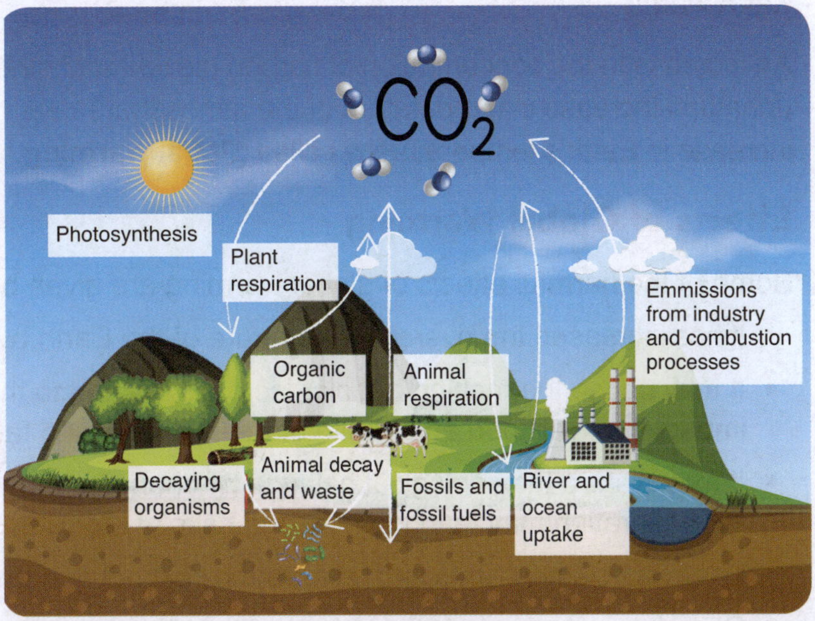

Fig. 9.17 Carbon dioxide cycle

Removal of Carbon Dioxide from the Atmosphere

Here are some of the processes that utilize carbon dioxin from the atmosphere:

- Photosynthesis
- Dissolution of carbon dioxide in water (when the amount of carbon dioxide in the air is more, the excess gas dissolves in water bodies and is utilized by aquatic plants to perform photosynthesis.)

GREENHOUSE EFFECT AND GLOBAL WARMING

Earth receives sun's heat, some of which is absorbed by its atmosphere while some gets reflected. Carbon dioxide and some other gases (such as methane, nitrous oxide and water vapour) present in the atmosphere can trap the heat rays reflected by the Earth's surface. These gases are called **greenhouse gases** and the trapping of heat rays reflected by the Earth's surface is called the **greenhouse effect** (Fig. 9.18). Greenhouse effect keeps the Earth warm.

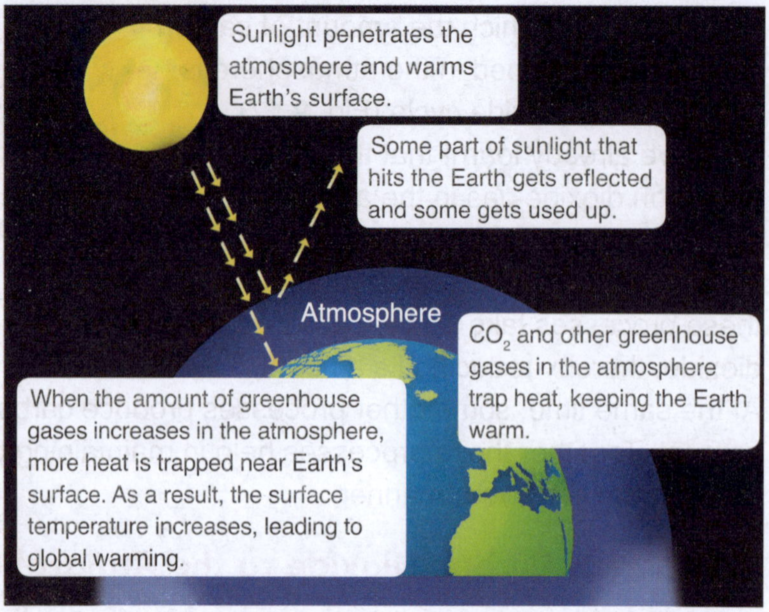

Fig. 9.18 Greenhouse effect

An increase in the concentration of carbon dioxide and other greenhouse gases results in an unnatural increase in temperature of the atmosphere near the Earth's surface. This unnatural increase in Earth's temperature is called **global warming**.

Effects of Global Warming

Some of the harmful effects of global warming are given below.

- It has increased the overall temperature of the Earth by 0.5 °C over the past 100 years.
- It may cause the melting of polar ice caps leading to the rise in sea level. This would impact the livelihood and health of the humans, and fauna and flora of coastal regions.
- It may disturb the ecological balance by changing the water cycle pattern in a region. This alteration may lead to increased risks of droughts, floods and biodiversity.
- Some species of plants and animals may extinct due to enhanced global warming.
- Global warming may lead to change in cultivation pattern.

Ways to Stop Global Warming

As the root cause of global warming is an increase in the amount of greenhouse gases in the atmosphere. By reducing the amount of greenhouse gases, mainly carbon dioxide, in the atmosphere, global warming can be controlled. Here are some of the ways to reduce the amount of carbon dioxide in the atmosphere.

- **Growing more trees:** Trees absorb carbon dioxide during photosynthesis and give out oxygen. Thereby, plants not only reduce the amount of carbon dioxide but also purify the air.
- Reducing the consumption of fossil fuels.
- Using alternate sources of energy such as solar energy and wind energy.

DO IT YOURSELF

What is Kyoto Protocol? Collect more information about this using the Internet and share with classmates.

CARBON MONOXIDE

Carbon monoxide is another compound of carbon and oxygen. It is highly poisonous in nature and may lead to problems such as headaches and nausea when inhaled in small amounts. When inhaled in large amounts, it may also lead to death. It is called a **silent killer** because its presence cannot be easily detected. Let us learn about the properties, sources and some of the uses of carbon monoxide.

Properties of Carbon Monoxide

- It is a colourless and odourless gas that easily mixes with the air.
- It is a highly poisonous and flammable gas.
- It is slightly denser than air.
- It is soluble in benzene and ethanol but sparingly soluble in water.
- It is a neutral oxide.
- It forms carbon dioxide on burning in the presence of oxygen.

Sources of Carbon Monoxide

Carbon monoxide is one of the products obtained by the incomplete combustion (combustion that takes place in insufficient amount of oxygen).

It is formed when the carbon containing fuels burn in an insufficient amount of oxygen.

$$\underset{\text{Carbon}}{2C} + \underset{\text{Oxygen}}{O_2} \longrightarrow \underset{\text{Carbon monoxide}}{2CO}$$

The exhaust of motor vehicles and burning of fossil fuels are the main sources of carbon monoxide gas in the atmosphere. Volcanic eruptions are also one of the sources of carbon monoxide in the atmosphere.

Carbon Monoxide Preparation in the Laboratory

In a laboratory, carbon monoxide can be prepared by the following methods:

- Carbon monoxide is produced by the dehydration process of formic acid with concentrated H_2SO_4.

$$\underset{\text{Formic acid}}{HCOOH} \xrightarrow{H_2SO_4} \underset{\text{Water}}{H_2O} + \underset{\text{Carbon monoxide}}{CO}$$

- By passing the carbon dioxide gas over heated carbon.

$$\underset{\text{Carbon dioxide}}{CO_2} + \underset{\text{Carbon}}{C} \longrightarrow \underset{\text{Carbon monoxide}}{2CO}$$

Uses of Carbon Monoxide

- It is extensively used as a fuel in the form of water gas and producer gas, thus known as industrial gas.
- It is a good reducing agent.

Carbon monoxide as a reducing agent in the extraction of iron: Carbon monoxide is a good reducing agent. It is a non-metal and forms gaseous non-metallic oxides on reaction with oxygen. Usually at high temperatures, being a strong reducing agent by itself, carbon monoxide can remove oxygen from the metal oxides to form metals.

Carbon monoxide is used in the extraction process of iron. It reduces iron(III) oxide and results in the formation of iron and carbon dioxide.

$$\underset{\text{Iron(III) oxide}}{Fe_2O_3} + \underset{\text{Carbon monoxide}}{3CO} \longrightarrow \underset{\text{Iron}}{2Fe} + \underset{\text{Carbon dioxide}}{3CO_2}$$

Harmful Properties of Carbon Monoxide (Asphyxia)

Haemoglobin is a component present in the blood that carries oxygen to the various parts of the body. When inhaled, carbon monoxide displaces oxygen and combines with the haemoglobin present in the blood to form carboxyhaemoglobin.

$$\text{Carbon monoxide} + \text{Haemoglobin} \longrightarrow \text{Carboxyhaemoglobin}$$

Carboxyhaemoglobin inhibits the reaction of haemoglobin with oxygen. This prevents the tissues from getting enough oxygen and results in the problems such as headaches, nausea and fatigue. When inhaled in large amounts, carbon monoxide poisoning may lead to a medical condition called **asphyxia** (suffocation) in which the body does not get enough oxygen, leading to death or coma, if untreated. Hence, it is unsafe to sleep in a closed room that contains burning coal.

Precautions from CO Poisoning

The first-aid treatment for carbon monoxide poisoning is given by

- moving the affected person to a place that has fresh air
- providing artificial respiration
- taking medical assistance
- ventilating the areas
- removing the source of carbon monoxide from the affected area

The traditional cooking methods, using firewood and cow dung, produce a lot of smoke and indoor pollution. This may lead to suffocation and even death in some cases. To control this, the government of India initiated a scheme called **Pradhan Mantri Ujjwala Yojna** on 1 May 2016. The aim of this scheme is to provide liquified petroleum gas (LPG) cylinders to women from below poverty line (BPL) households. This scheme will improve the health of women in rural areas and control the premature deaths caused by unclean cooking fuels.

CONCEPT MAP

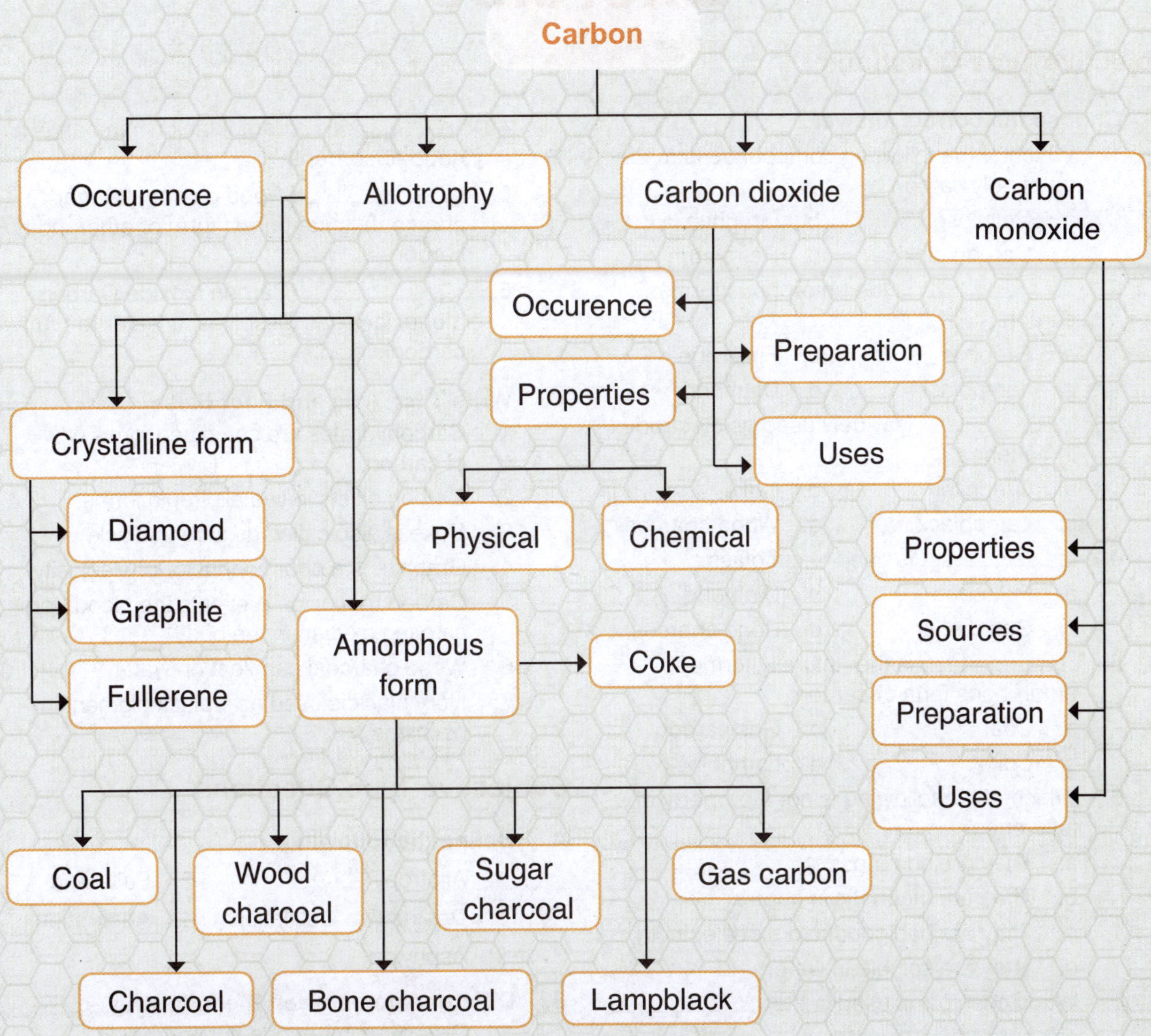

KEYWORDS

Allotropy: the property of an element to exist in various physical forms that have identical chemical properties but different physical properties

Crystals: solid substances in which the constituent ions, atoms or molecules are arranged in a regular, repetitive pattern with a definite shape in all dimensions

Fullerene: the crystalline form of carbon with a large number of carbon atoms; the number of carbon atoms can vary from 30 to 900

Hydrocarbons: organic compounds that are made up of only carbon and hydrogen atoms

Destructive distillation: the process of breaking down of organic substances by heating them at high temperatures in the absence of air

Asphyxia: a medical condition in which the body does not get enough oxygen, which leads to death or coma if untreated

Exercise

Objective Type Questions

A. Choose the correct answer.

1. Which of the following compounds is made up of only carbon?
   a. Cellulose b. Graphite
   c. Carbon dioxide d. Petroleum
2. ____________ is the amorphous form of carbon.
   a. Graphite b. Fullerene
   c. Lampblack d. Diamond
3. ____________ is widely used as electrodes in batteries.
   a. Graphite b. Coke
   c. Lampblack d. Wood charcoal
4. ____________ is used to cut glass.
   a. Fullerene b. Diamond
   c. Gas carbon d. Bone charcoal
5. ____________ is the naturally formed amorphous form of carbon.
   a. Coal b. Gas carbon
   c. Coke d. Lampblack
6. Which of the following is not a property of fullerenes?
   a. They are odourless.
   b. They are magnetic in nature.
   c. They are bad conductors of electricity.
   d. They are soluble in water.
7. Wood charcoal is used in the ____________.
   a. purification of water
   b. manufacture of tyres
   c. cutting of glass
   d. manufacture of coke
8. Which of these is not a property of carbon dioxide?
   a. Supporter of combustion
   b. Acidic in nature
   c. Colourless
   d. Odourless

B. Fill in the blanks.

1. The hardest known naturally occurring substance on Earth is ____________ (fullerene/diamond).
2. Charcoal is ____________ (a crystalline/an amorphous) form of carbon.
3. The substance used in the preparation of printer's ink is ____________ (lampblack/coke).
4. ____________ (Lampblack/Charcoal) is a good absorbent.
5. ____________ (Wood charcoal/Sugar charcoal) is the purest form of amorphous carbon.
6. ____________ (Carbon dioxide/Carbon monoxide) gas dissolves in water to form carbonic acid.

C. Write T for True and F for False.

1. Carbohydrates are combined forms of carbon.
2. Carbon exists in two allotropic forms.
3. Coke is also called as carbon black.
4. Graphite is a poor conductor of electricity.
5. Carbon monoxide prevents the blood from carrying oxygen in the body.
6. Wood charcoal can float on water.
7. Ivory black is used as a black pigment in paintings.

Subjective Type Questions

A. Define the following.

1. Allotropy 2. Fullerene
3. Destructive distillation 4. Adsorption
5. Asphyxia

B. Differentiate between the following.

1. Organic compounds and inorganic compounds of carbon
2. Natural diamonds and synthetic diamonds
3. Coal and coke
4. Wood charcoal and animal charcoal
5. Charcoal and gas carbon

C. Write the balanced equation for the following reactions.

1. Reaction of carbon monoxide with iron oxide
2. Reaction of carbon dioxide with calcium carbonate
3. Reaction of carbon dioxide with water

D. Answer the following questions in brief.

1. Differentiate between amorphous and crystalline forms of carbon.
2. Define allotropy. Give examples of elements that exhibit allotropy.
3. Mention two uses of diamond.
4. What happens when carbon burns in a limited supply of oxygen?

5. Mention the various uses of sugar charcoal.
6. What are the combined states of carbon?
7. Write the chemical equation for the reaction of calcium hydroxide with carbon dioxide.

E. Answer the following questions in detail.

1. Explain any four amorphous forms of carbon.
2. Distinguish between the structure of diamond and graphite.
3. Briefly explain the chemical properties of carbon.
4. List the chemical properties of carbon dioxide.
5. Explain the tests done to detect the presence of carbon dioxide gas.
6. Explain the properties and uses of carbon monoxide.

Application-based Questions

A. Ishita wanted to select one of the allotropic forms of carbon as a lubricant for fast moving machinery parts. Which material should she use and why?

B. Ram slept in a closed room in which coal was burned. Will Ram be affected with asphyxia?

C. Both diamond and graphite are made up of carbon. However, graphite can conduct electricity but diamond cannot. Similarly, diamond can cut glass but graphite cannot. Why?

Picture-based Questions

A. Look at the picture and answer the following questions.

1. What is this structure called?
2. Which allotrope of carbon has this structure?
3. Does this structure represent crystalline or amorphous form of carbon?
4. Name two properties the carbon allotrope having this structure will show.

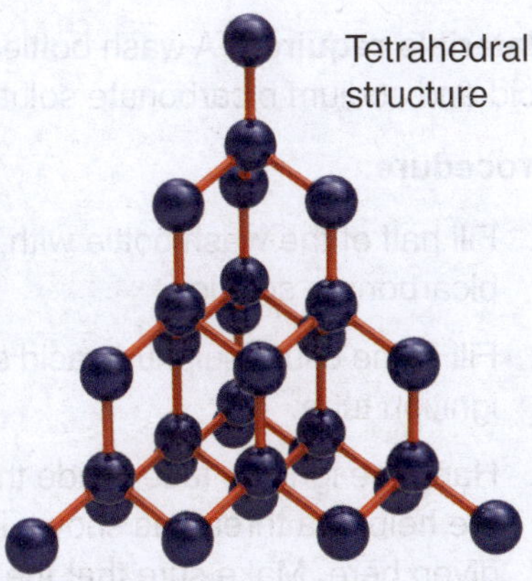

B. Mahira collected carbon dioxide gas produced during the burning of coke in the presence of oxygen in a gas jar. She inserted a burning candle inside it and covered the jar. Within a few seconds, the candle extinguished. Now, answer the following questions.

1. Why did the candle extinguish?
2. What will happen if this gas is passed through limewater?
3. Write the chemical reaction that takes place when coke reacts with oxygen.
4. Write one application of carbon dioxide gas.

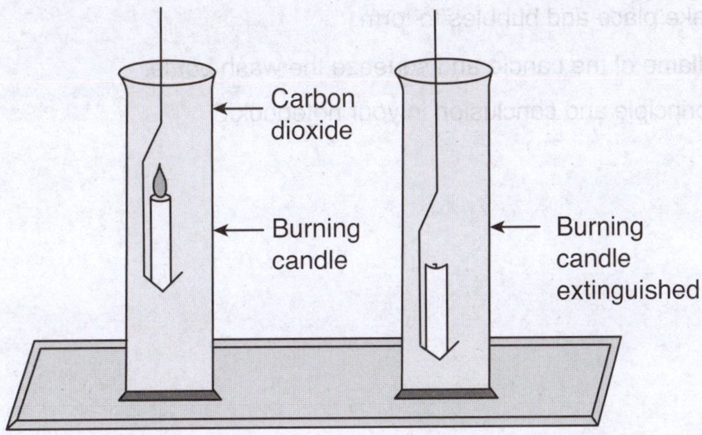

Skill Booster

A. **21CS:** Creativity and Innovation | **AL** | **BT:** Cognitive, Psychomotor

Using beads and sticks, make 3D models of the structures of diamond and graphite.

B. **21CS:** Information Literacy | **CC:** English | **BT:** Psychomotor

Collect information about conservation of non-renewable resources such as coal and petroleum. Write a report in 200 words in MS Word. Take a printout of the report and discuss with your classmates.

C. **21CS:** Critical Thinking, Creativity and Innovation | **EL** | **BT:** Cognitive, Psychomotor

Make soda-acid fire extinguisher

Materials required: A wash bottle, a small ignition tube, dilute sulphuric acid and sodium bicarbonate solution

Procedure:

1. Fill half of the wash bottle with sodium bicarbonate solution.
2. Fill some dilute sulphuric acid solution in ignition tube.
3. Hang the ignition tube inside the wash bottle with the help of a thread as shown in the diagram given here. Make sure that the ignition tube is not dipped in the sodium carbonate solution.

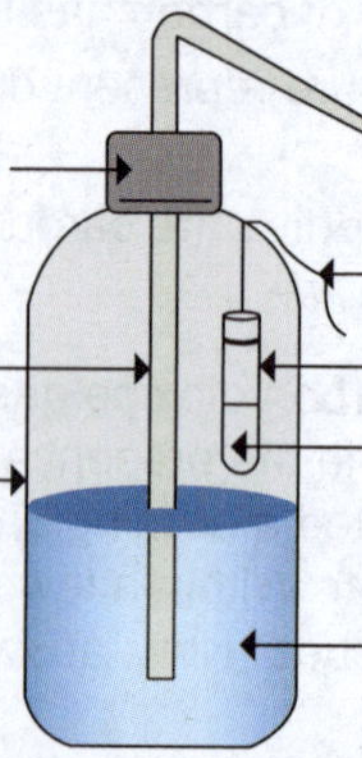

Making a soda-acid fire extinguisher

Working:

1. Light a candle and fix on a table.
2. Release the thread allowing the ignition tube to dip in sodium bicarbonate solution.
3. Allow the reaction to take place and bubbles to form.
4. Aim the nozzle at the flame of the candle and squeeze the wash bottle.

Write your observations, principle and conclusion in your notebook.

Worksheet 9

A carbon footprint is the total amount of greenhouse gases (GHG) released by an individual into the atmosphere. It is a measure of the impact of our day-to-day activities on the environment. A carbon footprint is the sum of two parts: a **primary footprint** and a **secondary footprint**.

The primary footprint is the direct emission of greenhouse gases (GHGs) into the environment caused by activities such as cooking with fossil fuels (for example, domestic LPG stoves) and transportation (for example, in cars and aeroplanes). We have direct control over these activities.

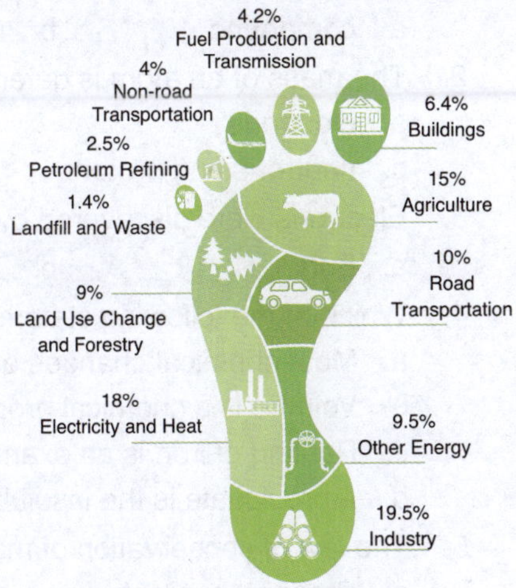

A secondary footprint is the measure of indirect emissions of GHGs into the environment during the whole lifecycle of the products we use, such as all the processes associated with the manufacture and final breakdown of a product. For example, all the processes involved, from the production of plastic till its decomposition.

My SEE Journal

What do you think will happen if the carbon footprint of all the people living on Earth doubles?

____

____

____

____

____

____

My SDG Journal

Make a poster of all the things that you can do to reduce your carbon footprint.

Review Corner

Review 1 (Chapters 1–4) Maximum Marks: 40

A. Choose the correct answer. **(5 × 1 = 5)**

1. A substance that contains two or more substances mixed together is a ______ .
   a. compound b. mixture c. element d. molecule
2. The mass of an atom is determined by the sum of the masses of ______ .
   a. electrons b. neutrons
   c. neutrons and protons d. electrons and neutrons
3. Electrons were discovered by ______ .
   a. Bohr b. Thomson c. Dalton d. Goldstein
4. Which of the following statement is correct?
   a. Most chemical changes are reversible.
   b. Volume is a chemical property of a substance.
   c. Rusting of iron is an example of physical change.
   d. A precipitate is the insoluble solid that forms during a chemical reaction.
5. The law of conservation of mass states that matter cannot be ______.
   a. changed or created b. burned or destroyed
   c. dissolved or disposed d. created or destroyed

B. Fill in the blanks. **(5 × 1 = 5)**

1. The interparticle space between the particles of ______ (gases/solids) is negligible.
2. The positively charged centre of an atom is called ______ (nucleus/proton).
3. Neutrons were discovered by ______ (Rutherford/Chadwick).
4. ______ (Sublimation/Vaporization) is a process of solids directly converting into gases.
5. ______ (Boiling of water/Baking a cake) is a physical change.

C. Write T for True and F for False. **(5 × 1 = 5)**

1. An element has two electrons in the M-shell. The atomic number of the element is 12.
2. Decantation is the best process for removing the tea leaves from tea.
3. The interparticle force of attraction between the particles of gases is maximum.
4. Acid rain damaging a marble statue is a physical change.
5. The fixed circular paths around the nucleus of an atom are called orbits.

D. Give reasons for the following. **(5 × 2 = 10)**

1. Some elements exhibit variable valency.
2. Atom is electrically neutral.
3. The mass of the products formed is equal to the mass of the reactants.
4. Salt dissolved in water is an example of homogeneous mixture.
5. Gaseous particles have more compressibility.

E. Answer the following questions. **(5 × 3 = 15)**

1. Briefly explain Dalton's atomic theory.
2. What are the different indicators of a chemical change? Justify your answer.
3. Write a short note on the discovery of electrons.
4. Name the different methods used to separate the components of a solid–solid mixture? Explain any two.
5. Write the postulates of the kinetic molecular theory of matter.

Review 2 (Chapters 5–9) **Maximum Marks: 40**

A. Choose the correct answer. **(5 x 1 = 5)**

1. __________ is the crystalline form of carbon that helps in the drilling of hard rocks and cutting of glass.
   a. Lampblack b. Diamond c. Graphite d. Fullerene
2. Reaction of hydrogen with __________ is also known as combustion.
   a. metals b. sulphur
   c. chlorine d. oxygen
3. __________ is used as a catalyst in Bosch's process.
   a. Copper oxide b. Iron oxide
   c. Calcium oxide d. Sodium oxide
4. Identify the chemical formula of calcium hydroxide.
   a. CaOH b. $Ca(OH)_2$
   c. Ca_2OH d. $(Ca)_2OH$
5. The reaction $AgNO_3 + NaCl \longrightarrow AgCl + NaNO_3$ is an example of a __________.
   a. combination reaction b. displacement reaction
   c. decomposition reaction d. double displacement reaction

B. Fill in the blanks. **(5 x 1 = 5)**

1. __________ (Coal/Lampblack) is the naturally formed amorphous form of carbon.
2. __________ (Graphite/Coke) is widely used as electrodes in electric cells.
3. The composition of water gas is __________ ($CO + H_2$/$CO + N_2$).
4. __________ (Oxidation/Reduction) is the process of addition of hydrogen to a substance.
5. __________ (Solute/Solvent) is the major component of a solution.

C. Write T for True and F for False. **(5 x 1 = 5)**

1. Purity of diamonds is measured in joules.
2. Hydrogen gas is acidic in nature.
3. Liquid hydrogen is used as a rocket fuel.
4. Pure water is a good conductor of electricity.
5. Al_2O_3 is an example of a neutral oxide.

D. Give reasons for the following. **(5 x 2 = 10)**

1. Graphite is soft and slippery in nature.
2. Carbon is widely used in the extraction of metals.
3. Hydrogen acts as a reducing agent.
4. Zinc oxide (ZnO) does not show any colour change with litmus paper.
5. Permanent hardness of water cannot be removed by boiling.

E. Answer the following questions. **(5 x 3 = 15)**

1. Explain the chemical properties of hydrogen.
2. Explain any five properties of water.
3. Distinguish between the structure of diamond and graphite.
4. Write a short note on decomposition reactions with the help of two examples.
5. Write down the steps involved in balancing a chemical equation.

Happy Accidents

Bakelite: The First Synthetic Plastic

Before the discovery of synthetic plastic, electric wires used to be coated with shellac, which prevented people from getting electric shocks. However, shellac was too expensive. Leo Baekeland, who decided to synthesize an affordable material to replace shellac, failed in his experiment. But his failed experiment resulted in the invention of the first synthetic plastic, Bakelite. Bakelite can be moulded into all kinds of shapes.

Let's make a bioplastic.

Note: *Perform this activity only under adult supervision.*

Things You Need

1. 10 mℓ distilled water
2. 1 g glycerol
3. 1.5 g cornstarch
4. 1 mℓ white vinegar
5. 1 to 2 drops of food colouring

Let's start!

1. 

Combine all the ingredients and stir together.

2. 

Heat on a medium-low flame. Remove the mixture from the heat when it becomes clear and thick.

3. 

Pour the hot plastic into the mould. Let it cool for two days.

4. 

Remove your plastic from the mould.

Your Task

Velcro was also invented accidentally. Read about it and write a short note on it.

Velcro straps are both reusable and durable. Design an activity on how to prepare Velcro straps.

Role of Science in Benefitting the Society

Preventing the Depletion of Ozone Layer

Mario Molina's research work led to the discovery of ozone depletion. He conducted numerous experiments on atmospheric pollutants and found that chlorofluorocarbons (CFCs) are one of the major causes of ozone depletion. CFCs rise into the stratosphere, where in the presence of the ultraviolet rays of the sunlight, they react with ozone molecules. Each CFC molecule can destroy up to 100,000 ozone molecules. CFCs may remain in the atmosphere for up to 150 years, depleting the ozone layer. For his work on the depletion of the ozone layer, Molina was awarded the 1995 Nobel Prize in Chemistry.

His findings led to an international movement in the late 19th century to limit the widespread use of CFCs. It is because of such restrictions on a global scale that the ozone levels started stabilizing by the end of the 1990s and began to recover in the mid-2000s.

Mario Molina
(1943 – 2020)

Who is your favourite science personality who has contributed to society through his/her work? Describe how the personality's work has advanced scientific knowledge and how it has helped society.

___

___

___

Collect some pictures related to your favourite personality's work and paste them in the space given below.